10541

BRITAIN YESTERDAY AND TODAY

WALTER M. STERN

BRITAIN
YESTERDAY AND TODAY

An Outline Economic History
from the middle of the Eighteenth Century

62

LONGMANS

LONGMANS, GREEN AND CO LTD
48 GROSVENOR STREET, LONDON WI
RAILWAY CRESCENT, CROYDON, VICTORIA, AUSTRALIA
AUCKLAND, KINGSTON (JAMAICA), LAHORE, NAIROBI

LONGMANS SOUTHERN AFRICA (PTY) LTD
THIBAULT HOUSE, THIBAULT SQUARE, CAPE TOWN
JOHANNESBURG, SALISBURY

LONGMANS OF NIGERIA LTD
W. R. INDUSTRIAL ESTATE, IKEJA

LONGMANS OF GHANA LTD
INDUSTRIAL ESTATE, RING ROAD SOUTH, ACCRA

LONGMANS GREEN (FAR EAST) LTD
443 LOCKHART ROAD, HONG KONG

LONGMANS OF MALAYA LTD
44 JALAN AMPANG, KUALA LUMPUR

ORIENT LONGMANS LTD
CALCUTTA, BOMBAY, MADRAS
DELHI, HYDERABAD, DACCA

LONGMANS CANADA LTD
137 BOND STREET, TORONTO 2

© WALTER M. STERN 1962
FIRST PUBLISHED 1962

PRINTED IN GREAT BRITAIN BY JOHN BELLOWS LTD, GLOUCESTER

TO MY WIFE

ACKNOWLEDGMENTS

We are grateful to the following for permission to reproduce copyright material:

Mrs George Bambridge and Doubleday & Co. Inc. for lines from 'Big Steamers' from *The Definitive Edition of Rudyard Kipling's Verse* and Mrs George Bambridge, Methuen & Co. Ltd and Doubleday & Co. Inc. for lines from *The English Flag* by Rudyard Kipling; the Controller of Her Majesty's Stationery Office for statistics from the Registrar General's Statistical Review of England and Wales and from the Royal Commission on Population.

PREFACE

The writer of an outline of economic history has to be a fairly brazen liar. So innumerable are the variations of life, so thick the underbrush of detail, that he cannot cover two centuries in 100,000 words without ruthless cutting, simplifying and straightening meanders of tortuous and slow-moving development, reducing an intricate landscape to a small-scale map by generalizations which verge on untruth. The present writer confesses himself guilty of this sin, but pleads in extenuation that he has done no more violence to truth than necessary to enable a stranger amidst the byways of British economic history to find his bearings. It is to this stranger, be he sixth-form pupil, student in or outside a university or just somebody curious about the past, that this book is addressed.

Apart from being a liar, a textbook writer is an inveterate borrower. Scores of scholars have by their researches lit up the past; he appropriates their efforts and embodies them in his book. Like many an improvident debtor, this writer tends to forget to whom he is indebted for what: teachers, colleagues and students have helped to broaden his knowledge and understanding until his debt has grown beyond all bookkeeping. Like the most hardened type of debtor whose affairs the Official Receiver seeks to disentangle, this writer can no longer account for all his obligations; hence he has eschewed footnotes for fear lest, by acknowledging debts he can recall, he show even baser ingratitude towards creditors who go unrecorded. This at least is the place for him to confess humbly how much he owes to those who have taught and befriended him.

There is one obligation which cannot be submerged in a general acknowledgment. Professor W. Ashworth went through the draft of this book and saved its writer from the worst of his follies, errors and excesses. For a scholar to spare time from his own work to read a lesser writer's typescript and submit it to constructive criticism is a sacrifice for which no expression of gratitude is adequate. Such merits as this book may have are largely due to his intervention. It need hardly be added that this does not saddle him with responsibility for blemishes and faults which remain.

A record extending to recent times reaches a point where its writer has no longer a right to speak as a historian. On the near-contemporary scene he casts like any of his fellow countrymen a partisan eye; his description is coloured by his convictions and prejudices. Alternatively he must refrain altogether from discussing recent events, merely recording them without comment—a cold and impersonal proceeding. Instead of submitting to such a self-denying ordinance, this writer has made no secret of his opinions; they are writ large on the last pages of most chapters. Experience teaches him not to expect readers to agree with his views, but he hopes they will credit him with stating them honestly; if he be guilty of faulty or hasty judgment, he shares after all a common enough failing.

W.M.S.

CONTENTS

CONTENTS

I | THE DEVELOPMENT OF BRITAIN

Much discussion today centres on under-developed countries. Up to the middle eighteenth century every country in the world was under-developed: no country, that is, had yet discovered, let alone opened up for economic use, the full natural resources with which it was endowed. Such resources can be of many kinds: soil of special fertility, a generous climate boasting adequate, but not excessive, rainfall, ample and accessible mineral deposits, easy routes of communication, a coast favoured by sheltered anchorages. Economists and geographers today survey countries for the purpose of ascertaining their natural advantages. In the past, such discoveries were left to those who hoped to put the resources to use.

It is the distinction of Britain, and in particular of England, to be the first country in the world which passed from the under-developed to the developed stage. This gives English economic history its singular importance: it traces a pattern of development without precedent. Many countries subsequently trod the path which England pioneered, some copying closely the English example, others deviating at an early stage because of different endowments and inclinations, but all were followers whither Britain led.

Why was Britain the first country to become fully developed? Many reasons have been adduced; all contain some truth, though in varying proportions. Whether British people in the eighteenth century were more ingenious and resourceful than their contemporaries elsewhere, is open to some doubt; that some, especially if educated at universities in Scotland, received a better grounding in the new natural sciences and in practical technology than dwellers in most other countries can be asserted with greater confidence. Non-conformists established their own academies. Though few who were not members of the Church of England obtained admission to Oxford and Cambridge, the only English universities then in existence, the rulers of the country in the middle of the eighteenth century tolerated, if they did not explicitly sanction, the existence of institutions of higher education set up for dissenters. Religious intransigeance leading to civil war and persecution had given way to greater tolerance. It did not yet extend to citizens of every persuasion, but mobilized a larger part of Britain's talent for the task of finding and harnessing her natural advantages.

Tolerance was one blessing which the country's rulers contributed to the common effort; good government was another. Not good government in the modern sense: popular representation in Parliament was ludicrous, taxation inequitable, jurisdiction a chapter of accidents hallowed by precedent, a true civil service as non-existent as a social policy. Yet compared to most countries, ruling power was exercised less arbitrarily, the sovereign had to carry with him a Parliament of a kind, taxation crippled nobody, nor was trade hampered by internal transit dues; above all, Britain had suffered no serious war on her soil for 100 years— these were substantial assets. By capitalizing them, Britain was the first nation to launch herself into a new type of development.

Britain's transition from an under-developed to a developed country is usually described as her Industrial Revolution. If taken literally, the title is misleading. Long before industrialization became widespread, England was a great trading nation, a rôle she had assumed in the seventeenth century. British agriculture embarked on new responsibilities when it began to sustain a growing population on food produced by a labour force increasing in a lesser proportion; methods of production improved in agriculture earlier than in industry. Britain's development was both wider and slower than the expression 'Industrial Revolution' suggests. Not only in industry did men think afresh about the business of gaining a living; science pervaded trade and agriculture as well. Nor was this at all the sudden process which a revolution seems to signify. When Caxton introduced printing to England in the fifteenth century, he made possible the dissemination among the many of what the few had thought and committed to paper. The effect was limited by general illiteracy; education had a heavy task to perform and took four centuries over it. The establishment in 1662 of a Royal Society for the Advancement of Science signified royal patronage for methodical thought along progressive lines, the highest in the land supporting the most ingenious. Almost a century elapsed before it was followed by a Society of Arts—art at the time meaning technique, the craft or method of making things, rather than fine or pure art. As regards speed, this was an industrial evolution rather than a revolution.

Yet there is a sense in which 'Industrial Revolution' does not sound an inappropriate description. Though slow, the change was all-pervading. It modified not only the manner in which people worked, but the way in which they lived. The man who had divided his working time between growing the family's food on his little patch and weaving cloth in a shed attached to his cottage had little in common with the man who started work at the sound of a whistle in a factory built and used only for industrial production, labouring with others all day at a rhythm set by mechanically propelled machines until his employer turned off the steam and released him. The patterns of their lives were completely different: the former with his family around him, helping or hindering him in his work; the latter but one of a family, all endeavouring to procure similar employment, all leaving their home early every morning, though not necessarily for the same place of work.

Though the change spread beyond industry, it was there that it was most radical and obvious, owing to the nature of Britain's chief natural resource: coal deposits. She had known and used them for centuries to warm the dwellings of her people and to achieve the high temperatures required by some manufacturing processes. But now her ingenuity invented a new use for coal: burnt to produce steam, it turned the wheels of machinery faster and more effectively than man, animal, wind or water. The development which Britain underwent between the later eighteenth and the middle nineteenth centuries was based first and foremost on steam power; it was the steam engine which gave Britain unquestioned superiority. Having conquered certain industries, the steam engine cast its shadow on agriculture and celebrated triumphs in transport. Britain achieved supremacy in many fields, but her industrial superiority was the most spectacular. Hence we may well speak of an Industrial Revolution.

The industrial revolution has been pictured as a blight spreading across 'England's green and pleasant land', a pall of smoke darkening the sky over her erstwhile lush pastures and

3

oppressing merry yeomen who had heretofore taken their ease and enjoyed their life in the intervals of bucolic pursuits. That is a warped view. Industrialization, especially the first industrialization which any country ever experienced, involved undoubted sacrifices. The strains and injuries ensuing from excessive working hours and unprotected machinery, the ugliness of unplanned urban sprawl, health hazards due to the absence of local government supervision and inadequacy of public services, failure to minister to the non-material needs of an industrial population—all these were very real. Yet they should not blind us to the fact that Britain's industrial revolution is first and foremost a success story. That a small, not very densely populated island, endowed with only few natural resources, made herself for a century the richest, the most productive and powerful nation in the world, setting the pace and providing the pattern which envious competitors sought to emulate, is nothing short of a miracle. If industrial revolution had spelt disaster, why were there—indeed, why are there—so many imitators? Because for the first time it gave everybody a chance of enjoying the good things of life in a profusion hitherto available only to the rich. Factories might belch smoke; they also poured forth streams of desirable goods at prices which were within the means of the common man. He had ceased to till his own plot of ground; neither was he tied any more to the soil of a village he hardly ever left, ignorant of all the world beyond his immediate neighbourhood. Variety became possible, variety of experience, of interests, of satisfactions, all because myriad wheels now turned at a speed never before achieved.

These blessings were not immediately apparent. To begin with, the yields of higher productivity were very unevenly spread: though all found life a hard struggle, some gained much, others little. Injustice was rampant; it needed another century to distribute the benefits more evenly, a century resounding with arguments over the sharing out of the national product, with labour disputes, with complaints by workers about cruel and grasping bosses, with industrialists' grumbles about eternally dissatisfied and predatory workers, a century of social research and fact-finding, followed by social and industrial legislation. While Britain was engaged in seeking social justice, she lost her lead; several of her foreign competitors first caught up, then left her behind, amid a hubbub at home of mutual recriminations over whose fault it was. Twice in thirty years the vast machinery fashioned to produce wealth and welfare had to be diverted to making armaments for use in the greatest and most destructive wars the world had yet seen. Not only did these war efforts yield no immediate economic benefits for her citizens to enjoy—we cannot put an economic value on intangibles such as national freedom or a sense of justice done—but they left much productive equipment overstrained, heavily worn and in bad shape; post-war production had to concentrate on repairs and replacements before resuming supplies of consumer goods. The sacrifices which war required from all members of the population added zest to the search for social justice; where all had suffered for the common cause, all had a right to the benefits which flowed from peacetime activities. But behind all the smoke and the disputes the wheels kept turning. Had they not produced more and more wealth, there would have been nothing to contend about. By turning they sustained Britain's claim to be the world's first fully developed country.

II | POPULATION

The Stage of Rapid Growth

Each country reaches a stage of development when population increases rapidly. Knowledge spreads and productivity rises, preserving life which previously fell victim to disease; a sufficiency of food, improved shelter against the elements, more suitable and abundant clothing all play their part. Of critical importance is a mastery of obstetrics: of the large number of babies born everywhere, the majority do not survive without adequate midwifery, and the fertility and lives of their mothers are endangered by unskilful deliveries. A country which succeeds in saving the majority of its mothers and babies is well on the way to population growth.

The middle eighteenth century marked this stage in Britain. It did not constitute a turning point in population history, merely the acceleration of an increase hitherto of moderate proportions. In the next 100 years population grew at an unprecedented speed. Some of the reasons for this increase have been indicated, but how far do they account for it? Medical science certainly made progress: midwifery was developed, lying-in charities multiplied. Agriculture provided more food and improved its quality; healthier diets were adopted. Industry furnished large quantities of cheap clothing, especially cotton underwear, and hygienic pottery rather than pewter tableware. Bricks increasingly replaced wood as a building material; water pipes enabled householders to draw water from an indoor tap instead of queueing at standpipes in the street. People could and did wash themselves and their clothes more easily and frequently. Hospitals and dispensaries were established to care for the sick; the government enforced quarantines more strictly. For these and other reasons, plague epidemics ceased to ravage Britain. All these improvements helped to raise the survival rate.

Yet improved facilities hardly suffice as an explanation of population growth. Many could be afforded only by the well-to-do. Most, especially the medical, were confined to towns; no hospitals or dispensaries served rural areas. On these grounds we should expect population to have increased in towns rather than elsewhere. True it is that the towns grew fastest; that however was due, not to natural increase, but to migration. In any case it would not account for population growth among Scottish crofters, Irish peasants or the inhabitants of distant European countries with little urbanization; yet there, as in England and Wales, the same tendency was at work.

We may never know the whole reason. Was it due to people having more children, as well as to more of their children surviving? Several scholars have explained Britain's population growth in terms of an increased birth rate in addition to the improved survival rate. There are good grounds why parents should have welcomed more children. At least from the end of the eighteenth century onwards, relief to the poor was proportioned to the number of dependants: the more children, the greater the sum of money allowed to the parents. If pauper parents did not actually consider themselves better off with a larger family, the system at least removed any restraints on the score of inability to afford additional children.

The belief that an increase in the birth rate was responsible for rapid population growth had a strong contemporary supporter, Thomas Malthus. His *Essay on Population*, first published in 1798, went through many editions and experienced a number of subsequent modifications. These did not alter the basis of his argument: if unchecked, Man multiplied faster than Nature could increase the supply of food. This doomed the country to periodical shortages of subsistence to redress the balance, unless wars, epidemics or other catastrophes intervened. Propounded in the middle of a war when food was scarce and dear and little could be imported, his views had a persuasive ring. For half a century the ghost of Malthusian overpopulation haunted Britain. By the time it was laid, science had shown ways of obtaining far greater yields from the areas under cultivation, and vast overseas territories stood ready to pour their abundant crops into this country.

It would be rash to seek an explanation of British population growth in terms of either an increased birth or an improved survival rate alone. Both contributed in varying proportions. We are unlikely ever to know these proportions with certainty. For not until 1801 did methodical ascertainment of population figures begin in Britain, after a previous attempt had been defeated in 1753. For the centuries preceding the nineteenth, we have to rely on the evidence of parish registers, supplemented from occasional estimates made by inspired amateur statisticians.

TABLE A

POPULATION OF ENGLAND AND WALES (MILLIONS)

1688	5·5	(Gregory King's estimate)
1760	6·5	(estimate)
1801	8·9	(census)

These enable us to determine with reasonable accuracy the general trend of population development, though not its details. Much public opinion opposed a census, partly on the grounds of its being contrary to God's will, partly because it would gratuitously disclose the strength of Britain's manpower to her enemies. Nor were the objects of enumeration anxious to cooperate: they had never known heads to be counted without being subsequently either taxed or conscripted. Even when opposition had been defeated, enumerators were difficult to provide: justices of the peace pressed into service overseers of the poor, churchwardens, vestry clerks, constables, village schoolmasters—anybody who could read and write: where all else failed, substantial householders had to act. Not until 1841 was this emergency force replaced by a hierarchy of registration officials.

The census of 1801 was inaccurate in the direction of understatement. Henceforth, a census took place every ten years; its reliability improved decade by decade, as people gained reassurance about its purposes. Originally only houses and numbers of either sex in a family were counted and a crude occupational classification attempted; later, its scope widened to include age, marital status, place of birth and occupational details. The history of the population census in Britain throws into relief the names of two distinguished statisticians: John Rickman, who had agitated for the introduction of enumeration, from the returns collected compiled the tables and reports of the earlier censuses;

Dr. William Farr, medical statistician in the General Register
Office, from the 1841 census onwards used the material for

TABLE B

POPULATION OF ENGLAND AND WALES, 1801–1851,
ACCORDING TO CENSUS RETURNS

	Total (millions)	Density (number per square mile)	Birth Rate* per 1000	Death Rate* per 1000
1801	8·9	152		
1811	10·2	174	37·5	23·9
1821	12·0	206	36·6	21·1
1831	13·9	238	36·6	22·6
1841	15·9	273	36·6	23·4
1851	17·9	307	33·9	22·4

*Birth and death rates refer to the decades between the dates shown in the
first column.

penetrating analyses of mortality and fertility—reports which the
Registrar General issued with the census returns. From being
the ascertainment of population figures, the decennial census
became the foundation of social policy.

The increased population was unevenly distributed. As
mentioned before, numbers grew faster in towns than in the
countryside. Industrialization based on towns needed people
from rural surroundings to take up employment in industry.
Though from the health point of view environment was much
more favourable and expectation of life higher in the countryside,
most people moved willingly enough; knowing the land as a
severe and irregular taskmaster which strained them beyond
endurance in season and found little use for their hands at
other times, they hoped for more regular and remunerative
employment from industry, quite apart from the lure of town
life. Not that these expectations were often justified in the earlier
phase of industrial development. They explain, however, how
the towns, notwithstanding a death rate higher than for the
nation as a whole, could grow faster than the remainder of the
country. Rural areas had hands enough and to spare, both for
their own work and to man the sheds and mills of industry.

Only a small proportion of people moved quickly or far. Most enterprising were the Irish, coming to Britain for seasonal work and returning home at the end of the harvest. They grew to know the areas which they visited and found it less hard to move permanently when economic conditions in Ireland deteriorated. Irish immigration forms a permanent feature of the English population landscape of the early and middle nineteenth century, rising to a peak after the Irish potato famine of 1846, but had probably been a factor even in the eighteenth. Highland landlords, dissatisfied with the revenues of the crofting system, drove many tenants from their lands in the 1820s; this added a Scottish wave to the Irish flood of immigrants. The magnets that drew people were London, the manufacturing North and the Midlands in England and in Wales the southern part based on the coalfield. But the state of communications did not enable many people to know where the streets were paved with gold. The labourer from the depth of the countryside might move to the market town. The man in the market town, wishing to better himself, would try his luck in the county town. From the county town where things moved slowly or not at all, men could be lured to an industrial centre by the demands for factory hands which manufacturers advertised in a boom. Thus, droplet adding to droplet, runnel passing into brook and brook swelling to river, grew the movement which distributed the population of Britain in response to the stimulus of economic opportunity.

The Fall in the Birth Rate

In the nineteenth century, the British population grew faster than that of France or of the Iberian peninsula; by 1900, nine per cent of the European population lived in Britain. This helps to account for Britain's standing and importance in the nineteenth century. Table C carries the statistics of the population rise for England and Wales from the middle nineteenth century to the eve of the first world war. Growth continued in absolute numbers; as a proportion of the total it slackened. Mortality fell further in response to ever-increasing medical knowledge and better social provision. But the birth rate sagged from the 1880s onwards. In every 1000 people, 14 more had been born than had died in the 1870s; that excess had fallen to only just over eight at the outbreak of the first world war.

The drop in the birth rate between the middle nineteenth and the earlier twentieth centuries forms the outstanding landmark in British population history of this period. It put an end to Malthusian fears; indeed, before the nineteenth century had run

TABLE C

POPULATION OF ENGLAND AND WALES, 1851–1911,
ACCORDING TO CENSUS RETURNS

	Total (millions)	Density (number per square mile)	Birth Rate* per 1000	Death Rate* per 1000
1851	17·9	307		
			34·1	22·2
1861	20·0	344		
			35·2	22·5
1871	22·7	389		
			35·4	21·4
1881	26·0	445		
			32·4	19·1
1891	29·0	500		
			29·9	18·2
1901	32·5	558		
			27·2	15·4
1911	36·0	618		
			21·8	13·5

*Birth and death rates refer to the decades between the dates shown in the first column.

its course, voices were asking anxiously whether Britain could hold her own in a world dominated by populous nations. Others, peering into the future, prophesied that the birth rate would eventually fall below the death rate, leaving the population to decline. For this extreme fear the figures gave as yet no warrant.

Had population in Britain continued to increase at the rate of the early nineteenth century, it would have reached 130 millions by the year 2000—a nightmare of overcrowding, of contending claims on food and land, recalling Malthus' worst fears. The slowdown in the rise of population was in the best interest of the country as a whole. But population is made up of individual families, making decisions for reasons of their own not in accordance with demographic considerations. In enquiring why the birth rate dropped, it is not therefore enough to suggest that such a movement benefited the nation.

Mention has been made of the influence which the age at marriage has on the number of children born to a couple. From

1850 to the end of the century the average age at marriage rose; the middle class man did not marry until he could maintain his wife appropriately, and we are driven to assume that many workers copied the example. But this would account for only a small fall in the number of children per family. That the average family in Victorian days had five-and-a-half to six children, but by the outbreak of the first world war between three and three-and-a-half, resulted from deliberate family limitation. It was the knowledge and practice of birth control which made this possible. In 1877 two people publishing in Britain an American book on this subject were prosecuted; their trial gave to birth control and its methods an amount of publicity which no printed matter had ever done. While prevention of conception in some form had always been known to some people, technical progress made it easier and safer, while propaganda spread it more widely. Many more people had the means of planning their families on a smaller scale at the end of the nineteenth century than at the beginning. We have to explain why they wanted to do so.

When the death rate had been high, parents of five children could expect only two or three to survive to adulthood. Once medicine held out prospects of all of them surviving, the eventual family would reach the same size if only two or three children were born. Nor did children continue to be the financial assets which they had been in the earlier part of the nineteenth century. Public opinion on child labour crystallized in factory legislation limiting progressively children's industrial employment. Compulsory education required attendance at school, thus postponing gainful occupation. Not only did children cease to swell the family income, they became a liability, having to be supported up to the age when the law at last permitted them to stand on their own feet. Parents looking upon their children from a less exclusively economic angle had even more reason to limit their numbers. A good start in life, especially a superior education, cost money; there might be enough to afford it for one child or two, but hardly for more. Paediatricians constantly improved standards of child care; parents wanting to do right by their children had to dip ever more deeply into their pockets.

Nor was family limitation practised only for the children's sake. The social position of their mothers had similarly changed. Up to the middle nineteenth century, they as well as their menfolk had looked upon pregnancies, however frequent, as their inevitable fate. Better education now gave them an insight into health problems; they learned that they had it in their power to space births more widely, even to avoid pregnancies altogether. Life held more in store for the better educated wife than to be merely the mother of her husband's children; she could also be his companion, share his interests, add some of her own, take up an occupation or engage in social work—a world of worth-while and absorbing pursuits opened before her, pursuits ill-adapted to constant child-bearing. Those engaged in gainful activities were equally concerned to avoid frequent interruption of earnings.

Not only the well-being of mother and child was at stake, but that of the family as a whole. Mr Quiverfull and his dependants always remained on shorter commons than those who had limited the number of their children; in addition to requiring more spacious accommodation, he had to pay higher rates because he occupied a larger house. Every increase in the family meant a smaller share of the good things of life, in extreme cases a less adequate ration of food all round. At a time when the standard of living was rising for the population as a whole, people with children found themselves left behind in the struggle for better conditions.

According to the 1851 census, approximately one-fifth of the employed population of England and Wales worked in agri-culture and two-fifths in industry, the remaining two-fifths providing transport, trading or other services. As against the past, this represented a considerable shift out of the agricultural sector. The movement continued: by 1881 that occupation accounted for only one-eighth of the employed population. Industry as a whole absorbed more workers in absolute numbers, but employed much the same proportion of the total as before. Within the industrial category, occupational change continued the geographical shifts of population described earlier. In particular, more men moved into coal mining and heavy industry: South Wales and the North East coast were the chief gainers. But the spectacular increase took place in the sector, neither agricultural nor industrial, which now accounted for only a little less than one half of all employment: services, whether domestic or retail, commercial or scholastic—services in which in the early twentieth century not only men but also women found employment. Bank and insurance offices multiplied; more doctors, lawyers and teachers were required; shops spread everywhere. Most of these services expanded in urban areas; people rendering them settled, not so much at the centre as at the periphery of towns, ringing them with suburbs. After the coming of short-distance transport whole dormitory towns sprang up near large centres.

Throughout this period Irish immigration continued, but was more than offset by emigration, chiefly to the United States, to a lesser extent to British Dominions and territories overseas. On balance, in no decade between the middle nineteenth century and the first world war did Britain lose less than 100,000 people through overseas migration, at most 800,000. Given the speed of her population increase, she could well afford the loss. Once Malthusians had thought of emigration as a form of medicinal blood-letting, a lowering of the pressure which threatened to burst the nation's safety-valves. Now people looked upon it as a means of spreading British influence, British trade and British engineering knowledge throughout the world—the most highly developed country making her resources, both human and material, available to her less developed sisters. Yet this surplus of emigration stamped its imprint upon Britain, not through numbers, but through composition of the population. The vast majority of emigrants were young men in the prime of life, enterprising, ready to seek adventure in other lands. Their going left the sex balance of the remaining population distorted, with an excess of women over men in every age group. This unbalance was tragically enhanced by the loss of life suffered through the first world war.

Twentieth Century Development

If every married couple aims at two children, population will diminish, because this average provides no replacements either for children who die before they reach marriageable age or for people who remain single or childless. For a population to remain stable, those who marry must have enough offspring to replace the unmarried as well as themselves. In Britain after the first world war, the average number of children per family fell to 2·2, where it remained for some 20 years. Even that figure left a small deficiency—so small, however, that it would take many years to translate itself into an actual decline in numbers. Meanwhile, population continued increasing, because the reproductive generations themselves were still children of larger families and accordingly more numerous and because mortality had continued on its downward path.

TABLE D

POPULATION OF ENGLAND AND WALES, 1921–1951, ACCORDING TO CENSUS RETURNS

	Total (millions)	Density (number per square mile)	Birth Rate* per 1000	Death Rate* per 1000
1921	37·9	649	21·8	13·5
1931	39·9	685	18·3	12·1
1941	41·7†	720†	15·3	12·4
1951	43·7	754	17·3	12·3

*Birth and death rates refer to the decades between the dates shown in the first column.
†Estimate.

Wars create highly abnormal conditions of life; not much can be deduced about the permanent trends of a population from any period which includes a major war. However, not only the birth rate, but also the literature and the fashions of the interwar years made it clear that family limitation had come to stay. Indeed, whereas pre-war couples had reduced the number of their children, many post-war couples decided to do without children altogether, preferring a life unencumbered by parental responsibilities. All the reasons in favour of the smaller family which had operated before the war continued in force. In addition, insecurity, political and economic, dominated everyday lives; explosive foreign dictators threatened every now and then to engulf Europe in war; economic crises at intervals jeopardized employment and cut earnings. Were people to bring children into the world to serve as cannon fodder in the intervals of standing in dole queues? It meant giving unnecessary hostages to fortune. Town-dwellers preferred labour-saving flats to houses, but flats restricted accommodation to the indispensable minimum, providing neither room nor rooms for children, whose romping would call down upon parents the outraged remonstrations of disturbed neighbours.

It came therefore as a considerable surprise when births in the early 1940s suddenly increased over those expected as the result of the previous trend. At first opinion inclined to attribute it in one way or another to the war, the more so as government policy during the war had done much to ease the burden of parenthood. However, the tendency continued beyond the end of the war; for the first time in 70 years, the birth rate of a decade was higher than that of the preceding one, while the death rate, after briefly reflecting war casualties, resumed its downward course. Though Britain in 1941 was too exclusively occupied fighting for her life to hold a census, the interpolated figures are reliable enough for demographic purposes.

Some of the grounds which might determine couples to have more children did not cease to operate when the second world war came to an end. One of them in fact preceded the war: after having risen up to the 1911 census, the age of marriage began to fall again and dropped lower than it had been at any period for which records exist. Psychologists had begun even before the war to paint a very black picture of the state of mind of the only child. Perhaps it took time for such theories to be disseminated among the population at large, but the fashion of having no children came to an end; though the small family remained the rule after the war, large families became less exceptional than they had been. The full employment engendered by the war led to much greater prosperity in the 1950s; few people had reason to fear that they would be unable to feed the children they had brought into the world. The government helped this development by income-tax rebates in respect of each child, family allowances paid for every child but the first, and by transferring the cost of all education and medical care from the parents' shoulders to the broad backs of the tax and rate payers. While definite conclusions on future population can be drawn only after a decade or two, it seems probable that post-war birth and death rates at least offered the prospect of an approximately stable British population for some time to come.

While mortality is high, large numbers of children may be born, but many die after a short span; at the other end of the scale, few people survive to old age. The young will therefore predominate in a population at this stage. When medical knowledge reduces mortality, both of children and adults, a considerable increase takes place among the very young and among the old. Not until the birth rate begins to fall is the proportion of the very young in the population reduced; so long as the death rate continues to decline, the aged form a growing percentage of the total.

The significance of the age structure to the economic and social historian is that he divides population into producers and dependants. In other words, some of the population make goods or render services, others only consume them. It is customary to look upon people between the ages of 15 and 64 as producers, those under 15 or over 64 as dependants. This is an over-simplification, taking account neither of the boy who at the age of 13 delivers newspapers before school nor of the prime minister who graces his office at three score years and ten; not everybody between 15 and 64 can or has to work, nor are people outside these age groups necessarily idle. Moreover, the producers of goods and services are themselves also consumers. The distinction, however, works satisfactorily enough on a rough and ready

TABLE E

POPULATION OF GREAT BRITAIN
AGE DISTRIBUTION PER 1000 PERSONS

Year	0–14	15–64	65 and over
1851	355	598	47
1891	351	601	48
1911	308	639	53
1939	214	697	89
1947	215	681	105
1957	229	653	118

basis: workers produce more than they consume, while dependants statistically figure purely as consumers. Bearing these reservations in mind, we can say that on the proportion of producers to consumers depends the standard of living which the community as a whole enjoys.

Some time in the eighteenth century medical knowledge began, and in the nineteenth it continued, to save the lives of many children in Britain; much more slowly it succeeded in prolonging the lives of adults. The burden of dependency on workers therefore grew heavier; excessively long working hours become more understandable when we remember how many more mouths had to be fed. Table E shows that even in 1851, 600 producers had to provide for 400 non-producing consumers; by 1939, 700 workers had to supply only 300 dependants. The total number of children in the British population increased to a maximum in 1911; as a proportion of total population, however, children diminished from 1851 onwards, showing an upturn only as the result of the rise in the birth rate in and after the 1940s. Old people on the other hand as a percentage of the total have steadily increased. So long as generations born in the decades of falling birth rates moved up the age scale, this was in itself inevitable; better geriatrics merely accentuated the effect. Expectation of life at birth in Britain by the end of the nineteenth century was approximately 20 years longer than at the beginning; it had reached 65 years when the Royal Commission on Population reported in 1949.

Numbers and proportions paint a vivid picture, but do not tell the whole story. In adopting the age groups of Table E, we look at history through the eyes of the present. Neither before nor in the nineteenth century were children dependants up to the age of 14; they obtained employment much earlier, engaged in heavier and more productive work, attended school either not at all or for fewer hours a day, for fewer years of their lives and up to a lower leaving-age. Nor did retirement pensions exist before 1909, except under private arrangements; people had to go on working as long as their strength and opportunities lasted. Once they ceased to earn, their savings had to maintain them; the great mass of the population who had no savings, unless relatives took charge of them, had to look to the cold comfort of the poor law to keep them alive and bury them thereafter. All these factors cause Table E to under-state the changes which have taken place over the century covered. Dependants at either end of the age scale functioned as producers earlier and later in 1851 than in 1957; they also consumed on a far less generous scale, particularly the old. To that extent, the burden of dependency on the working population increased heavily during the century.

The age structure of the population explains certain changes in the British economy after the second world war. There are always some industries which contract, while others expand. The former need less labour than hitherto, the latter more. To transfer labour from one industry to another is rarely easy; it requires adaptable workers willing to make the change and train for their new employment. In an economy where the young and the old abound, adjustment is smoothed by old workers retiring from the contracting industries, who need not be replaced, while young people entering the labour market are directed towards expanding occupations. In the British economy, particularly after the second world war, it proved comparatively easy to take the sting out of the reduction to which some industries were doomed; the high proportion of old workers who retired in the natural course of events rendered large-scale redundancy rare among those seeking to retain employment. Far more difficult proved the task of manning new and expanding industries, because not so large a proportion of young people came forward. To that extent the British economy had grown more rigid and found adjustment to changing needs a stiffer problem. But altogether the heavier burden of dependency made it desirable to retain at the oars any hands willing to continue pulling. Older people, though entitled to retire at 65, were tempted to remain at work, partly by raising the retirement age in many occupations, partly by creating a category of semi-retirement: work for fewer and more convenient hours, where possible in pleasanter surroundings, with some of the most burdensome tasks transferred to younger hands. In these ways Britain after the second world war tried to adapt her economy to the changing age pattern of her population.

Migration in the years after the first world war showed trends very different from those which had dominated the nineteenth century. Then it had been a movement towards the industrial areas; now, particularly in the 1930s, workers fled from them. Or rather, the description had become inappropriate; the depression concentrated unemployment in the areas of the old staple industries: the Scottish Lowlands, the manufacturing North of England and South Wales. Such industries as suffered less had located themselves in the South of England or the Midlands; thither workers migrated in search of employment, occasionally helped by government transfer schemes, usually on their own initiative.

In the same way overseas migration did not follow precedent, at least not after 1931. Once doubts existed whether population would continue to replace itself, there might have been no case for facilitating emigration at all. As against this, interwar governments held that the maintenance of the British Commonwealth of Nations depended on a preponderance of British stock in its overseas members. Compared to Britain, these territories were very thinly settled; their need of population was greater than the home country's. The government therefore, in cooperation with Commonwealth countries, continued to assist emigrants from Britain to settle in those territories, at least until 1933, and assisted emigration schemes for selected settlers were resumed after the second world war.

This did not prevent the balance of overseas migration swinging the other way after 1931. For the first time since statistics had been collected, a decade of overseas migration added to Britain's population. Nor was the addition numerically unimportant: of the total population growth of the 1930s, the 650,000 surplus immigrants constituted over 30 per cent. The majority consisted of former emigrants hit by the worldwide depression and compelled to return to Britain from the countries in which they had attempted to settle. Their ranks were swelled, as ever, by Irish immigrants, but newcomers in the inflow were refugees from political and racial oppression in different countries of the Continent of Europe. Britain had a proud tradition of offering asylum to such refugees; but—with the exception of Jews driven from Russia and Poland by the pogroms of the 1880s—most nineteenth-century political refugees had been only too anxious to return to their homelands once their enemies had been overthrown. It was different in the 1930s: these refugees had cut all bonds with their countries of origin and wanted to settle permanently and start a new life in the country of their adoption. This proved to be the enduring pattern of political emigration in the twentieth century.

No clear picture of overseas migration emerges from the 1940s, a decade of which the first half passed in the shadow of the second world war. The overall result was a small inward balance, composed on the one hand of the discharge into the British civilian population of large numbers of allied soldiers, who preferred settling in Britain to coming under the sway of political régimes which had usurped power in their erstwhile home countries, on the other hand of the necessity for Britain to keep a much larger part of her own armed forces than formerly serving overseas. The 1950s saw a strong inward movement from the non-white countries of the Commonwealth. Britain enjoyed prosperity with full employment; she had difficulties in staffing comparatively unattractive occupations and was driven to recruiting displaced persons on the Continent of Europe. In many Commonwealth countries the employment situation was far less favourable; from the West Indies, from Asia and from Africa men and women poured into Britain to supplement a labour force whose natural increase had considerably slackened since 1939.

III | AGRICULTURE

The New Husbandry

Man's basic needs in temperate zones consist of food, clothing and shelter. Before the coming of modern technology, agriculture was the only source of the first and almost alone provided the raw materials for the two others. To supply the necessities of an age of low productivity, it had to employ by far the largest number of people in every country. There was not then any sharp distinction between the activities of urban and rural areas; though towns attracted what industries there were, they also grew within their walls part of their own food. Men and women could be spared for other occupations only in proportion as agriculture could afford to do without them. Most industrial workers downed tools at harvest time to help with the crops. This fitted the rhythm of agricultural production which requires much labour at peak periods and employs far fewer hands at other times. Governments reserved the right to recall to the plough or other agricultural work all the able-bodied, should a famine threaten.

The farmer is thought of chiefly as a supplier of food. However, for centuries, industries have relied on him for the raw material they require—not only industries processing food like milling or brewing; while all branches of textiles needed starch, the most important and largest in Britain up to the end of the eighteenth century spun and wove wool; tallow (made of grease scoured from sheep's wool) formed the basis of most candles, while leather went into footwear and equestrian equipment as well as into components of machinery. All these industries depended on the quantities and prices of materials which agriculture made available. Fluctuations in agricultural production thus had repercussions throughout the industrial economy.

Activities which supply this variety of products constitute not so much an industry as a range of industries; we over-simplify when we lump together the silviculturist, the grazier and the corn grower under the generic description of 'theagriculturist'. Unlike other industries, agriculture has to work with varying inputs. Most industrial producers use standard materials, but each farmer contends with different climatic and soil conditions. Worst of all, he can never foretell what the weather will be, but has to make his decisions on the basis of forecasts which are little more than guesses. Having acted on these decisions, the grower is committed; he may turn his land to other use when he has harvested his crop, but not before. This hazard is greater in Britain, an island at the mercy of sea winds, than in countries surrounded by continental land masses. To the town dweller the annual vagaries of the British climate may be a joke; they represent a serious business risk to the British farmer.

Agriculture began at a time when each man produced for himself all the necessities of life. This meant mixed farming, procuring enough of everything for the needs of the family. Gradually, agriculturists had specialized, as indicated above, in accordance with local soil and climatic conditions, but while they shifted the emphasis, theirs remained mixed farms; especially, small farmers continued to supply their own needs as far as possible, selling only a surplus. What surpluses would sell and how well, depended on the market. No two villages were in the same position. Before the coming of improved transport the agricultural market in Britain was not, could not be, organized on a national, barely on a regional scale; most agricultural commodities were bulky, hence difficult and expensive to shift. Livestock, it is true, could be moved on the hoof, but lost condition through long treks and had to be fattened up again near its destination. Each farmer therefore, when deciding on his output, had to ask himself not only what he was best situated to produce, but also what and where he could sell. The answer might differ not only from village to village, but also from year to year.

Having decided upon a line of production, the farmer did not find it easy to change. Crops could be varied annually, but a breeder of livestock had to finish his animals to saleable weights and ages before he recovered his outlay; decisions regarding woodlands committed owners for a generation or more. Meanwhile prices changed, chiefly because supplies proved abundant in some seasons, scanty in others, whereas demand for necessities remained steady. The price of food, especially of bread, played a large part in determining general standards of living; to the farming community it might mean affluence, survival or ruin. That it was subject to constant fluctuations exasperated consumers and producers alike, but resulted from the nature of the agricultural economy.

If crops were poor, food prices would be high, leaving consumers with little money to spend on anything but necessities. Yet this did not always benefit farmers, especially not little men whose saleable surpluses were small, nor those who did not supply staple foodstuffs, but semi-luxuries like fruit, eggs or poultry; both had to pay dearly for the necessities they themselves had to buy, while neither sold enough to compensate for the expenses of their purchases, the little men because they had not enough to sell, the purveyors of specialities because they could find no customers. Similarly, in a year of abundant crops, prices often fell below costs of production. So the small farmer stood to lose at both extremes of the price scale; his prayer was for a reasonably good harvest selling at a middling price. However, all agricultural prices did not move in unison, nor was there any reason why they should. A farmer who produced both meat and wheat might recoup on one what he lost on the other; indeed, the sheep grazier necessarily offered a combination of mutton, wool and tallow, the cattle raiser of beef and leather, and though neither could quickly abandon livestock production, he could within limits vary the proportions of the joint products which he put on the market. This was his traditional reaction to price fluctuations.

Prices were most volatile in the South, particularly in the London area, a large consuming centre for whose custom agriculturists, even foreign ones, competed over a wide region. Whereas a certain amount of imported food reached England, especially from Ireland, some of the barley grown in Southern and Eastern England went to provision the breweries and distilleries of Holland; there was a two-way traffic in agricultural produce, but up to the middle eighteenth century Britain on balance was a supplier, especially of grain, of which exports reached a peak round 1750. Much of it was wheat grown on the heavy clays of the Midlands, whereas the damper North and West specialized in cattle and spring-sown grain; from the Trent northward, oatmeal rather than wheat constituted the staple foodstuff. The North and West had less traffic in agricultural commodities with the outside world, either in or out; its food prices varied neither as much nor as fast as those in the South.

Ever since the late seventeenth century, knowledge of better methods of cultivation had been reaching Britain from the Dutch, then pioneers in many arts and crafts. These improvements owed remarkably little to theoretical science; the age of soil biology and veterinary progress had not yet dawned. They were the results, partly of observation and experiment, partly of geographical discovery, of attempts to establish outlandish plants in home soils, to assimilate to domestic agriculture practices first encountered elsewhere. Man had not in earlier centuries known how to grow grass, but had relied on Nature clothing with grass any land which he left unworked. Now the technique of artificial grasses spread: clover, sainfoin, lucerne and others were sown. Such leguminous plants extracted nitrogen from the air and restored it to the soil which hitherto had had to lie fallow one year in two or three after cereal crops in order to regain its fertility. Alternating roots and cereals formed a rotation which allowed crops to be taken from the land every year. Not only did this increase the productivity of the soil by one third or one half; whereas hitherto much livestock had been slaughtered each autumn, owing to lack of feedingstuffs, root crops now provided good winter feed.

More animals all the year round produced more dung to manure the land. So more livestock yielded better crops, ampler grasses fed more beasts; each stimulated the other in a snowball growth. From the Dutch, England also learnt about the fertility inherent in fen land, if drained, and about deep ploughing. Enterprising landowners put these lessons into practice and experimented with others. Improvements were made in ploughs and other implements. Jethro Tull invented a horsehoe and a seed drill which obviated broadcast sowing. Thomas Coke, Earl of Leicester, improved the quality of light Norfolk soil by an admixture of finely ground clay (marling), thus gaining the benefit of the clay's fertility without the drawback of its heaviness and impermeability. Viscount Townshend earned the nickname of 'Turnip Townshend', not by introducing to England the root of that name—this had happened much earlier—but by contributing to its popularity as an animal and—as some misguided people would have it—human food. Nor did the livestock branch of agriculture lag behind. Robert Bakewell and many disciples, by selective inbreeding, improved cattle, horses and sheep through maximum development of those parts of the animal which had commercial value. The products of their efforts, while aesthetically deplorable, achieved considerable success.

We cannot put a date to many of these improvements, often because we do not know who first introduced them, but particularly because, once introduced, they took a long time to spread. Different soil and climatic conditions required different methods; successes in one part of the country could not always be transplanted unadapted to others. From the late seventeenth to the end of the eighteenth century there is a pattern of progress expanding very gradually—certainly not a revolution as regards either speed or spread. In the latter part of the eighteenth century support was forthcoming from the Board of Agriculture, an unofficial body of enthusiasts enjoying however patronage and grants from the government. Its president, Sir John Sinclair, and its secretary, Arthur Young, were prolific writers on agriculture; Sinclair concerned himself with scientific aspects, whereas Young, a journalist and indefatigable traveller, toured the country and reported on cultivation, propagated new methods and exposed bad and wasteful practices. Among great landowners improved agriculture became the fashion; George III personally supervised the home farm at Windsor and was known as the 'farmer king' at a time when he earned little praise for any other exercises of his royal functions.

Though only a small sector of the agricultural community had taken to new techniques to improve productivity before 1750, the greater supplies forthcoming created a glut before the market in its turn expanded by an increase in population. Agriculture in the 20 years preceding the middle of the century experienced a depression, owing to the low prices which its produce realized. Different areas and different branches were not equally affected, the worst sufferers being the clay lands of Central England where wheat was expensive to grow. Many farmers there changed over to grazing as a better way of using the heavy soil. The lighter lands of Southern and Eastern England found adaptation less hard;

it was here that most of the improvements in cultivation were pioneered, associating especially with the name of Norfolk a typical crop rotation. Around big urban centres, above all London, farmers concentrated on dairying and market gardening in order to produce fresh vegetables, fruit and milk for the town dwellers. The demand for these foodstuffs never flagged; these branches of agriculture continued to flourish, even during the depression of the earlier eighteenth century.

In the second half of that century, market conditions changed rapidly. Population now grew by leaps and bounds; new mouths required food. Having earlier in the century expanded ahead of demand, agriculture now failed to keep step. Nothing short of a thorough revolution could have made it supply all the food required. Most first-class land for grain growing was by this time in use; increased quantities of corn were more likely to result from intensifying cultivation of the area already tilled than from bringing further acres under the plough. Though knowledge how to produce it existed in the country, it had not penetrated sufficiently far to revolutionize general practice. This was the fault of neither the agricultural pioneers nor the Board of Agriculture; the small man on the land retained his traditional conservative attitude. Mostly unable, always unwilling to read, he could not be reached by literature. Though a few large landlords established model farms and held demonstrations, many of their small neighbours even at the end of the eighteenth century obstinately continued farming methods handed down to them by their fathers and grandfathers.

The lag of agricultural production behind increased demand reflected itself in food prices. After remaining stable or falling during the earlier part of the century, they rose in the second half, first slowly, then more rapidly, when population increase got under way, at the end of the century exceedingly steeply under the impact of war. Several livestock epidemics accentuated the effect upon meat which increased in cost more than grain, though improvements in the standard of living may also have enabled consumers to demand protein foods rather than starch. Agricultural production did increase, but the home market required all it could put forth. From a maximum in 1750, grain exports declined, to be replaced by import surpluses from 1766 onwards. A momentous stage had been reached: Britain had ceased to feed herself. As yet the deficiency was but small, hardly noticeable in good years. From 1773 onwards corn laws fixed two prices: an upper limit beyond which imports became duty-free, and a lower below which exports earned a bounty, but above which they were prohibited. The bounty soon became a dead letter because prices never dropped low enough to make it operative; so great was the need for imports in years of bad harvests and throughout the wars with France that the corn laws had to be suspended. The delay with which agriculture responded to its opportunity may well have determined the attitude of the investor in the later eighteenth century, when he chose whether to venture his savings in industry or agriculture; by preferring industry, he kept agriculture short of capital for almost 100 years.

Enclosure

Agriculture has three aspects: markets and cultivation we have discussed; it remains to speak of landholding. The personnel of agriculture in Britain, more than in any other country, is characterized by a threefold division into landlords, farmers and agricultural labourers. Of these, the landlord owned not only the land, but also the fixed capital, chiefly buildings. Though he might farm part of his land himself, more typical was the landlord who let his estate to one, often to several tenants. The farmer usually therefore owned only the working capital, consisting of implements, livestock and seed; he was in the economic sense of the word an *entrepreneur*, conducting business at his own risk with the help of much hired capital. Not only was he the *entrepreneur*, but also the manager, deciding what, when and how to cultivate, so far as the lease did not impose restrictions; he also functioned as the employer of such labour as the farm required. That labour was first and foremost that of his own hands, next that of his family; almost one half of all English farms, probably far more of all British ones, employed no other labour at all. Only the bigger establishments could afford hired hands, either farm servants on a long-term engagement or daily or weekly labourers for seasonal work. Such farm hands, if occupying cottages, might own smallholdings, growing a little of their own food, even keeping a cow, a pig or a couple of geese; on the whole they lived by wage labour.

This threefold division was the product of centuries during

which land had conferred upon its owner political power and social prestige. Landowners dominated Parliament—the House of Lords entirely, the Commons by a large majority. The trader or lawyer who wanted to climb the social ladder retired from business and bought land. If he spent enough, he might become a great estate owner; a more modest purchase would turn him into a country squire. Once he had acquired land, his next concern was to extend his property. Purchase required money. Marriage proved a suitable device: by linking himself or his son to a landed heiress, many a small owner doubled or trebled the estates and laid the foundation of a landed family. To prevent loss, he resorted to entail, a legal device by which at his death all immovable property descended undivided to a single heir. Such land, once in one hand, could be added to; it could never diminish.

A system which secured all landed property to a single heir, mostly the eldest son, bore hard on the others. Neither the Church nor the army had been designed as relief organizations for dispossessed younger sons, though they provided employment for any whose talents lay in either direction. However, these young men had grown up on estates; the land was in their blood. If they could not become landowners, the nearest they could come to that status would be as large tenants. Thus, many farmers were the landowners' younger sons who had no prospect of inheriting estates, so would take farms on a seven, 14 or even 21-years' lease. Landlords liked them as tenants; they had sprung from the same background as themselves, were of their own class, knew all about farming. If they had lived on a progressive estate and took on a good-size farm, they could be expected to make use of their knowledge of up-to-date methods of cultivation, work for higher yields, improve the value of the land. Landlords' preference for this type of tenant expressed itself in the increasing size of holdings frequent in the later eighteenth century.

Farm labourers came from two sources: small cultivators who had fallen on bad days and lost their land or tenancies, and people who had never played any other part in agriculture. The latter had usually drifted to a village from elsewhere, 'squatted' on land which had not been claimed by anybody else, built themselves cottages, with gardens or smallholdings around them, which they worked in their spare time. They were allowed to cut turf or collect firewood in the common forest, sometimes to pasture a head of livestock on the common meadow.

Common fields, meadows and forests existed in the large part of England cultivated on the open-field system. The details of this system varied from region to region, sometimes from village to village; a typical example must suffice here. The arable was divided into three fields, one laid down to a crop in winter, one sown in spring, the third fallow. A farmer's holding consisted of a number of strips in each field. Not only did he have strips in different fields; his strips in any one field would not adjoin, but alternate with the strips of others. If the landlord possessed a home farm, it might consist of a consolidated piece of land or merely of a number of similarly scattered strips in the common fields. This meant that, though each cultivator remained responsible for his strips, fields could be cultivated only in common, laid down to an agreed crop, harvested at the same time—all the more since the livestock were let in on the stubble as soon as the crop had been taken. Beyond such temporary grazing the village possessed common meadows. Where they were ample, villagers might be left free to pasture as much livestock as they liked; if a danger of overgrazing existed, the number of animals to which each villager was entitled would be fixed in proportion to the size of his holding in the common field. Similarly, common rights existed in the woods belonging to the village. These rights appertained only to owners and tenants. So far as cottagers and squatters shared the benefits, they had been admitted on sufferance.

This system had never prevailed over the whole country. It suited a type of cultivation where arable predominated and land was rich enough to repay tillage in comparatively small units. This had never applied to most of Scotland and Wales nor to the peripheral areas of England. Moreover, a good deal of enclosure of erstwhile open fields had taken place in the course of time. By the eighteenth century the open-field system occupied chiefly a broad belt stretching southwards through the centre of England from Yorkshire to Hampshire and Dorset. The men who first cultivated land in this manner knew why they did it; the system had its advantages and did justice of a rough kind as between farmer and farmer. By the eighteenth century men mainly noted its drawbacks. It was wasteful of the cultivator's time spent walking between his strips, wasteful also of land in that strips had to be separated by small earth banks (balks); it needed a network of footpaths to give men access to all their strips. But above all, it slowed the progress of cultivation to the speed of the most supine or obstinate farmer. What good did it do any man to weed his strips if his neighbours allowed weeds to spread outwards from theirs? How could he drain his land—and the damp climate of Britain rendered drainage the chief problem of land improvement —except by carrying his surplus moisture away over or under his neighbours' strips? Most of all, open fields did not lend themselves to experiment. They afforded no scope to the grower who wanted to try a new crop, any more than to the breeder who wanted to practise selection; crops in common fields, like cattle on common meadows, had to take their chance with the rest. When agriculture had to expand its output and adopt more intensive techniques of land cultivation, the open-field system was doomed.

Not that all enclosure promptly led to better farming. Arthur Young on his travels often observed enclosed fields without finding evidence of cultivation having been improved. Enclosure, while providing an opportunity for new and better techniques to be applied, did not in itself effect any improvement; enclosed land could be farmed as wastefully and inefficiently as open fields. Some landlords enclosed their estates because it had become the fashion to do so and showed awareness of the demands voiced by the leaders of progress in agriculture. Many more followed suit because enclosed land enabled cultivation to be rendered more profitable, thus yielding higher rents. In times of rising prices and costs, estate owners could not afford to neglect this opportunity of increasing their incomes.

Conversion of open fields into consolidated holdings is the chief, but not the only process which we call enclosure. In addition, enclosure could and usually did involve hedging and ditching of the new holdings created, the division of common meadows and the extinction of rights of common over woods or wasteland. These operations were often performed as a single process, begun by the decision to enclose. Unless it could be done by agreement of all owners concerned, enclosure required coercion, and this could be achieved only by a private Act of Parliament. Most enclosures in the eighteenth century started in the form of a petition to Parliament, followed by a parliamentary

31

committee of enquiry. If the committee recommended it, the Act would be passed, appointing two or three men with knowledge and experience of land as enclosure commissioners. They would have to throw all the land together, calculate the share of each owner, then divide it out in consolidated units proportionate to these shares. It was a long and by no means cheap process: in addition to incurring parliamentary expenses, beneficiaries had to remunerate the enclosure commissioners. The fact that the Act usually stipulated for hedges and ditches to be made round each new holding added to the cost. Yet such was the pressure of demand for agricultural produce, such the lure of higher rents— or perhaps in the case of some supine estate owners merely the desire to follow the fashion—that between 1760 and 1803 Parliament passed 2000 enclosure Acts.

There was nothing inherently unjust in enclosure. It consisted of a transmutation of one set of property rights into another which preserved as accurately as possible the owners' relative positions. But whereas the principle did not offend justice, many of the individual operations lent themselves to abuse. Parliament would take notice of a petition of enclosure, provided it represented three-quarters of the land surface involved. But three-quarters of the land concerned might well be owned by one, two or three large landlords who could thus set in motion a process utterly detested by all the small men in the district. Nothing prevented these small men from opposing the petition in Parliament—nothing but the difficulties small men always experience when required to observe complicated legal formalities, incur the expenses of attending to matters in London, far away from their own homes, and of briefing barristers to plead on their behalf. In a Parliament composed of large landed proprietors full of sympathy for the landlord who wanted to enclose and improve, a committee was easily packed with petitioners' friends, naturally predisposed in favour of enclosure. When the enclosure commissioners started redistribution, tenancies had to be prematurely terminated, of course against compensation, but not every tenant with cash in his pocket could find another farm. Holdings proportionate to previous rights left the small man, heretofore grazing an animal or two on the common meadow, with a piece of pasture the size of a pocket handkerchief on which his cow could hardly turn round; the balance of his agriculture had been disturbed. As the holdings were proportionate, so also the common costs; often the small owner could not afford them, before he even started to count the separate costs of hedging and ditching his property. In order not to lose his rights, he had to sell and get out. Worst of all was the plight of cottagers and squatters. Justice as meted out by enclosure commissioners meant compensation for all existing rights. Squatters had been part of the village community not by right, but only on sufferance; they had no title of which enclosure commissioners were empowered to take notice; so they went away empty-handed. In the nineteenth century, Parliament often gave instructions to enclosure commissioners to provide some compensation for squatters; in the eighteenth this rarely happened.

Owing to the fact that enclosure benefited large men more often than small, it has been subject to much impassionate censure from later commentators. They have looked upon it as a legal trick to dispossess the yeomen of England, upon enclosure commissioners as tools of large landowners to cheat their smaller neighbours out of their inheritance. Careful research has borne out none of these extravagant claims. Enclosure undoubtedly was a tragedy for many farmers. However, without enclosure agricultural progress would have been impossible, leaving the country inadequately fed until improved transport enabled large-scale imports; the alternatives to enclosure were under-nourishment and famine. Nor is it true, as was believed at one time, that enclosure depopulated the English countryside. Census figures— when they appeared in the nineteenth century—disproved this assumption. Small men might sell, but there were other small men able to buy. Whatever caused Oliver Goldsmith's 'Deserted Village', it was not enclosure. Where owners enclosed as a prelude to better cultivation, on the contrary, they required more labour, first to make hedges and ditches, then to drain, weed, plough and sow more intensively. Enclosure was not an unmixed blessing to contemporaries; steps on the road to progress rarely are. It formed part of the price they were called upon to pay for adapting agriculture to the rôle assigned to it in modern Britain.

The Repeal of the Corn Laws

Britain began the nineteenth century in a blaze of war. For a decade and a half British agriculture had to feed almost single-handed her population and armed forces, quite apart from helping Britain's allies whose crops had been laid waste in Peninsular campaigns. In rising to its opportunity, agriculture strained every nerve. Grasslands were ploughed to bear cereal crops, women, children and old people drawn into employment to replace the men who had joined up. Enclosure proceeded apace; by the time war came to an end, not many open fields remained. All this did not stop food prices from rising to famine levels on several occasions and remaining high throughout the war; in one of the worst years, 1810, Britain was reduced to importing grain from the enemy, knowing well that Napoleon levied a war duty on every ton allowed out of France to swell his campaign fund. Many tenant farmers believed that prosperity for agriculture had come to stay; where they could persuade landlords to sell, they bought their land. They could not usually pay cash, so borrowed the purchase price, mortgaging the land as security for the loans.

Fighting stopped in 1814, flared up again and came to a definite close in 1815. Prosperity for arable farmers had ended even earlier. Throughout most of the war, harvests had been bad. That of 1813 produced an ample crop at a time when the market anticipated the coming of peace and the resumption of unrestricted imports. Agricultural prices came tumbling down, wheat falling from 126s. 6d. a quarter in 1812 to 65s. 7d. in 1815, other grains in proportion. Not for 20 years had cereal growers known such a disastrously low price level. Hastily they allowed the land ploughed up during the war to revert to grass. War economy had fostered overproduction of cereals, above all wheat; agriculture had to readjust to the peacetime pattern of demand. But by itself this could not save it. Distress reigned everywhere, especially among those tenants who had so confidently turned owners by means of heavy mortgages on which they now had to default. Answers to a questionnaire from the Board of Agriculture in 1816, reports of select committees of Parliament in 1821, 1822, 1833 and 1837, all told a tale of mortgages foreclosed, land abandoned, villages depopulated, because cultivation had ceased to pay.

Parliament did not remain idle. It consisted after all chiefly of landowners who, if they did not suffer first hand as farmers of estates, felt the backwash of agricultural depression at least as receivers of rent. If anything, they were only too prone to identify the welfare of British agriculture with the well-being of the country as a whole, to consider food producers' interests to the exclusion of consumers'. In the year which saw an end to the war, Parliament passed a law which prohibited imports of grain unless the price of wheat rose to 80s. a quarter (whenever laws in this connection mentioned the price of wheat, they also fixed corresponding prices for the other cereals). This was drastic legislation indeed. Only once in the eighteenth century before the French wars had wheat climbed to 80s.; that had been in 1709 during another war. To keep out imports until the price level indicated famine, did not prove practical policy in a country whose population was rapidly growing and in any case resenting its exclusion from parliamentary representation. In the 1820s the corn law had to be amended to establish a sliding-scale of duties; tariff rates diminished in proportion as corn prices rose.

Parliament thus attempted to steer a middle course between the interests of producers and consumers. In effect, it satisfied neither. Given that agriculture had a claim to protection in a country where industries grew up behind tariff walls, the law operated far too clumsily. Corn prices were determined once a quarter, the level ascertained on the appointed day determining the rate of duty for the ensuing three months. Dealers in any market, if they know that much depends on the price ruling on a particular day, have means of making that price conform to their wishes. If they had foreign corn in hand, a high price on the appointed day would secure for them three months of sales at a low duty. Nor did the corn have to be shipped from foreign ports. It was already in the country, lying in bonded warehouses in London, Liverpool and Hull; dealers only had to pay the duty for the sheds to be unlocked and the supplies to flow whither their owners directed them. Had the farming community benefited, the system might have had something to recommend it. But farmers rarely had space or means for storing produce in anticipation of a rise in prices. They sold as they harvested, to shift the crops off the farm and obtain some money. It was the corn merchants and factors who 'played the markets' and reaped the benefits of higher prices—men well able to look after themselves without help from the law.

In spite of the corn laws, the arable sector of British agriculture from 1815 to the end of the 1840s remained semi-depressed, the Cinderella of British economic life. Its gloom is exaggerated by comparison with industries which soared to world domination in those years, buoyed up by generous infusions of capital—capital which might well have flowed into agriculture, had not industry held out far more alluring prospects. British agriculture was not really inefficient; the Continent of Europe in the first half of the nineteenth century even regarded it as a model of progressive farming methods on the arable as well as on the livestock side. Only in contrast with industry did it present a picture in sombre hues, growing darker up to 1837; from then to mid-century agricultural prosperity improved slowly.

It is impossible to determine to what extent the corn laws raised the price of the people's bread. All that can be said with certainty is that that price remained higher than it would otherwise have been and fluctuated more than it would have done, had not the law tempted men to interfere with natural price formation. Contemporary opponents grossly exaggerated the effect of the corn laws, being infuriated by bread prices which were rarely low and never steady. The standard of living of many urban workers remained depressed in the early nineteenth century. At a time when they had large families to feed, they felt the pinch severely; much depended on the price of the quartern loaf of bread. The corn law constituted a convenient scapegoat for the lack of purchasing power from which the urban masses suffered. Moreover, the population of England and Wales by the 1840s was producing 500 new mouths a day to fill with bread. There could be no question of British agriculture, whatever its efficiency, coping unaided with this increase in demand.

That corn laws had some effect, is beyond doubt because a bad harvest in Britain up to the middle of the century still raised bread prices. The late 1830s and early 1840s saw a series of poor crops. It was during those years that the Anti-Corn-Law League was born, an association of all those who, as consumers of bread, stood to gain from duty-free corn imports. The men who took the initiative in establishing and leading the League were Northern and Midland manufacturers, John Bright of Manchester and Richard Cobden of Birmingham; they rallied their chief support among industrial workers. But their courage and conviction drove them far afield. League speakers invaded the enemy's territory when they impressed upon agricultural labourers in Southern England that they, too, had everything to gain from lower bread prices; they even assured farmers that they stood to benefit more from selling high-value foodstuffs to a prosperous industrial population than from keeping up the price of bread. True though this might be, campaigners did not even seek to understand the agriculturists' point of view; while sincere in their opinions, they over-emphasized the benefits of 'untaxed bread' as much as their opponents the innocuousness of the corn law. But though numbers might be evenly matched, the Anti-Corn-Law League commanded the greater talent; its invective, though violent, kept skilfully on the right side of the law. Day in, day out, within and outside Parliament, it preached the repeal of the corn duties.

Its success came in 1846. Not because the country as a whole had as yet been persuaded; an emergency fortuitously tipped the balance. Parliament at Westminster was responsible for the administration not only of Britain, but also of Ireland, which at the time formed a customs union with the remainder of the British Isles. The Irish peasants' basic diet consisted of the potato, a plant which of all the staple foodstuffs has the shortest gestation period. Potatoes of the cheap variety cultivated by the Irish are liable to pests, and one such destroyed the 1845 crop and threatened Ireland with a famine of unprecedented proportions in 1846. All harvests were bad that season; only by buying corn as cheaply as scarcity permitted wherever it could be obtained and rushing it to Ireland could the government avert wholesale disaster. Duties would have enhanced the cost; wheat imported into Ireland could not be kept out of Britain. The Duke of Wellington inelegantly attributed the repeal of the corn laws to 'those rotten potatoes'. But without the constant burrowing of the Anti-Corn-Law League, the walls might have withstood even that blast.

The repeal of the corn laws exposed British agriculture to the cold winds of foreign competition—or so British farmers thought. For the time being they were wrong. Corn and flour imports increased from 4·8 million quarters in 1846 to 11·9 million in 1847, settling down to an average 10 million quarters a year for a decade before rising again. Given the need to feed the rapidly growing population adequately, repeal had come only just in time.

But shipping of corn over long distances, though feasible, was not as yet cheap; while British farmers no longer enjoyed tariff protection, the cost of transport had the same effect. Britain needed all the corn she produced, as well as what she imported. Having repealed the corn laws, the government felt that it owed agriculture compensation. It judged correctly that what British agriculture suffered from was lack of capital—that capital for which industry had successfully competed. So the government financed a scheme of State aid to agriculture by means of capital loans on favourable terms. Its success was surprising and sustained, so much so that, when the State scheme ended, commercial investment companies took it up as a private venture. Agriculture, no longer starved of capital, shed Cinderella's rags.

What agriculture did with the capital put at its disposal was sensible rather than spectacular. Though it experimented with new ideas, with reaping and mowing machines and steam ploughs, with imported fertilizer, the scale of the innovations remained small. Of far more importance was the general spread of improvements which had been known for at least half a century, the extension of drainage, the erection of better buildings to house produce and livestock. The difference between the best and the worst farm narrowed considerably; fewer cultivators lagged behind the standard generally accepted as desirable. The third quarter of the nineteenth century has been described as 'the age of high farming'. This signifies farming with an eye to maximum yields from the scarce factor of production. Agriculture in different territories is subject to different scarcities; in an island like Britain, with a limited surface, some unsuitable for cultivation, much dedicated to other uses, the scarce factor is land. High farming in the British context implied apportioning capital and labour so as to work for the highest yield per acre of farm land— a very profitable pursuit, always providing producers could be sure of a sale for all their output. In the third quarter of the nineteenth century they needed to have no fears on that account.

Agriculture after 1850

Agriculture in the third quarter of the nineteenth century brought prosperity to the British farmer. Much of it, via rent payments and the rise in land values, spread to landlords. It failed conspicuously to bestow similar blessings on the third partner in the agricultural trinity, the labourers. Why had they been left out? Primarily because there were too many of them. We have previously referred to the rhythm of agriculture which requires a larger labour force at peak time than it can keep busy all the year round. Farm hands employed during the harvest cumbered villages at other times, offering services which nobody wanted. Public opinion held that they should move to the towns where employment awaited them. This happened in the North and Midlands where farmers had to raise wages in step with the general level of prices lest they lose all their labour to industry. Agriculture in Southern and Eastern England was far from industrial areas; nobody but the farmers were likely to employ labourers whose wages consequently did not keep pace with rising prices. As regards accommodation, agricultural labourers fell between two stools: their employers who, if anybody, had reasons to keep them contented, were farmers, whereas responsibility for the erection and upkeep of their cottages lay with the landlord. Cottages, especially in the South, were a disgrace; though housing in the country, owing to the smaller numbers involved, never became the scandal into which it degenerated in towns, house for house the rural cottage was often considerably worse than its urban counterpart. Agricultural workers and their wives had augmented their wages by spare time occupations. One by one these now fell victims to the march of progress: the ironmonger in the nearest town stocked many of the commodities which village blacksmiths had hitherto supplied; textile factories made cheaper and better fabrics than the cottage industry; even bread and beer now became articles of large-scale production.

Inexorably the net closed on Hodge and his family. Undesirable forms of peak labour made further inroads on his livelihood: agricultural labour gangs, mobile forces of women and children hired out by a contractor who paid them by the hour, but was himself remunerated per job, became the rule in East Anglia until legislation impeded and eventually stopped them in the 1860s. Of the more energetic agricultural labourers, many had made their escape, into railway building when the iron roads were laid into the countryside, or by emigration. But this required a good deal of initiative. Those who remained were usually too much weakened and dispirited by bad conditions to discover a way out. Nor could they educate their children to different pursuits; no schools existed in the countryside where these could have learnt something better.

Not until the 1870s did agricultural workers find the answer to their plight: combination. Local attempts at organization had been pursued in the late 1860s, but the successful move came in 1872 in Warwickshire where Joseph Arch formed a union and by means of a strike obtained a minimum wage for his fellow workers. Arch had two advantages as a leader: he was no ordinary labourer, but a skilled hedgecutter, who could not easily be replaced; as a Methodist lay preacher, he knew how to address and handle men. For two years a national union, sprung from Arch's Warwickshire movement, counted 100,000 labourers among its membership and achieved some improvements, carried on an undercurrent of public sympathy. But in 1874 it suffered a serious reverse, when union members were locked out by their employers all over the country as the result of the Suffolk branch demanding a 1s. a week rise in wages. The agricultural workers' defeat did not put an end to the union, but it remained under a cloud for a number of years. Of all kinds of labour, agricultural is one of the most difficult to organize, because of its dispersal in small numbers over many farms which cannot be picketed in disputes; at least for some of the less skilled jobs, strike breakers are easily recruited. But what really defeated the union were not these permanent features of agricultural employment. It was the date at which it had tried to improve wages. By 1874 the great agricultural depression had started.

Farmers up to the middle nineteenth century had been a self-reliant community. Economically they depended of course on the townsfolk to whom they sold their produce and from whom they bought what manufactured goods they needed, but as regards their work they stood alone. Over the next hundred years this self-sufficiency yielded to an ever greater dependence on a variety of outsiders who brought scientific and technical knowledge to bear on the production of agricultural commodities. Liebig, a German, studied the connection between soil composition and plant nutrition, laying the foundations of agricultural chemistry. One of his British disciples, Sir John Lawes, in 1834 acquired Rothamsted, an estate which he soon turned into the first agricultural research station, and in 1843 it acquired a chemical laboratory. Artificial fertilizers were discovered and applied, making yields rise beyond the dreams of even the most optimistic Anti-Malthusians. In the wake of chemists and biologists followed pathologists who studied and eventually eliminated most plant diseases, evolving strains which resisted infestation. On parallel lines, veterinary science in the latter part of the nineteenth century conquered many livestock diseases which had decimated herds in earlier decades. Engineers added their contribution. Not until a machine had been designed in the 1840s for the mass production of cylindrical clay pipes did underground drainage of agricultural land become cheap enough to be applied on a large scale. Men with experience of industrial machinery re-designed and produced agricultural implements the shape of which had undergone little change since the days of the New Testament. Threshing and winnowing machines, though known in the eighteenth century, had hardly been used. A number of British engineering inventions reached British agriculture via the United States, reapers among them; mechanical ploughs also came in the 1850s, mowers in the 1860s, combine harvesters still later. They substituted horse power and steam, in the twentieth century even petrol and oil engines, for man-power. Architects designed improved farm buildings, constructing them with the use of materials not known in earlier times. From being a solitary fighter in the battle of food production, the farmer turned into a frontline soldier supported by a whole host of specialist reconnaissance and intelligence troops.

Among these supporting forces must be counted the State. Education, training, research and encouragement were the fields in which it helped agriculture. The English Agricultural Society, founded in 1838, enjoyed royal patronage from 1840 onwards; it began in 1839 the issue of a journal and the practice of holding shows to record and publicize agricultural achievements. The first agricultural college was opened at Cirencester in 1845; its successors at the end of the century obtained their finances from public funds. Drainage and other capital improvement loans which the State made available in the two decades after the repeal of the corn laws have already been mentioned. Experimental stations and laboratories multiplied in the twentieth century; universities opened agricultural departments. Agricultural advisers paid by the government which put their services at the disposal of all farmers first made their appearance in the 1914–18 war. When it came to taxing and rating assessments, the State granted agriculture preferential treatment.

Though some of this State support had its roots in the middle of the nineteenth century, much dates from the periods of depression of which agriculture had more than its fair share. Its golden age terminated abruptly in the 1870s. A series of unusually bad harvests characterized that decade, but the cause of depression lay deeper. Heretofore, in years of bad crops, farmers had recouped on the swings of prices at least a certain amount of what they lost on the roundabout of volume, thus shifting to the shoulders of the consumers some of the impact of poor output. From the 1870s onwards, bad harvests ceased to have significance for the community, who made up from abroad any shortfall in home supplies of foodstuffs. The nightmare which had haunted farmers at the repeal of the corn laws had now become reality. Cheap deep-sea transport enabled growers of grain, not only in Central and Eastern Europe, but across the Atlantic and in India, to compete with British agriculture, preserving and freezing techniques the ranchers of America and the sheep graziers of Australasia to invade the British meat market. Already in the middle 1850s Britain had been the world's most substantial food importer, buying more than three-fifths of all butter, one half of all minor grains, one-third of all wheat and one-fifth of all meat which entered world markets. But then these purchases had supplemented home supplies; now they replaced them.

From the 1870s to the end of the century British agriculture attempted to adjust itself to the changed situation. From grain, where competition was earliest and fiercest, it switched to meat; there at least it retained a quality advantage. It intensified livestock farming, especially animals for breeding purposes, and established herd books. Hard-pressed even in this field when chilling techniques developed, it turned to vegetables, fruit and milk—lines depending on freshness in which the foreigner could compete only after the coming of aerial transport and quick-freezing at the close of the second world war. The shift to non-competitive fields helped to soften the blow; yet agriculture's loss can be measured by its share of national income which fell from 17 per cent in 1867–69 to seven per cent in 1911–13. It sustained a rearguard action, though by 1878 half the bread and a quarter of the meat Britain ate were of foreign origin. In 1900 Kipling could sing:

For the bread that you eat and the biscuits you nibble,
The sweets that you suck and the joints that you carve,
They are brought to you daily by all us big steamers,
And if any one hinders our coming, you'll starve.

Not until the outbreak of the first world war did this prophecy reverberate in the ears of the poet's contemporaries.

To the landowners' failure to retain political power, the repeal of the corn laws had borne eloquent witness. Socially they remained a distinct class at least to the end of the nineteenth century, with their own ways of life and their own sense of duties incumbent upon them. They continued hunting and shooting, as their wives continued distributing soup and blankets to the village poor and their daughters teaching in the Sunday schools. Depression reduced rents; most landowners could have obtained a better reward from their capital by investing in industry. Far from withdrawing from the land, large landlords extended their estates by purchasing any adjoining land which came into the market. By the 1870s an influential section of the public feared that land in Britain was rapidly becoming the monopoly of a few noble families. Of many remedies canvassed, land nationalization, as advocated by the American Henry George in the 1880s, was only the most radical; less extreme land reformers tried to turn into small-scale owners both tenant farmers and agricultural labourers; such was the idea underlying the Birmingham Radicals' slogan of 'three acres and a cow'. The government went some way towards supporting this agitation; it allowed strict covenants keeping land in a single family to be broken, if courts of law judged it to be in the public interest; it granted tenants increasingly stronger protection *vis-à-vis* landlords and pursued a policy of providing allotments for agricultural labourers. In this way it tried to check the 'drift from the land' which reduced the regular farm labour force in England and Wales from 937,000 in 1871 to 472,000 in 1938. But it was death duties rather than settlement policy which after 1918 broke up the large estates and had by 1960 made owner occupiers of

43

half the farmers of the country—almost a rebirth of the peasantry, were it not for the size of the holdings.

Even before the first world war, disturbances all over the world and the fear of food shortages had revived the market for agriculture. The war itself meant cutting imports to the irreducible minimum, giving the British farmer an implicit guarantee of sale for anything he produced, supplemented in the later war years by explicit price guarantees to encourage the growing of wheat and oats. The agricultural worker came into his own and had his wages regulated by the government to prevent a complete dwindling away of the labour force; women had to be recruited into agricultural work. In terms of output, all this effort added a mere 30 to the 125 days a year for which home produce in 1913 would have fed the British population. The State promised to maintain cereal prices and agricultural wages after the war, but the slump of 1921 prevailed upon the government to buy itself out of this promise. Prices and wages were left to drift, the latter until 1924, the former until the end of the decade, when over-production of most agricultural commodities in most countries assumed the proportions of a worldwide catastrophe. The return of protection in 1931 brought a change; in addition to tariffs, marketing boards were established in many branches of agriculture, associations of producers which had statutory powers to restrict output and maintain prices. They shared out what remained of the market in an economy generally short of purchasing power; they were less successful in increasing it. The lean years left their imprint on arable agriculture. Soil fertility deteriorated in many parts of many farms. Relying chiefly on livestock for their income, farmers lost through disuse their skill in arable cultivation. The agricultural share of the national income fell by 1939 to $3\frac{1}{2}$ per cent or slightly above.* The legacy of the interwar years faced agriculture with problems at the outbreak of the second world war which it had not encountered in 1914.

The lessons of the first world war might have been disregarded in the interwar years; they had at least not been forgotten. Agriculture in the second world war organized itself for

* This figure does not bear strict comparison with those quoted on p. 43, owing to the omission of Southern Ireland, a chiefly agricultural producer, from the national income figures of the United Kingdom.

effective action far more quickly and successfully than in the first. Much the same policies had to be applied: concentration on cereals which, owing to their bulk, would have required most shipping space to import; sharp reduction in the pig and poultry populations which competed with humans for cereal food; price guarantees, this time for most commodities; wage maintenance plus the drafting into agriculture of women, prisoners of war and for seasonal labour schoolchildren and anybody else who could be mobilized. In conjunction with price guarantees, the government every year fixed production targets, armed with powers to enforce them. The government carried this programme of annual reviews of prices and output for agriculture into the post-war period. The farming community remained mistrustful: having been abandoned to world competition after one war, would they not suffer the same fate after another? The government this time kept its promise. Ability to vary price supports as between commodities enabled it to evolve an overall policy, favouring certain outputs, discouraging others; the temptation lay in using it as a weapon to thrust upon consumers what some nutrition expert or other considered good for them rather than what they demanded. Against annual re-negotiation of guaranteed prices, the farming community stressed its need for long-term planning; subsidy changes in any one year had to be limited to give producers time to adjust to variations in policy. Britain stood committed to maintaining her agriculture at a substantial level, whatever its competitive strength in world markets. The price exacted from the taxpayer in subsidies was heavy and showed no tendency to lessen as the years rolled on, though the government could claim, with at least some plausibility, that it purchased for him as consumer a certain degree of three benefits: preservation of the countryside which provided not only food, but also health, recreation and a holiday area for the population at large, immunity from world food price fluctuations and independence of imports in the event of another war.

In two directions, British agriculture had made a new start between the wars: stimulated by government subsidies, it had taken up large-scale cultivation of sugar beet, and it had supplied increasing quantities of fruit and vegetables to bottling and canning factories. The government looked upon sugar beet chiefly as a measure to combat unemployment: it fitted well into the agricultural rotation and required much labour at times when other crops could spare it; what was left of the beet after the extraction of sugar made good cattle fodder. But the drain on the public purse was heavy; it went into refiners' rather than growers' pockets; among growers the large benefited more than the small. The policy had many critics whose voices were stilled only at the outbreak of war when the volume of sugar produced at home could be measured in terms of shipping space saved. There could henceforth be no doubt that sugar beet had become a permanent feature of the British rural landscape. Bottlers and canners preserved and eked out food supplies during the war; subsequently they were joined by quick-freezers. Agriculture discovered an unexpectedly large new market, but a market with distinct peculiarities of its own. Grading became essential so that customers, buying by description, knew what quality they would obtain. Not only quality, but standardization—all produce to be of similar colour, size, shape, taste and ripeness. It wanted supplies to be staggered seasonally so as to keep factories busy all the year round. Livestock raisers tapped a similar market, first chicken breeders, then others, when shop windows began to display their poultry and meat already cleaned, cut, roasted and transparently packed in quantities selling at standard prices. These processers put a farmer under contract to produce for them, guaranteeing to buy all his high-quality output; only the rejects had to take their chances through the customary outlets. In adjusting to this twentieth century type of demand, agriculture was relieved of its chief risks of sale, at the price of achieving a high and unvarying standard of output.

IV | INDUSTRY

Industrial Revolution: Labour-Saving Inventions

The key to industrial organization is power. Men work singly as long as the prime mover consists of human or animal muscles. Large numbers are not harnessed for combined production unless considerable economies result from working on a greater scale or their joint output exceeds the result of individual efforts, individually performed. Not until a source of power was discovered which moved wheels faster and farther than human exertion, was there any reason for British industry to change its traditional ways. Here and there, from the Middle Ages onwards, forces of nature had provided prime movers; hence wind and water mills ground corn, slit iron, fulled cloth and performed a number of similar simple operations. Such power however was at the mercy of capricious elements; its use, up to the middle eighteenth century, constituted the exception rather than the rule.

While industry adequately met consumers' demands, the incentive towards improvement remained weak. If shortages occurred, the rise in prices caused by the scarcity tempted producers and capital into the field; more men, using a larger volume of equipment, soon filled the gap, at the expense of resources in some branch of the economy whose output had proved less popular. Why, then, did any major improvement ever come about, either in the middle eighteenth century or at any other period? Partly because men's thinking changed: the habit of scientific reasoning spread. To say that manufacturers associated with scientists could be misleading; the most progressive manufacturers were scientists, as much at home in the laboratory as in the workshop where they scrutinized the methods of production employed by industry from time immemorial. Discussion in their societies and clubs turned as easily to a new method of bleaching as to the implications of the law of gravity. Driving them towards reform was their awareness that industry's traditional reaction to increased demand had ceased to satisfy current needs, though the reasons were not the same in all industries affected.

Industrial producers had started as independent craftsmen. They had bought their raw materials; by means of their own tools, they had transformed them into finished products for sale. The proceeds had remunerated the makers and paid for the purchase of further materials. Two phases in this cycle of production stand out as making disproportionate demands on the producer's time and talents: the purchase of raw materials and the sale of finished goods. A maker of fine cloth, for instance, using high-quality wool, had to know where sheep with suitable fleeces were reared and at what time of the year he would buy his wool on favourable terms. He would have to leave his loom for a long spell to inspect and buy his wool and carry it home. Sales imposed similar tasks, not if he produced for local consumption, but—to continue our example—high-quality cloth was sold in distant markets, much of it abroad. Goods would have to be displayed to prospective customers and prices ruling in different areas ascertained; if he concluded a bargain abroad, the seller would even have to be knowledgeable about foreign money, lest he lose on the roundabout of currency exchange what he had gained on the swings of the transaction.

Marketing experience, both of raw materials and finished goods, could be acquired, but at considerable sacrifice to craftsmen whose skill consisted in the making of goods; the weaver wanted his time to be spent at his loom, not in a search for either the most suitable wool or the most profitable outlet for his cloth. If these indispensable, but troublesome stages of industrial life could be performed by specialists, he would remain free to devote his full energy to the job he did best, that of actual manufacture. Even in the Middle Ages, to an increasing extent in subsequent centuries, the economy required not only craftsmen who produced, but merchants who procured their materials and effected their distant sales. These functions were distinct and specialized; they entailed more than ordinary business risks, rewarded by opportunities of unusual gain.

Once a craftsman bought his materials from a merchant specialist and sold his output to another, he lost touch, both with the sources of his materials and the consumers of his products; unless he continued to do at least a certain amount of purchasing

from the one and selling to the other direct, he would in the end
not even know any more whence his material came or whither his
output went. The specialists on whom he relied became indispensable to him. His independence suffered even further
jeopardy, if the merchant who bought the raw material also sold
the finished goods. He would hardly exact money for the materials, only to pay back as much and more as soon as these materials,
converted into goods, returned to his keeping. Far simpler to
give credit for the materials to be set off against what he paid for
the finished article. Legally, this system of accounting merely
simplified the money part of the transaction without varying the
relationship between independent contracting parties. Yet it
meant that a merchant now supplied a producer with a quantity
of material to be turned into saleable merchandise at a remuneration equal to the difference between the value of the goods in the
raw and in the finished state. In other words, in economic reality
the merchant had become an employer paying a piece rate to a
worker for an agreed job to be performed. Industry, instead of
being practised by independent craftsmen, had begun to differ-
entiate between men who worked and men who gave out work.

The development was hastened where industries employed
complicated and expensive equipment. Craftsmen had not the
means, nor often the desire, to own a shipyard, a glass casting
hall or a coal mine, sometimes not even a weaving loom or a
stocking-frame. Technical progress over time raised the cost of
equipment in more and more industries, helping the system to
spread. In such trades, it became customary for the financially
more substantial employer to own the apparatus and for the
craftsmen to hire or use it on agreed terms. This fastened the
fetters of dependence more securely to the producer's wrists; he
had ceased to be even the proprietor of his tools of trade.   A
mere worker, he provided only labour and received a fixed
remuneration in return.

The system under which a man performed work on another
man's materials for an agreed remuneration has become known
as the 'domestic system'. The description is regrettable because
it stresses an unessential feature, the place where work was
performed. Textile, metal-using and a number of other trades
employed techniques which did not call for separate workshops;
producers laboured in their own cottages. When it came to

mining, shipbuilding or agricultural work, the misnomer is more obvious: these jobs could not be performed in a setting of domesticity; yet the system was applied to them. Essentially it meant that the employer 'put out' work to be performed by another. The latter assumed the risk of production: he received payment only in proportion to the quantity and quality of finished goods which he delivered up. 'Putting-out system' therefore describes the character of the arrangement more adequately than 'domestic system'.

Though the putting-out system can be traced back to the beginning of modern times, spread progressively in industry up to the eighteenth century and has not disappeared entirely even in the twentieth, it never became all-embracing. Where a producer could buy his materials or sell his output locally, he had a strong incentive to retain his independence. When material was too expensive to be entrusted to labouring men to take home, as in the case of gold, silver and silk, the employer had the work done under his own roof in order not to surrender custody of his property. He sometimes adopted the same method for the finishing of goods put out in the earlier phases of manufacture; once they had reached the stage of saleable commodities, he wanted to run no risk of their being embezzled by dishonest workers. The method of production of some articles, notably firearms, required a coordinated effort because components had to fit accurately, when assembled. If manufacture required a multiplicity of hands working under single management on large-scale equipment, such as in a soap-boiling or sugar-refining establishment, a chemical or iron works, it could be undertaken by a partnership, but as often as not a master hired journeymen on an agreement which constituted a contract of employment in law as well as in economic reality. The putting-out system itself proliferated a variety of arrangements, some regulating the use of equipment, others concerned with modes of calculating and effecting payment. The system signifies the principle governing production, while affording scope for a multitude of differing details.

The system's chief advantage from the employer's point of view consisted of the freedom he enjoyed. He had no fixed costs, no establishment to keep up; if trade were bad and he could see no prospects of sale, he gave out no work, hence had nobody to pay. Nor was he tied to particular producers, but picked and chose at will, exercising his preference in the direction of the most highly skilled craftsman or the lowest rate of pay. Where his income derived not only from trading profits, but also from equipment hired out to men working on his materials, he maximized the flow of rent tributes into his coffers by spreading employment over as many producers as possible.

On the other hand, much of his time and energy had to be spent distributing materials among, and collecting finished goods from, workers dispersed over a large area or having these errands performed at his expense. The quality of work done without any supervision often left much to be desired; methods of controlling it were difficult to devise. Nor could he be certain of the work being completed when he called; a man labouring on his own and remunerated merely in proportion as he handed over finished goods worked at his own speed. He might even have found an opportunity of serving another employer, hence be unwilling to accept the job which the merchant came to put out. Moreover, men had to live while they laboured. Embezzlement of goods entrusted to their custody constituted a perpetual temptation to workers not entitled to payment until they had completed an assignment. Alternatively, the employer had to advance money on account. Hence merchants needed to incur credit risks which grew in proportion to the circle of men employed.

Workers had reason to bless the putting-out system for providing them with employment which they could not otherwise have obtained; this must have been particularly true of many producers of high-quality goods necessarily destined for distant sale. Capital costs of equipping himself would have barred many a gifted craftsman from the trade of his choice, had not the merchant employer bridged the gap for him. Moreover, whatever his economic reliance on the merchant, the worker remained an independent craftsman in the conduct of his life. On any one day he chose to work or not to work at his trade, to limit the number of hours he devoted to his job, to spend some of his time growing food, drinking or gambling. He laboured alone or employed members of his family; he could even hire journeymen if the work and the state of his purse warranted it.

Irregular working hours may have served to buttress the worker's conviction that he remained his own master. They could not have been good for health, neither his own nor that of those who assisted him, least of all that of his children. Nor were the results of irregular work edifying; irregular output implied irregular payment. This did not matter to workers with adequate resources, but where employers had to extend credit, workers became demoralized by a state of permanent indebtedness; every time they received payment, the advances already obtained had to be deducted, so that their earnings did not suffice to keep them going without new credit until next settlement day. An employer or his agent who had hired out equipment would give preference to craftsmen who paid him rent; this discouraged men from preserving their independence to the extent of purchasing their own equipment. Because the rent recipient saw his advantage in spreading employment thinly over the largest possible number of workers, men did not suffer so much from unemployment as from under-employment; everybody had something to do, but except at times of good business, nobody had enough.

In industries organized on putting-out lines, labour costs rose in the eighteenth century, partly because of the abuses to which the system lent itself, partly because it left workers free to pander to their natural disinclination for hard work. Up to the third quarter of the eighteenth century, as we saw in discussing agriculture, food prices and the cost of living remained stationary or declined; just before the middle of the century the fall was quite steep. A drop in the cost of living enhances the worker's purchasing power, provided his earnings remain unchanged. He can use this incremental benefit to buy either more goods or more leisure, the latter by reducing his working effort; economists describe this inclination as 'leisure preference', though eighteenth century pamphleteers called it by less squeamish names. Once they and their families had an adequate supply of the necessities of life, workers had good reason to prefer leisure to commodities, because contemporary industry did not produce many consumption goods to tempt them. Strong drink there was always in abundance, but as its large-scale consumption soon impaired earning capacity, purchasing power exerted in this manner proved self-liquidating. Textile and other employers tried to obtain undiminished output from workers whom the putting-out system left free to reduce their efforts; the attempt sent labour costs soaring. Industries could meet consumers' demand only at an ever-increasing expense—in unfavourable contrast with the general price level. This dilemma could be resolved only by innovations economizing in labour.

We cannot trace labour-saving inventions in every industry afflicted with the putting-out system; the example of textiles must suffice. The most glaring disproportion existed: weaving was men's work, women spun, children prepared the material. This family division of labour would have worked satisfactorily, had not a single weaver used as much yarn as three or four spinners could provide, reducing weavers who lacked an adequate number of female dependants to the necessity of employing unattached spinners (spinsters) to make up the deficiency. Logically, therefore, the industry called for an innovation in spinning technique. But history is not always logical. The first major invention did not affect spinning, but weaving; it was the flying shuttle which John Kay, a Bury cotton weaver, patented in 1733. A shuttle is a wooden box containing the weft, threads which pass under and over the warp, yarn tautened across the loom to provide the basis of cloth; broadcloth had hitherto needed two weavers, one to throw the shuttle across, the other to return it. Kay attached to the shuttle a weight which returned it by gravity, dispensing with the second man, doubling a weaver's output and proportionately increasing his need for yarn as well as improving the quality of the cloth. The effect on the industry would have been greater, had not weavers countered the threat to their livelihood by smashing flying shuttles wherever they appeared, so that Kay went in fear of his life and eventually died a poor man. Yet a speed-up of spinning was badly needed and came in the middle 1760s when James Hargreaves' jenny enabled a cotton spinner to spin six to seven threads simultaneously, where hitherto she had spun only one. The spinning jenny underwent subsequent modification until the number of threads spun in a single process rose to 80. Its yarn proved too soft for the warp, but suitable for the weft.

Neither the flying shuttle nor the spinning jenny were revolutionary inventions; while increasing the productivity of their operators, they remained gadgets rather than machines, designed for use in cottages where these trades had traditionally been plied. The next spinning invention, Arkwright's frame, took the industry out of the cottage into the mill; it was a machine which proved too heavy for human motive power and had to be driven by a water wheel. Arkwright may have invented or merely stolen from the real inventors the principle of spinning by rollers rotating at different speeds; his name became attached to the water frame which he turned into a great commercial success after 1771. It spun threads unsuitable for high-quality cotton textiles, but adequate for the warp of cheap calicoes, for which a linen thread had hitherto been used; Arkwright's innovation therefore signified the first introduction to England of cloth made entirely of cotton and the emergence of cotton as the most important and prosperous of the country's industries for a century. Not only did the frame require water power; cotton manufacture used much pure water free from lime. These combined water requirements located spinning mills where water of the quality demanded fell steeply enough to provide a head: the river valleys of North Lancashire, Cheshire and Derbyshire, at the time a remote and under-populated region.

If Kay and Hargreaves had sketched a mere preface to the Industrial Revolution in cotton textiles, Arkwright wrote the introduction. Yet while transcending the strength of human exertion, his frame depended on a traditional source of power. The Industrial Revolution of the eighteenth century derived eminently and decisively from steam. Not until James Watt had perfected a steam engine to drive productive machinery, could that revolution transform cotton manufacture. This happened in 1778. Samuel Crompton invented the mule, a cross between a jenny and a frame. Steam-driven mules rendered spinners independent of water power and the inconvenient locations which it dictated; the source of energy now being coal, mills established themselves on the Lancashire coalfield.

Successive inventions had speeded up the production of yarn to a degree where it exceeded the capacity of the industry's weaving sector. Such was the scarcity of workers that, though it had traditionally been a men's preserve, now women invaded it, at least for the coarser grades of textiles. The last 20 years of the eighteenth century are known as 'the golden age of the fine handloom weavers', the period when their skill commanded a scarcity price. It did not last long. In 1785 Edmund Cartwright had invented a 'weaving engine', as the first power-loom was called. Cartwright, an ingenious man, had done it for a bet; his invention required 20 years of improvements before it became fit for practical work, quite apart from the violent reactions of the weavers. When in the 1830s it conquered one Lancashire weaving shed after another, the cotton industry had undergone a radical industrial revolution.

Machinery transformed the worsted and woollen industries much more slowly. The reason is partly mechanical: the woollen fibre, being softer than the cotton one, cannot withstand the same degree of strain; a machine must reach a higher standard of perfection before it can work on wool. The long-stapled combed fibres employed for worsted yarns could be mechanically spun and woven earlier than short-stapled wool. But woollens were also a much older industry, hampered by guilds and their restrictive legislation, all aiming to preserve traditional methods, exclude innovation and prevent men from outgrowing their competitors. Not until the middle of the nineteenth century did the woollen industry reach the stage of mechanization which characterized cotton by the 1830s.

Industrial Revolution: Capital-Saving Inventions

Revolution overtook some industries because their labour costs had risen too far. It engulfed others whose labour costs had undergone no noticeable change. Here other causes were at work to bring about reorganization, causes of a technical rather than economic nature. In its development, an industry may reach a stage where further expansion cannot be achieved on established lines, merely by increasing the scale of operations, but requires a new departure. Bottlenecks may be encountered, restricting freedom of movement, until the industry regains flexibility by adopting new methods of production. Agriculture for instance, hampered by the open-field system, changed to more intensive forms of cultivation which presupposed enclosure, thus achieving an output which neither more ploughs nor more farmers could have produced along traditional lines. In step with the revolution in industry, some writers have called this an agricultural revolution, but changes in agriculture were neither fast nor widespread enough to assume revolutionary proportions. More genuinely revolutionary was the transformation of inland transport by engineers who, instead of patching and mending rutted roads, embarked in the eighteenth century upon the making of modern surfaces, supplemented rivers by canals and in the nineteenth invented railways to displace stage coaches. This was indeed a revolution; we consider it in more detail below.

Revolutions occur in response to some pressing need, to prevent an industry's development from being stifled. Necessity may be the mother of invention, but some women remain sterile. In other words, while revolution occurs only as a consequence of need, not every need produces a revolution. Of muffled reaction to need, the coal industry affords a good example, all the better because it furnished the raw material on which the Industrial Revolution was based. Coal had been mined for centuries to warm dwellings and to produce heat required for cleansing wool, fulling and dyeing cloth and for some chemical processes. Deposits had been discovered where they outcropped on the surface, so that simple digging or tunnelling into the side of hills won the mineral, but long periods of working had exhausted the more accessible deposits, compelling miners to pursue the coal to lower layers. When in the eighteenth century shafts reached depths of 200 feet, problems of ventilation, lighting, drainage and transport arose. Gas is trapped underground; coal deposits harbour firedamp, a particularly inflammable type of gas. The industry failed to provide the improved system of ventilation needed to safeguard miners' lives. It achieved greater success in lighting the workings. Hewers had to be able to see; yet any kind of fire or spark entailed risks of explosion. Between 1813 and 1815, two inventors, Sir Humphry Davy and George Stephenson, independently hit upon identical solutions, the miners' safety-lamp.

Drainage as a problem was not confined to the coal industry; any type of mine reaching a certain depth encountered water intrusion, sometimes in proportions threatening to flood and drown the workings. Unless the water could be pumped away, it paralysed mining operations. Two engineers who had experienced this difficulty in the Cornish tin and copper mines had around 1700 devised machinery for keeping the water at bay; to Thomas Savery's pump Thomas Newcomen had added a 'fire' engine operating by means of atmospheric pressure. A steam pump of a kind existed therefore, a vertical cylinder containing a piston which moved up and down as the result of expansion and compression. To keep the engine working, the cylinder had to be alternately heated and cooled. Coal mines, with abundant fuel on the spot, found this no hardship, but it caused excessive expenditure to Cornish metal mines, far from any source of heat. It was in response to their need that James Watt made the first of the two great inventions associated with his steam engine by creating the condensation in a separate vessel which did not have to be heated and cooled in turn. This vastly improved the steam pump, even though for some time after its invention in 1765 it made its appearance alongside rather than in place of Newcomen's engine. Only the second of Watt's inventions, the conversion of reciprocating into rotary motion in 1781–2, put his steam engine into general rather then pumping service. The coal industry's last bottleneck, transport, had two aspects: mineral had to be moved laterally from the face to the pit bottom, then raised to the pithead. Primitive methods varied from wooden sledges dragged by men to pit ponies employed in the Newcastle coalfield in the middle eighteenth century; Scotland made use of women and youths to carry coal in baskets and other containers on their backs all the way from the face to the surface. Though rails were laid to facilitate the passage of tubs, underground transport of coal remained one of the most obstinate problems which the Industrial Revolution conspicuously failed to solve.

To make pig iron, ore had to be smelted in a blast furnace. A small sector of the industry, the ironfounders, made castings direct from the furnace, but cast iron was too brittle and hard for most uses. Where the metal had to be in a malleable state, it required fining in a forge. Wrought iron constituted the form in which the smith used the material; bar iron could be passed through rollers in a slitting mill and cut into rods for conversion into sundry iron products. The iron industry suffered from various difficulties throughout much of the eighteenth century. Though iron ore deposits were plentiful, providing an adequacy of raw material, much British ore could not compete in quality with Swedish mineral. The operation of bellows and hammers depended on water power; this precarious source of energy entailed irregularity of working. Each stage of manufacture required the heating of metal to a very high temperature, because it could be worked only in a molten state. Charcoal (wood heated in special kilns) alone could be used for the purpose because the impurities contained in mineral coal combined with the metal and spoilt it. This rendered the industry dependent on timber of which only certain types made good charcoal. Above all, this was a transport problem; if timber had to be carried over distances in excess of ten miles, fuel costs made iron production uncompetitive with the imported product from Sweden. Timber can be replaced by reafforestation, but this is a long-term policy which affords no relief in the short run. However favourable the location of their furnaces, ironmasters sooner or later exhausted the timber supply within reach of their works and then had to move on in search of convenient areas. From the Weald of Sussex and Kent where the industry had been situated in the sixteenth and seventeenth centuries, it had shifted to the as yet luxuriant forests of the Midlands (Cannock Chase, Shropshire) early in the eighteenth; though abundantly supplied with fuel, these locations created difficulties in transport, communications and labour supply and saddled the industry with increasing production costs. Ordnance orders kept it going, but the combined effects of foreign competition, irregularity of power supplies and difficulties of keeping within economic distance of fuel resources put severe limits on its profitability.

Abraham Darby had actually had success in smelting with coke at the end of the first decade of the eighteenth century. Working at Coalbrookdale in Shropshire, he took advantage of a particularly suitable type of coking coal mined locally, smelting in a very tall furnace with an unusually powerful draught. Pig iron made by Darby's method could be satisfactorily cast, but not fined. As a Quaker, Darby refrained from boasting; as a business man, he did not advertise his discovery to his competitors. Deprived of his particular local advantages, these might anyhow not have been able to emulate his example. However that may be, not until the middle of the eighteenth century did the industry as a whole become aware of the possibility of smelting by means of mineral fuel. When the new process became general, blast furnaces and foundries left the woodlands and moved towards coalfields, sources of the new fuel. In general use cast iron, cheapened by the new smelting method, was substituted to some extent for wrought iron. This happened at the time of the Seven Years' War (1756–63) which greatly stimulated the whole industry and revived it from a long spell of depression. Experiments continued at Coalbrookdale to adapt mineral fuel to fining, the branch of the iron industry which had remained dependent upon charcoal. Some success attended these efforts in the middle 1760s, but the real breakthrough came with the puddling process, discovered by Henry Cort 20 years later, wherein the metal was stirred throughout fining, thus oxidizing the impurities. When forges had at last been delivered from the thraldom of charcoal, they could join furnaces and foundries to form the integrated ironworks which characterized the modern industry. This revolution turned iron for the first time into a cheap commodity available for a variety of new purposes: elegant iron bridges spanned rivers, graceful iron balconies adorned Georgian houses. Machines, hitherto consisting of wood or leather with only their working edges made of metal, could now be constructed wholly in iron; this added much to the precision of their functioning.

This account of changes in a few industries illustrates that there never was a general Industrial Revolution to which we can assign precise dates. Transformation took place, assuming revolutionary proportions in some instances, remaining far more modest in others; a number of industries were completely untouched by it, among them one of the largest of all, building. The picture of British industry as it emerges in the middle nineteenth century is not one of a highly advanced and progressive branch of the economy, but of a large number of manufactures, all at different stages of development, some having passed through, others not even having entered upon, a revolution, while in yet others the process was in full swing.

For a few outstanding industries we have traced the course which revolution took and the inventors responsible for it. Yet this paints an unbalanced picture. Without the genius to whom the divine spark in a flash reveals the solution to an urgent problem, invention would never occur; without the *entrepreneur* at his elbow, it would never be translated into practice. Inventors of the day may have been as much at home on the production floor as in the laboratory; they rarely acquired equal familiarity with the counting-house. The inventor's share in progress can be presented in vivid hues. How unlike the drab story of the business partner who provided the wherewithal to pay for experiments, working models, patents, successful or otherwise, who had to risk capital in advance of knowing whether the invention could ever be put to commercial use! It took nine years to translate Watt's steam engine from the drawing-board to the first production model, much longer to establish its success, confound doubters, remedy imperfections, introduce it to potential users. A man lacking robust health and self-confidence, Watt would never have persisted, had it not been for the patient help, first of John Roebuck, but more particularly of Matthew Boulton, the man who believed in him to the extent of committing his whole fortune to Watt's success, adding his wife's when his own did not suffice. The spotlight of history plays on inventors, but their business partners have remained dim outlines in the background of the stage. Yet without their persistence, organizing ability, attention to detail and patience in taming volatile genius, few sparks would ever have turned to flame.

In industries which had undergone a revolution, the mode of work was radically transformed. On the day in 1771 when Arkwright opened his first water mill at Cromford in Derbyshire with 300 employees, the factory system was born. The man who had felt his own master under the putting-out system found factory discipline not only strange, but irksome beyond bearing. Few workers succeeded in bridging the gap; as craftsmen went out, a new generation manned the factories, men who had no experience of earlier working methods, no nostalgic regrets. But yet transition could not be frictionless; craftsmen did not die out as fast as machinery displaced them. The misery of the handloom weavers—which could be paralleled in nail making, razor grinding and a dozen other trades—bears witness to the hardship which the Industrial Revolution inflicted on those whom it failed to carry. Had they been eliminated at one blow, their sufferings would have been more acute, but less prolonged. Instead, manufacturers accepted all orders placed with them; the surplus with which machinery could not cope was sub-contracted out to craftsmen. Thus the latter in boom periods obtained a certain amount of employment and retained the illusion that they could survive; yet at other times they had no work. Moreover, to remain competitive, they had to lower prices in step with their mechanized competitors, regardless of the fact that the mechanical improvement which had lowered manufacturers' costs had not affected their own. If the Industrial Revolution had to be purchased at the expense of much suffering and deprivation, it was not because of its dramatic speed, but on the contrary because of the slowness with which it came.

The Reign of Steam and Steel

Steam, more than any other common denominator, had been the symbol of the Industrial Revolution; by harnessing its power, industries had substituted mechanical propulsion for human or animal energy. By the end of the eighteenth century, only a few industries had progressed far on this path. Steam's greatest triumphs belonged to the nineteenth, when on the one hand whole industries conformed to patterns traced by their pioneers, on the other steam power conquered entirely new fields; railways secured for overland transport pride of place among nineteenth century industries converted to steam. Once begun, mechanization ranged farther and farther. Electricity, introduced for lighting purposes in the early 1880s, occasionally powered the prime mover in the 1890s, hampered by the large size of generating equipment required. Not until the coming of steam turbines of moderate dimensions around 1910 was this form of power more generally adopted, and the first world war hampered its spread. Up to the 1920s, steam remained king.

The Industrial Revolution had relied on steam for power and looked to iron as a material, substituting it for wood, leather and non-ferrous metals when technical progress diversified and cheapened its use. King iron, however, reigned more briefly than king steam; in the second half of the nineteenth century, his sceptre passed to steel. Up to that time, steel had been a very costly high-quality derivative of iron, used sparingly for cutting edges of tools, razor blades and other articles where quality counted more than cost. Converting haematite ore (that is, iron ore free from phosphorus) into high-quality bar iron, then heating it for another seven to eight days, produced shear steel of great tenacity. Not only did this process take much fuel and time, but ores of the requisite purity occurred in Britain only in two areas, Lancashire and Cumberland, neither endowed with very rich deposits; better haematite ores were imported from Sweden. In the 1740s, a clockmaker—the precision engineer of his day—Benjamin Huntsman, had produced cast steel, harder

61

and more uniform in quality than shear steel, by melting it in crucibles, clay vessels within the furnace, but this did not cheapen the process. For 100 years no decisive improvement in steel-making followed Huntsman's; though more durable, tough and resilient than iron, steel was too dear to replace it in most uses.

The paper read by a metallurgist, Henry Bessemer, to the British Association meeting at Cheltenham in 1856 *On the Manufacture of Malleable Iron and Steel without Fuel* caused a major sensation. He did not mean it literally; his steel-making process did not dispense with fuel, merely with additional fuel. From the blast furnace, he ran the molten pig iron into a tipping vessel, known as a Bessemer converter, through which compressed gas could be forced, thus raising the temperature beyond levels previously attained. Not only did he substitute air pressure for fuel, saving fuel costs; though not without significance, this economy did not impress mid-nineteenth century Britain where coal was plentiful. He cut the process of steel-making from seven or eight days to half an hour, an enormous saving in production time. Yet contemporaries were in no hurry to adopt Bessemer's process. He was too good a business man to underestimate the value of his discovery; steelmakers considered his patent fees excessive. They found the quality of steel produced in the Bessemer converter disappointing. Above all, Bessemer's process succeeded only where pure haematite ore was used; he himself had made his experiments on such ores, and patentees using phosphoric ores suffered failure. The initial sensation past, steelmakers continued along traditional lines. Bessemer found it very difficult to shake their unadventurous attitude. To prove his invention, he set up his own steel works at Sheffield. For a period of 14 years this enterprise yielded a 100 per cent profit every two months, convincing his fellow steelmakers that he could substantiate his claim. In 1859 John Brown, a famous Sheffield firm, adopted Bessemer's process; the army ordnance switched over to Bessemer steel in 1863; railways made their first experiments with steel rails in 1864.

Even before Bessemer had achieved full recognition, another discovery had taken steel-making a stage further. It came from William Siemens, member of a famous German family of engineers and inventors, who had settled in Britain because of his dissatisfaction at the inadequate protection afforded to ingenuity by the patent laws of the various German States. He first used in 1857 the regenerative furnace—a method of heating in which he substituted, for solid fuel, gases made from inferior fuels and re-circulated inside the furnace at ever higher temperatures. This dispensed with closed crucibles and left the steel exposed; Siemens' furnace was known as an 'open hearth'. Not only was the quality of the product higher than Bessemer's, but inspection enabled it to be controlled and accurately proportioned to the intended purpose, avoiding the expense of a higher grade steel than the customer needed. Siemens' method achieved economies not only of fuel; it enabled the re-use of iron and steel scrap by re-melting and substituting it for scarce iron ore up to a maximum of 80 per cent. Compared to Bessemer's, the open-hearth process suffered from only one disadvantage: it extended the time of steel-making from half an hour to six or eight hours. But Siemens found British industry no more enterprising than Bessemer had done. To introduce to steelmakers the open hearth, he too had to join their ranks, establishing a regenerative furnace in South Wales in 1869. Two years earlier the railways had consented to an experiment: along the customary iron rails, the Great Western Railway laid steel rails outside Paddington Station where all would be subjected to equal wear. When 11 years later both sets of rails were taken up, the steel rails had survived the test in very much better shape than the traditional ones; thereafter all permanent way replacements substituted steel for iron. Railway workshops had meanwhile adopted open-hearth steel in 1868; the first merchant vessel made of this material took the sea in 1877.

These discoveries still left a fortune to be claimed by the man who could remove the last stumbling-block on the path to really cheap steel by making ordinary phosphoric iron ore available for steel manufacture. That this had to be the next step on the road of progress was well-known to the industry as a whole; yet metallurgy owed the discovery not to a professional, but to a spare-time amateur who earned his living as a police-court shorthand writer. Sidney Gilchrist Thomas, with the assistance of a chemist, his cousin Percy Gilchrist, in 1879 invented the basic process. 'Basic' is the name which metallurgists give to a heat-resisting material rich in metallic oxides.

Thomas lined his furnace with basic bricks; to keep this lining intact, he added more basic, silica of limestone, to the metal during the heating. The basic dephosphorized the material, leaving steel as pure as any of the other (acid) processes had done. This discovery was not an alternative, but an addition to Bessemer's and Siemens'; either Bessemer's converter or Siemens' open-hearth or his subsequent electric furnace could be so lined, so that henceforth steel, classified according to methods of manufacture, could not only be Bessemer or open-hearth steel, but also acid or basic steel.

Foreign rather than home steelmakers extended a whole-hearted welcome to the new invention. In the 1870s and 1880s, westward progress enabled the United States to open up iron ore deposits of a richness unparalleled in the world which the basic process made available for steel-making. Germany had wrested from France in the 1870–1 war the minette fields of Lorraine, another source of phosphoric iron ore; Gilchrist Thomas' invention enhanced a hundredfold the value of the prize. Both the United States and Germany, as a result of this British invention, in the early 1890s overtook Britain in steel-making. British industrialists proved as lethargic over basic as they had done over Bessemer and open-hearth steel. Its quality did not match that of acid steel. Though Britain had by this time worked her own haematite ores to the point of near-exhaustion, the industry had provided against a shortage of raw material by investing extensively in non-phosphoric ore deposits in Spain and Sweden and establishing transport links to those fields; it deprecated developments which detracted from the value of these investments. Only 17 per cent of British steel was produced by the basic method in 1901; it needed the cutting of shipping lanes in the first world war to bring home to British steelmakers the debt of gratitude which they owed to Gilchrist Thomas.

Steam providing power, ferrous metals the chief materials, these were the characteristics of nineteenth century technology. But neither of them alone nor even their combination could have given industry an uplift comparable to that which it had experienced in the later eighteenth century. The significant and peculiar contribution to industrial development of the period from the middle nineteenth century to the interwar years was the coming of mass production. This meant a change in the nature of machinery. The machines which men like Watt, Crompton or Arkwright had invented assisted in achieving with greater accuracy, ease and dispatch operations hitherto performed by hand. They helped, but did not displace skilled craftsmen; at most, they enabled them to dispense with unskilled assistants. The human hand remained employed to feed machines with raw materials, to guide operations, to effect quick repairs where a machine tore or broke the stuff on which it worked. In speaking of a skilled workman, people no longer meant a craftsman whose hands deftly fashioned beautiful or intricate patterns, but a man able to operate and service with a minimum of interruption and breakdowns delicate and complicated machines. To this new type of skilled man, the machine, far from being a substitute, acted as an auxiliary. His output of standard pattern goods was greatly increased by this helpmate which reinforced his muscles by the power of steam, but it had not nearly reached proportions of mass production. This needed machinery capable of acting on its own, operating autantically and fed mechanically, machinery to which the worker was no longer operator and manipulator, but merely supervisor. Steam and steel were well adapted to provide such machinery, but it required a new technology to construct it.

When Boulton and Watt undertook to supply a machine to a customer, they sent it with an engineer who supervised the erection, demonstrated the operation and did not return to the makers until he had satisfied himself that the customer's employees had learnt how to work it and to effect minor repairs. If a major fault developed, however, whether the machine had been erected in the proximity of their Soho works, in London or in far-away Cornwall, there was no help for it: an engineer from the makers had to travel to the place, because they alone had detailed knowledge of machinery of their manufacture; if a component had broken or worn out, the replacement could be made only by the factory responsible for the original machine. This was no peculiarity of Boulton and Watt; up to the middle nineteenth century the whole engineering industry worked on this basis.

For progress towards automatic machinery to be made, this possessive attitude of industry towards its product had to change. Far from each firm considering every machine it had made as its preserve on which no rival engineer might poach, there was need for standardization, if not of machines, then at least of components common to them all, of bolts, nuts, screws, hinges, shafts, cogs and the hundred and one parts which go into most machines. To be able to buy and fit spares on the spot in London, whether a machine had been manufactured at Birmingham, Newcastle or Glasgow, was an indispensable condition of the new technology —a condition which imposed unprecedented accuracy and precision. Standard output could be produced only by tools standardized themselves within narrow limits of tolerance. This was the message preached throughout the earlier nineteenth century by two far-sighted engineers, Henry Maudslay and his even more famous and eminent one-time employee, Joseph Whitworth. They did more than preaching; their own inventions showed the way. Maudslay improved lathes, especially the screw-cutting lathe, and invented the slide-rest; the measuring machine designed by him registered one ten-thousandth of an inch, a record bettered by Whitworth's which registered one two-millionth. To Whitworth the industry owed the achievement of perfectly plane surfaces; he it was who suggested in 1841 the standardization of screw threads, put into general effect by 1860. Maudslay and Whitworth were protagonists of a new industry making machines to make machines, the machine tool industry, which held the key to the new technology. By the end of the century, the initiative in many of its aspects had passed from British engineers to their transatlantic colleagues; apt pupils to begin with, they soon outstripped their masters. But our concern here is with the British side of the story.

Mass Production

Mass production suggests output of a standard commodity produced in a continuous flow on a very large scale. This flow implies the necessity for the article to move while it is being made and assigns a key rôle to transport in the course of production. The devices employed for this purpose, be it the endless belt, the Archimedean screw, the bucket conveyor or the crane travelling on overhead rails, were none of them new in the 1840s; some had been used for centuries, some in the recent past, though not necessarily in the service of industry. But industrialists now adapted them to purposes of flow production, turned them into standard devices of up-to-date industrial technique.

Nor did an assembly line constitute a novel departure, insofar as it could be a purely human line, grouping workers in the sequence in which they had to perform operations on a product which in the process of production passed from hand to hand. The novelty consisted in the combination of both techniques, of the human assembly line with the mechanical transport of the product, of arranging both machinery and workers in sequence of operations required while the commodity passed at a speed just sufficient for them to perform their own parts of the process before it moved on to the next stage. Manchester machine-tool factories which in the 1840s pioneered the new production technique went further: distances between work benches were calculated to afford each man just the requisite elbow-room, while eliminating all unnecessary portage from bench to bench; materials required were conveyed by trucks running on rails, obviating every superfluous effort on the part of the worker. As machinery and flow production acquired greater perfection in the twentieth century and self-acting machinery conquered further sectors of industry, more and more manufacturers could boast of standard outputs 'untouched by hand', be it of 50-gross cases of matches boxed and labelled, of loaves of bread coloured and flavoured to taste, sliced and wrapped, or of double-shell bath units, cast iron outside, enamel inside.

The scientific study of the working process, begun in the middle nineteenth century, reached a much higher stage around 1900. In *The Wealth of Nations* published in 1776, Adam Smith had illustrated by the example of a pin manufactory the division of labour. Although unaware of it, he had described the end of an era, division of labour between man and man; the division of the future then lay between man and machine. Now a new division of labour emerged, that between the man who worked and the man who told him how to work. To use abbreviated language, it was a division of labour between brawn and brain.

What had made a man the 'boss' of an industrial enterprise? Usually ownership, seniority or efficiency at the job. Any of these attributes might constitute a good reason for entrusting him with the organization of production; none furnished conclusive proof of his suitability for management, of ability not only to perform the work himself, but to lead other men in its performance. That this function required gifts not unlike those of a general in war, directed however to productive instead of destructive purposes, became gradually recognized. Around 1900 the fashion of scientific analysis spread in many fields: Alfred Marshall at Cambridge, the Austrian School on the Continent of Europe, reached heights of refinement in economics; Sigmund Freud plumbed the depths of the human mind. The industrial working process was subjected to similarly refined dissection, largely at the initiative of Americans, men like Frederick W. Taylor and Frank Gilbreth, who became known as work study specialists; a few years after the turn of the century, the invention of the motion camera brought visual evidence to their aid. If the movement of a man's working limb flowed easily and effortlessly, the performance could not be bettered; if it was ragged or hesitant, he misapplied his strength and skill and could do better if the operation were thoroughly examined and modified. New materials, especially steels hardened by adding alloys, enabled work study specialists to devise jigs, tools designed for the particular job in hand, instead of the all-purpose tools hitherto used. Work study aimed at conservation of strength: either undiminished output produced at a lower cost in exertion or undiminished effort rewarded by higher output. After each of two world wars it could achieve reintegration into industry of war-disabled men, provided job analysis pinpointed occupations in which their disabilities did not affect their competitive strength.

Work study was not the only function of the professional manager. Management itself became sub-divided: alongside the production manager, who had a bevy of foremen and progress chasers to assist him, appeared the chief of personnel, supported by a staff welfare organization, the financial director, relying on information made available by costing clerks and accountants, and a variety of specialist buyers, graders and designers. Outside experts could be put under contract to perform functions like designing or marketing, but the most successful concerns tried to have specialist staffs in all these fields.

Early industrialists had manufactured one article or a few commodities. In addition, they 'produced' a certain amount of refuse, waste which emerged in the course of manufacture and might assume embarrassing proportions, as did the tips of spoil disfiguring the landscape of mining areas. If possible, waste was disposed of or allowed to escape from working establishments as inconspicuously as possible: it might in the form of black smoke ruin housewives' washing over a wide area or as industrial effluent muddy and heat streams and poison fish; the refuse of certain metallurgical processes sterilized the soil and deadened vegetation for decades. The more responsible industrialists realized that such waste disposal deprived the community of amenities in the interests of private profit, but until science and technology had reached a certain level, amends were not easy to make. Even to less public-spirited manufacturers the idea occurred that in the shape of industrial refuse they were throwing away substances not needed for their own production, which yet might have value in some other use. Instead of removing them from their factories in whichever way proved least conspicuous, industrialists investigated what could be done with them. Soon 'waste' ceased to be an appropriate description; they became 'by-products', valued either by their own or some other branch of manufacture. From this change of outlook to the point where meat canners utilized 'every part of the pig but the squeal', development proceeded along a straight line punctuated by experiments, some of which proved abortive. Enthusiasm around 1850 for the uses of gas passing at pressure through a narrow channel led to the pleasing, though hardly epoch-making invention of the soda water syphon before finding a more important application in the Bessemer converter, but though successfully employed by an Edinburgh doctor in baking bread at record speed, neither Scottish nor any other palates tolerated the outcome. The coking of coal gave rise to a range of by-products which in subsequent industrial development threatened to engulf and displace the main output: gas, tar, chemical dyestuffs, oil. Slag yielded by the making of basic steel revealed itself as a major artificial fertilizer. Industrialists by these discoveries not only got rid of a great embarrassment, but opened up prolific sources of additional revenue.

Utilization of by-products improved the output side of an activity upon which we can look simply as a method of converting input into output. Curtailing unnecessary inputs, whether measured in materials, fixed capital or human effort, was an equally fruitful source of economy. The early industrialist kept books in a rough and ready manner, surveying stock in hand and cash till or banking account at the beginning of the year and again at the end to ascertain whether or not he had worked profitably. As industry grew more complex and each factory produced a greater variety of commodities, industrialists needed more detailed information; they wanted to ascertain, not only whether production paid as a whole, but whether every branch of their manufacture paid for itself; otherwise one department of their factory might unwittingly serve to subsidize another. Not only departmental accounts could be isolated, but investigation could elucidate whether any one component of a composite commodity ought to be produced on the premises or bought ready-made from an outside source, possibly a manufacturer who concentrated all his resources on the production of a single article, supplying users everywhere and therefore turning out quantities which justified installing the largest machinery available. Many industrialists in the twentieth century—motor-car manufacturers are the most conspicuous example—became little more than assemblers of parts prefabricated by a variety of specialist works. But before industry reached this stage of complexity, it had to create the apparatus which isolated and supplied the necessary information; cost accountants with their modern techniques of book-keeping and balancing established themselves as a new profession in the 1880s.

Industrial innovation depends on invention and discovery; the temptation is great to treat them as synonymous. But the inventor is rarely the man responsible for the invention from start to finish; more often, he represents the final link in a chain stretching from the man who first formulated the problem via those who experimented, but were baulked by some practical difficulty, those who, coming from different industries, suggested the application of known techniques to new fields, to the designer who put the solution on the drawing-board, but could not translate it into metal and wood or bricks and mortar. Up to the end of the nineteenth century, such men usually worked in isolation, often knowing, sometimes generously invited to utilize, each other's achievements; only in a few instances did isolation result in acrimonious disputes about the merits of particular discoverers. While no human contrivance can replace or provoke the spark which brings a long search to a brilliant conclusion, industrialists in the twentieth century realized the value of facilitating ignition. As science developed, discovery depended more and more on a multitude of systematic experiments, completely covering a field of possibilities—a form of research much less laborious to a team of scientists than to an individual working in isolation. So industry—the largest firms by themselves, the smaller manufacturers in cooperation—equipped laboratories and staffed them by groups of scientists, formulating problems to which they wanted answers. This was what the twentieth century termed 'the invention of inventions'.

Division of labour not only among workers, but among management specialists, an organization on a scale sufficiently diversified to take advantage of its by-products and of economies of size, works-owned laboratories employing teams of research scientists, all pointed to larger and larger industrial units. Whenever a boom stimulated activities, manufacturers competed for scarce raw materials and fuel; the incentive to secure supplies by establishing ascendancy over their owners led iron and steel producers to integrate the antecedent manufacturing stages of the metal and the coal mines into their enterprises by purchase, the film exhibitors to buy up distributors and producers. If on the other hand a slump paralysed business, manufacturers doubted the willingness of independent sellers to focus consumers' attention on their own product to the exclusion of rival commodities, especially if expert servicing was needed to keep customers satisfied. So shoe and sewing machine manufacturers, instead of selling through ordinary retail outlets, opened shops of their own; brewers possessed themselves of 'tied houses' which served only the proprietors' brands of beer. These are examples of vertical integration, a form of industrial combination bringing under unitary control various stages in the passage of a commodity from the raw state to the hands of the ultimate consumer. Its counterpart, horizontal integration, occurs when manufacturers performing similar operations or supplying competing commodities agree among themselves to restrict output, raise prices or impose identical conditions—usually on the purchasers of their goods, occasionally on the suppliers of their materials; the first instance in this country to become well-known, though by no means the first ever to achieve its purpose, occurred in the 1880s when 64 manufacturers of salt, controlling 90 per cent of the output, amalgamated into a union which quadrupled its price within two years. Such industrial concentration remained confined to a few sectors of the economy, but where it involved the production of an ever-increasing output of goods by an ever smaller number of productive units, it raised urgently twentieth century problems of industrial monopoly power and the function of the State as protector and champion of unorganized consumers. To keep within bounds monopolies and restrictive practices became one of the recognized duties of government in Britain; where combination had proceeded too far for competition to be re-established, nationalization was advocated as a means of ensuring that power would be wielded by responsible hands. Industrial agreements transcended even national boundaries; international combinations of producers prepared to do battle with States which disapproved of such monopolies.

The Old Staples

Around the middle of the nineteenth century, Britain led the world in several industries: first and foremost cotton and woollen textiles, but also coal, iron and steel, shipbuilding and engineering. These pillars of the British industrial edifice are often collectively described as the 'old staple industries'. The shapes and sizes of the pillars varied. Cotton claimed pride of place: in 1840, 50 per cent of the total value of British exports consisted of cotton goods; if woollens and worsteds are added, textiles in 1850 accounted for more than two-thirds of Britain's home-produced exports. Though demand for fuel grew in proportion to installed steam power, coal mining's period of maximum expansion had still to come. Railway and steamship construction was just stimulating the iron, and somewhat later the steel, industries to growth at an unprecedented rate. Shipbuilding has no claim to inclusion among the range of peerless British industries while wooden clippers dominated sea lanes, but steamships carried it to success in the 1860s and 1870s.

A category of old staples does less than justice to some industries, either because they are half in and half out or because a major industry of long standing does not share many of the characteristics which old staple industries have in common. The latter is the case of building and construction, developing along its own lines; though periods of greater and more limited expansion alternated, the phases rarely coincided with corresponding movements of industry as a whole. The more difficult instance is illustrated by engineering, once a single industry, but branching out into a variety of trades and skills from the later eighteenth century onwards, when contractors and builders established civil engineering. Diversification of tasks in the early nineteenth century made clockmakers and millwrights adopt the more modern designation of mechanical or constructional engineers; towards the middle of the century all-purpose mechanics specialized by becoming fitters or turners. Machine builders who had designed any type of machinery to each customer's specification, in the last quarter of the century limited their output to machinery for particular trades; in 1889 the Society of Telegraph Engineers gave recognition to its members' enlarged scope by re-christening itself the Institution of Electrical Engineers. Branches of engineering producing steam engines and railway equipment have every claim to be included among the old staples, whereas some of the most promising sectors, such as the construction of road vehicles and the production of electrical and gas equipment belong to the new industries of the later nineteenth and early twentieth centuries. A similar and in the long run no less important division applies to textiles: old staples continued to make use of traditional materials, whereas a wholly new industry arose on the basis of man-made fibres.

Most old staples produced capital or semi-finished goods, though a proportion of cloth went direct from the factory to household consumers and small quantities of coal heated domestic hearths. Staple industries, apart from coal mining, relied heavily on overseas materials, cotton exclusively, but even the woollen industry progressively, as British land originally devoted to pasture was put to other uses; by 1860 more than one half of all wool consumed in England came from overseas sources, Australia foremost among them. Equally was this reliance on overseas supplies true of iron ore using industries, their appetite for Spanish and Swedish haematite ores increasing; of all pig iron made in Britain in 1913, 50 per cent was smelted from imported ores. Old staple industries looked to other countries as furnishers of materials, but equally as customers for their products. Many of the staples, cotton above all, for three-quarters of a century found an easier sale abroad than at home and owed their expansion to foreign even more than to domestic demand. Only gradually did this apply to coal or ships, though it is worth recording as a historical curiosity that up to the late 1860s Prussian warships were built on Thamesside to the specification of the British Admiralty's chief constructor.

The old staples had grown up in an atmosphere of free competition; where associations of traders had existed, as for instance the Newcastle Coal Vend, effective transport in the form of railways had emasculated and ultimately destroyed them. It made coal mining the textbook example of a competitive industry, but in cotton spinning and weaving also the trend ran away from, not towards, combination. Units of production were controlled by individuals or partnerships; not until the last quarter of the century did staple industries adopt joint-stock organization on any scale. In textiles, the number of women workers exceeded that of men; all other old staples employed a high ratio of male to female labour.

All old staples continued to expand down to 1914, whether we use as an index their volume of output or the size of their labour force (the latter remained stationary in woollens and worsteds). Some grew faster than British industry as a whole, most of them at about the same rate; textiles increased rather more slowly. Wherever foreign countries industrialized, they always began by establishing their own textile industries, because cloth making lends itself to mechanization even in conditions of imperfect technology. British textile manufacturers experienced in foreign markets not so much the intrusion of successful rivals, but the increasing self-sufficiency of former customers, usually fostered by protective tariffs. The British woollen industry certainly owed its expansion after the 1860s to the steady growth of the home market alone; cottons, particularly handicapped where foreign competitors could locate mills alongside cotton fields, found themselves pushed out of the European market first of all, while after the American Civil War the United States produced her own piece goods. Colonization came to the industry's rescue by opening up large new markets in more distant territories. The minor textiles fared worse than cottons and woollens.

Comparison with foreign achievements at the Paris International Exhibition of 1867 generated a wave of misgivings and self-criticism in Britain, especially in the iron and steel industry, much of it not fully—or at least not yet—justified by the facts. The industry as a whole did not lose ground, though changes

74

within it served as danger signals for the future. British plant, expensive to erect, hence designed to last decades rather than years, had been constructed for the iron age; when users substituted steel for wrought iron, Britain lost orders. Whether it be Bessemer's converter, Siemens' open hearth or Gilchrist Thomas' basic process, German and United States steelmakers took up new production methods faster than the industrialists in whose country they had been discovered. Foreign iron and steel works, having been established at a later date, had British experience to guide them; they could install the most up-to-date and largest plant, make use of the most recent metallurgical discoveries.

The second half of the nineteenth century was truly 'the age of coal'. Coal mining enjoyed buoyant markets both at home and abroad. Nor could the coming of electricity endanger its sway in a country where water power plays only an insignificant part; like steam and gas, electricity had to be generated by coal. Up to 1914, the coal industry underwent continuous expansion: expansion of the labour force, whether in absolute numbers or as a proportion of working population, expansion of output in volume and value. As miners penetrated farther underground, progress in depth compelled them to hew coal in a hotter atmosphere and transport it a longer distance to the pithead; maximum output per man was achieved in the 1880s at the rate of 400 tons per year, declining thereafter. But so great was hunger for fuel, especially Welsh steam coal suitable for bunkering, that consumers shouldered such increased costs of mining up to 1904. They were helped by economies in coal utilization; even where fuel cost them more, they learnt how to make it go further. The seemingly insatiable appetite for coal prompted fears lest Britain unthriftily exhaust her coal reserves, expressed as early as 1865 by Stanley Jevons, the outstanding economist of his day, in his book *The Coal Question*. He pointed to the nature of coal, a wasting asset which no human ingenuity could replace, and warned that it was always mined in conditions of increasing costs: pits worked their best seams first and attacked the poorer ones only when the easiest and most worthwhile deposits had been exhausted. The prophecy that Britain might find herself denuded of accessible coal resources within a century illustrates the danger of peering too far into the future through the mist of contemporary conditions.

Severe trials lay ahead of all staple industries, but exhaustion of their natural resources was not among them. Much as their supply side suffered from the first world war when equipment, however worn out or obsolete, could not be replaced, far more painful and sustained were the blows to demand. Productive facilities had been adapted to military needs and required re-adjustment, but this caused only transitional difficulties. Old staples concentrated on the production of comparatively simple goods, basic necessities or semi-necessities, in a world where demand shifted away from their output to more complex and elaborate manufactures. The change in the nature of consumers' requirements would have made itself felt in any case, but while industry can contract in response to a gradual diminution of orders, hostilities had converted what would have been a back-ward slide into a headlong fall. During the war British industry could not supply overseas customers because erstwhile buyers had become enemies, naval action had severed trade routes, or resources could not be spared to manufacture commodities not essential to the war effort. Whatever the reason, foreign con-sumers of British goods had to buy elsewhere or make arrange-ments to manufacture for themselves. Having once built up a new trade connection or started industrialization, they did not revert to British sources when the state of the world permitted it.

Old staple industries saw their exports in the interwar years curtailed for two different reasons: their share in international trade diminished, sometimes because their output was no longer in great demand; pig iron for forges, foundries and acid steel, ships propelled by steam rather than diesel or electric trans-mission, high-quality rather than cheap cotton goods; sometimes because foreign countries had developed industries enjoying advantages of location denied to their British competitors. American coal seams were closer to the surface, more horizontal, less faulted and not nearly so heavily worked out; India, the United States, Japan and China had raw cotton supplies close at hand; the ore deposits of the United States and Germany were richer in iron content. International trade as a whole shrank, particularly in the 1930s, through pursuit by most countries of national self-sufficiency; less commerce remained to be divided among participants.

The livelihood of a large number of people depended on the old staple industries. The decline of their markets affected a circle wide enough to engage the attention of the nation in general and call for action by the government. Derating of industrial premises could be no more than a minor form of first aid to alleviate the shock when the slump of 1929 brought the long-heralded crisis to a head. Bad industrial relations singled out the coal industry for scrutiny by two Royal Commissions, one which immediately after the war by the narrowest of majorities recommended nationalization of coal mines, the other which tried unsuccessfully to avert the labour dispute leading to the general strike of 1926. The latter's recommendations took belated effect when the industry was reorganized in 1930 as a nation-wide cartel, divided into districts for selling purposes. Government intervention in the iron and steel industry followed similar lines: the Import Duties Advisory Committee, established in 1931 to guide the Board of Trade in the imposition of tariffs, undertook to protect the industry from foreign competition on condition that it formed a national combine and negotiated on a basis of equality with foreign iron and steel interests, consisting of cartels and trade associations of long standing. As a weapon in this fight over the division of such markets as remained, the government imposed import limitation by quotas where tariffs did not prove effective enough. In return, the Import Duties Advisory Committee expressed a hope that the industry would reorganize itself by eliminating high-cost producers and transferring activities to works operating most economically. High-cost producers were reluctant to go out of existence at a moment when tariff protection brought them orders which in conditions of free competition would have been placed with foreign rivals. But the future looked bright for this industry; armaments for at least the first three years of the second world war required every inch of floor space, every furnace and every pair of hands it could muster; cost of production in such circumstances hardly mattered at all.

In spite of objections in principle, the government had resorted in practice to monopoly formation in order to put the heavy industries back on their feet. Individualistic tradition proved too strong for effective combination in the cotton industry, even when an eminent economist like John Maynard Keynes impressed upon manufacturers the impossibility of reconquering their former markets or competing with foreign rivals without establishing control of output. As this industry did not yield to persuasion, the goverment eventually forced a reduction scheme on the spinning section and had obtained a statute applying the same remedy to the weaving side when the outbreak of the second world war rendered the Act ineffective. Shipbuilding on the other hand undertook its own concentration with some financial help from the government and subsidies to selected sections.

If one world war deprived the old staple industries of their markets, the second sapped their productive capacity. While war lasted, output was limited only by their ability to secure raw materials and labour, repeating a pattern familiar from the first world war. But whereas the latter had brought in its wake after a brief replacement boom 20 years of bad trade, the sellers' market engendered by the second world war endured for the better part of a decade. Industries which had worked 24 hours a day for the war effort, many in old-fashioned and unattractive premises, using obsolescent equipment subject to the excessive wear and tear of war time, were worsted in the competition for scarce labour of the post-war period. Quick re-equipment along up-to-date lines might have enhanced their attraction to the labour force, but required foreign resources for which Britain, weakened financially as well as materially by her struggle for survival, could not afford scarce gold or dollars. Limitations of capital investment compelled industries to hasten slowly, however good a case they could present for large-scale reconstruction. Meanwhile not only the home market, but foreign countries everywhere thirsted for goods which had been rationed, if not completely unobtainable, for six years; staple industries, accustomed to being unable to sell what they made, found themselves in the novel situation of being unable to make even half of what they could have sold. The industry which weathered the situation best was iron and steel; by undertaking a considerable investment programme financed largely from internal reserves accumulated in war time, while maintaining the Iron and Steel Federation in control, it achieved greater competitive strength *vis-à-vis* its foreign rivals than at any time since, if not before, the first world war. Shipbuilding maintained an intermediate position, overtaken in, but not crowded out of, world markets by its American, Japanese and German competitors. If the woollen industry barely held its own, its danger did not stem from foreign competition, but from artificial fibres which threatened cotton even more. Neither in cotton nor in coal could the post-war boom conceal the industry's fundamental weakness; though there would be room in the world for a British cotton industry, never again would it be the world's cotton industry. Planned and subsidized reduction in capacity proved unavoidable; a smaller and more efficient industry alone could hope to survive. Far more desperate was the position of coal, displaced in favour of a fuel cleaner, cheaper, more economical and convenient in use, namely oil, when even more revolutionary changes in power supply could be discerned on the horizon. A well-ordered industry might have presented a united front to this threat; bad labour relations in coal mining maintained an unhappy tradition which even nationalization did not affect. The unfortunate taxpayer was forced to underwrite the losses which no amount of mechanization enabled the industry to wipe out, leaving its outlook as bleak as the landscape pitted by spoil heaps which had formed its setting in the days of its prosperity.

New Industries

From the point of view of the old staples, British industrial history since the first world war presents a sombre picture. It is brightened by industries—and by branches of the engineering industry—which grew up just before or in the twentieth century. Higher standards of living from the middle of the previous century onwards had changed the nature of demand. Once they no longer went hungry, people required not more, but more palatable, food, nor did they want just clothing, but better, more attractive, more varied, clothes. Convenience of social life called for better communications, whether in the form of public transport or private cars and cycles or cable and telephone lines. Men and women adequately housed, fed and clothed wanted to be entertained; they demanded games and sports goods, theatres and films, gramophones, radio and television sets; they read more and larger newspapers and periodicals, more novels, in the quest of knowledge even more textbooks. The modern housewife had had an education which gave her interests beyond her household; at the same time she could neither afford nor obtain domestic help. To live a full life and yet do her duty by her family, she had to rely on a variety of labour-saving devices with which new industries equipped her home: vacuum cleaners, washing machines, electric irons. Heat in the house, once bought at the expense of laying fires and cleaning grates daily, could now be commanded at the turn of a gas tap or an electric switch. Food as supplied by the agriculturist required much cleaning and preparing; by interposing the processing industry, the same food could be delivered to her tinned, dehydrated or frozen, cut, boned and cleaned, ready for pot or frying-pan. To save her much time spent in buying food in small quantities, industry provided the housewife with a refrigerator; however extensive her purchases, they could be kept fresh until wanted. Another industry, that of advertizing, grew up to advise her—and her menfolk—on their choice of purchases. Thus consumers' preference might be guided by, or might itself be the guide to, new manufactures: women's demand for apparel possessing particular qualities prompted the woollen industry into devising unshrinkable cloth; their refusal to pay the inflated prices of menthol and natural perfumes stimulated the growth of synthetic substitutes.

Most of the new industries ministered direct to the consumer, many furnishing not goods, but services. As they did not supply necessities, but semi-luxuries, consumers exercised a real choice, not only whose output they bought, but whether they bought at all. Sales of new far more than of old industries reflected prices on the one hand and the state of the consumers' purses on the other. The average factory price of a motor-car in 1912 was £308; 176,000 only were in use in the United Kingdom. 2·1 million cars crowded the roads by 1936 when their price had fallen to £130. In 1920 rayon yarn cost as much as raw silk; by 1933 it not only sold at half the price of raw silk, but was cheaper than raw wool. Not having grown up in the days of British industrial supremacy, new industries never swept export markets; usually their counterparts in foreign countries had developed at the same time. They had therefore to place their chief reliance on the home market, some because they were in their nature 'sheltered' industries, such as electricity supply, road transport or personal services; the majority grew or settled down to a smaller scale than their American counterparts, typically motor-car manufacture and food canning. Though the United Kingdom was the foremost producer of rayon in 1913, she had fallen to fourth place in 1929. Yet to these generalizations there was one spectacular exception: the motor-cycle industry exported nearly 40 per cent of its output between 1927 and 1929, and Britain accounted for 66 per cent of the world's export trade in motor-cycles in 1934.

Unlike the old staples, new industry had inherited no individualistic tradition, but adopted industrial concentration early in life, if indeed it had not from the outset been confined to one or two firms. Giants like Imperial Chemical Industries in dyestuffs or Unilever in margarine and detergents overshadowed the whole field; in some industries there reigned oligopoly, as in motor-car manufacture, in others even a dyarchy eventually resolved by amalgamation, as when Courtaulds and British Celanese joined forces after the second world war to explore all methods of making rayon. Only intervention by the Board of Trade prevented the J. Arthur Rank Organization from bringing the vast majority of the country's cinemas under one management. Sometimes a larger number of manufacturers sank their identity in an attempt to reap benefits of scale: 12 makers of metal containers became the Metal Box Company in the 1920s; 15 beet sugar factories formed the British Sugar Corporation in 1935. Ill-devised wartime controls speeded concentration: the Custodian of Enemy Property, having at the outbreak of the second world war appropriated a parcel of Siemens Brothers' shares owned by Germans, sold it, and with it the company's independence, to its chief competitors, Associated Electrical Industries. Amalgamation sometimes led to public ownership, as when four struggling air lines in 1924 became Imperial Airways, or when the London Passenger Transport Board was constituted by Act of Parliament in 1933 successor to 18 underground railway, 60 other transport companies and the passenger transport departments of 14 local authorities. Yet other new industries were entrusted to public corporations, such as the British Broadcasting Corporation in the 1920s, followed after the second world war by some old industries removed by nationalization from their erstwhile owners: coal mining, electricity and gas generation, rail and—for a period—road transport. However, even among new industries some set their face against concentration. Food canning could best be carried on by factories scattered where their raw materials grew in the country; increase in scale promised little advantage to an industry whose optimum size could not exceed the capacity fully employed on processing the volume of crops coming forward in every season. Advertizing rendered highly individual services; the larger an agency, the more difficult to preserve its characteristic imprint by which it commended itself to clients.

In their heyday, the old staples had scorned government help and prided themselves on their ability to stand on their own feet, even if free trade exposed them to world competition. New industries grew up in a less independent atmosphere; many indeed would never have grown up at all, had government support been withdrawn at any stage. Sugar beet and civil aviation were examples of beneficiaries from direct public subsidies; most new industries, unless sheltered by the nature of their activities, enjoyed protection in the form of tariffs, import quotas or licences. Some, such as food canning, received government help in research and grading. Where industrial training had been given at all, the standard method had been apprenticeship; new industries preferred the more intensive and systematic tuition provided by technical schools or colleges. However, they tried altogether to scale down their requirements of skilled labour by substituting capital; intricate and elaborate machinery enabled them to operate with fewer workers, many of them without previous training for the job. The skill involved had been transferred from the worker making the goods to the engineer who designed the machinery and the manager who supervised its operations.

Transition would have been smoother if new industries had grown up in places where the old had contracted or decayed. At no time have workers brought up to one trade found it easy to get accustomed to another, but at least their children might have faced a brighter future with expanding opportunities close at hand. That no coincidence of redundancy and vacancies occurred, was particularly unfortunate for the Scottish Lowlands, the English North East coast, manufacturing areas of Lancashire and Yorkshire and the South Wales coalfield; wherever old staples had existed in the nineteenth century, the end of the 1914–18 war left a 'depressed area'. New industries established themselves in the Midlands and South of England, partly by sheer accident of location, but often drawn there by rational choice: they valued proximity to places of concentrated purchasing power, close to the dwellings of those most likely to buy their products. Light engineering, the basis of several new industries, had always flourished in the Midlands where its skilled labour force was domiciled. Before industrial derating, the rate structure favoured the choice of a site in a prosperous community, where even a low rate provided the local authority with a product which a poor area could secure only by levying a much higher rate. Once upon a time, all these considerations, much as they were in industrialists' minds, would have been outweighed by the cost of transporting coal to the works; power had been the magnet irresistibly drawing old staples to the coalfields. Now, however, power could be conveyed to factories anywhere in the form of electricity which cost little to transmit and enabled manufacturers to disregard expenses of power supply in choosing a site.

Geographical maldistribution between industries able to expand and labour seeking employment left interwar governments with the choice of transferring workers to work or taking the work to the workers. The former commended itself on economic grounds: if manufacturers had chosen their location with their eyes open, persuasion or coercion to settle elsewhere saddled them with the permanent costs of unfavourable location. However desirable economically, transfer of workers was socially difficult. It meant abandoning social capital sunk in towns like Bishop Auckland or Merthyr Tydfil, towns which had once had a *raison d'être*; it created problems of housing and of adaptation for men and women who resisted separation from relatives and friends. So, apart from very half-hearted attempts in the middle 1930s to subsidize the transfer of individual workers out of the distressed areas, governments opted for the policy of bringing industries to the regions which the decline of the old staples had left derelict. The government established trading estates and built factories ready for letting or sale on favourable terms to industrialists willing to move there. Rate and tax remissions and government loans served as baits to tempt them; port, transport and communication facilities were improved to minimize disadvantages

83

of location. Where alien immigrants applied to establish industrial enterprises in Britain, permission was rendered conditional on their settling in the special areas, and when rearmament required the expansion of industrial capacity in the later 1930s, the government directed thither one-quarter of all new war factories. Diversification of industry aimed at diminishing an area's dependence on a single line of production; a number of light industries now existed side by side with what remained of the old staples. This policy proved very successful, indeed embarrassingly so. The lighter industries provided work not only for women in areas traditionally employing only male labour, but their up-to-date premises and easier processes attracted away from the old staples even men whose employment had not been in jeopardy. Especially after the second world war, when all industries enjoyed a long period of full employment, the older ones could not recapture their labour force and had to rely more and more on foreign workers imported to man unpopular occupations. Diversification of industry, however acceptable to areas formerly depressed and workers once upon a time unemployed, made it harder than ever for the old staples to continue playing their part in the national economy.

The end of the second world war was hastened by the dropping of two atomic bombs. To the uninitiated, this constituted the first intimation that man had succeeded in harnessing a new source of power through splitting the atom. The search for new power generators had never been given up: unavailing attempts had been made to harness the heat of the sun or the movement of the tides. This, however, represented the first success; though the bombs were of American manufacture, their design owed much to British cooperation. British scientists knew enough about splitting the atom to repeat the process at home. For a number of years the political consequences of this discovery displaced its industrial potentialities in the minds of most people, but not of the British government. From 1945 onwards it fostered research into the peaceful uses of nuclear power. This policy bore fruit in the 1950s when manufacturers' demands for energy were jeopardized by shortfall of coal output and the political vagaries of oil-producing countries. As yet, methods of generating atomic power were untried and unsafe; when first harnessed to industrial purposes, its cost exceeded that of power obtained from traditional sources. These however were clearly but the childish ailments of a new giant whose full girth nobody could as yet discern. Even at the time of writing no more than a guess can be hazarded that the effect on industry of this new form of power will be more far-reaching than that of its predecessor, steam, two centuries earlier.

Another major British industry was raised in, rather than as a result of, the second world war. A negligible quantity of oil had been refined in Britain before 1939; by 1959, an 18-fold increase in capacity had made the United Kingdom the fourth-largest oil refiner in the world. The industry made available yet another source of energy—relying on imports, hence vulnerable; but catalytic cracking at least freed it from dependence on crude oil of a particular chemical constitution. At a cost of one-thirtieth of the manpower, the industry in 1959 contributed only a little less than a third of the total output of the coal mining industry, calculated in coal equivalent, to British energy resources. Beyond making available power supplies, oil refiners found uses for their surplus gases. In collaboration with chemical manufacturers they developed petro-chemicals, a new industry in which the United Kingdom became the leading European manufacturer, yielding products as diverse as fertilizers, industrial solvents and detergents. Petro-chemicals were typical of a range of hybrids formed by the joining of forces on the part of two hitherto separate industries; other intermarriages led to such post-war offsprings as electronic engineering and chemical metallurgy. The chemical industry in particular partnered others in giving birth to new types of output: plastics and man-made fibres, though they had their scientific beginnings in the nineteenth century, did not transform the British industrial scene until after the second world war.

Transformation is not too strong a term to apply to the change. Not only were there once again industries in which Britain, if not the largest, was at least one of the world's leading producers and exporters, but even her old industries, so much weakened by lack of demand in the years between the wars, recovered in the van and wake of the new ones. Only traditional textiles failed to benefit from this industrial revival: in 1958 for the first time Britain imported more cotton cloth than she sent out of the country. Such was the demand for power by post-war industries that annual coal output in the 1950s hardly fell short of what it had been in 1938; crude oil imports necessitated a large tanker fleet, keeping shipbuilding in the later 1950s busier by one-third than before the war; iron and steel was required in large quantities by engineers building power stations, both nuclear and conventional, and oil refineries. The hum of the wheels was once again changing to a higher pitch; British industry made full use of its capacity and endeavoured to find new methods of raising productivity and saving labour which had become unobtainable.

Such labour-saving devices in the 1950s were often summarily described as automation. The term covered a number of different processes. The simplest, derived from the assembly line of the later nineteenth and early twentieth centuries, concerned itself with continuous mechanical handling of materials in the course of manufacture. It included fork-lift trucks, conveyors and other weight-lifting and transporting apparatus which came into general use after 1939. But beyond mere carrying, machinery could be used for the automatic assembly of electronic products: as a plastic board was carried past a number of machines, they attached to it electric circuits and other components. Even more complicated devices by means of sensitive equipment 'scanned' production processes and took appropriate action to maintain or restore a given set of conditions. Finally, electronic 'brains' made complicated calculations at a much greater speed than their human counterparts; by feeding into a computer constructional details of an article in the process of manufacture, engineers made it record the production programme on magnetic tape. The tape, fed into the control unit of a machine tool, acted as a master plan guiding and controlling the tool in its production activity. Thus as the 1950s gave way to the 1960s, more and more did the most advanced sectors of industry replace hand labour by immensely intricate machines designed by the most highly skilled technicians and scientists ever engaged in productive effort, while furnishing each remaining worker with a steadily growing amount of capital equipment under his control and at his command.

V | INDUSTRIAL RELATIONS

Working Conditions

Many industrial occupations can never have been healthy. Some required people to work in an atmosphere saturated with noxious, sometimes even poisonous fumes, or simply unnaturally hot or humid. Others forced them to adopt unwholesome postures owing to cramped space; men spending their working lives underground rarely saw daylight, let alone the sun. Most occupations were performed in people's houses and carried industrial dirt and dust into the home. Housewifery, in the face of such conditions, must have been heartbreaking; had more working class women possessed the literary ability to leave written records, this aspect of industry would have received more attention.

These hazards to health however were traditional. People had grown up with them and accepted them unquestioningly as part of the immutable order of things. Bad working conditions attracted attention only if they were new, if they entailed risks not previously incurred, if the yoke irked owing to the unfamiliarity of the harness. Hence working conditions aroused little dissatisfaction before the coming of mechanically propelled machinery and factories. This new form of production, taking place on the employer's premises, exposed employees to unfamiliar dangers: keeping up the speed determined by machinery caused fatigue and carelessness, thus facilitating accidents; these might also be promoted by unfenced machines catching in workers' garments, particularly the voluminous clothing worn by women; employees were often unfamiliar with the exact layout of the premises. Demands arose for factory workers' protection, not because conditions in factories were inherently much worse than in home industry, but because they were new.

But how and by whom could workers be protected? The only agency with power to intervene between master and employee was the State. Though the State had power, the majority of educated opinion around 1800 denied its right to such inter-position. A contract of employment had been freely entered into by master and workman, both with their eyes open: neither need have clinched it, had he considered it disadvantageous; either could give notice if he grew to dislike the conditions. People presumably accepted employment on the stipulated terms because, after weighing all circumstances, they preferred it to the alternatives available; interference by authority could only prevent their making the best possible contracts for themselves. An employer who offered bad conditions would soon find himself without labour and compelled to improve his terms to the level set by his competitors.

This is not the place to discuss the merits of a theory of the free employment contract which, taking a purely legal view, assumes equality of bargaining strength between a master em-ploying 30 men who may, or may not, add a thirty-first, and a worker faced with possibly protracted unemployment if he does not accept the terms offered. The wide currency which the theory enjoyed among social philosophers and economists in its day rendered any attack on bad working conditions very difficult. Workpeople themselves were mostly too inarticulate to give effective expression to objections; protests reached the public from medical men practising in industrial areas, whose surgeries provided visual evidence of the toll taken by the new manu-facturing system. It was a voluntary medical organization in the heart of the industrial region, the Manchester Board of Health, which first set itself to find a remedy for the bad working con-ditions which its investigations had disclosed.

To avoid the charge of interposing between man and man, forcing people into less favourable contracts than they could have made for themselves, early factory reformers concentrated their attacks on the conditions of children working in factories. However capable a man to determine his best advantage, the same discretion could not be presumed in a child, least of all in a child deprived of its natural protectors, such as an orphan or foundling. As for a pauper child, its parents had demonstrated their inability to earn their living on any terms. To interfere on behalf of such children was not open to the objections raised against regulation of adults' employment. Concentration on children accompanied naturally the phase during which cotton spinning mills establishing water frames in the river valleys of the North West required a labour force recruited mainly from women and children. The area was thinly settled, but work-houses in large towns—London in particular, but also Edinburgh and Glasgow—sheltered more women and children than would ever find local employment. Parishes responsible for their maintenance were only too glad to respond to the cotton spinners' appeals for labour; women and children found themselves set to work at unfamiliar occupations in strange surroundings. The water power phase in the development of the manufacturing system did not last, but left its imprint on factory reform by presenting it in a false light: contemporaries thought of it as an appendage to the poor law, a measure required merely to protect pauper apprentices.

Manufacturers were by no means indiscriminately opposed to factory reform as far as it concerned child workers. Under a system of sub-contracting, such children rarely worked for the owners, more often for people who, though in fact employees, performed certain jobs under contract with the owners and employed their own helpers. In any case, large manufacturers often were enlightened as well as generous enough to prefer good working conditions, but feared the competitive advantage which might accrue to their small and less reputable rivals from wringing the last ounce out of their labour; factory reform could be made acceptable only by being enforced on all men, large and small alike. This meant recourse to the law. The Health and Morals of Apprentices Act of 1802, the first piece of legislation in this field, sponsored by one of the largest cotton spinners of Lancashire, Sir Robert Peel (father of the statesman), concerned itself chiefly with pauper apprentices. Its detailed provisions are not important because, though it constitutes evidence of Parliament's benevolent intentions, it achieved no practical effect, having entrusted enforcement to the voluntary efforts of two local 'visitors', a magistrate and a clergyman. Its scope extended to working hours and instruction of apprentices and certain minimum requirements of hygiene in establishments to which it applied.

During the next two decades Peel in collaboration with Robert Owen, head of a model cotton spinning mill at New Lanark, attempted to render factory reform more effective. Peel obtained the ear of Parliament for a bill drafted jointly by Owen and himself; but many of the medical witnesses heard at Westminster argued against it on *a priori* grounds without practical experience. The Act of 1819 emasculated the proposals, leaving little of any importance; it applied only to cotton mills and again failed to make effective provision for policing its regulations. Nor did two subsequent amending measures change the situation.

Effective reform of children's working conditions owed much to the search by landed interests in Parliament for a weapon to hit back at Radical manufacturers attacking the corn laws. In 1830 a chance visit to a Bradford woollen mill so impressed Richard Oastler, steward of an estate in the neighbourhood, that he addressed seven letters on 'Yorkshire slavery' to the *Leeds Mercury*. He contrasted the urgency with which humanitarians and Radicals demanded the abolition of slavery in the British Empire with their indifference to the conditions of women's and children's employment in English factories. No longer was this a matter of pauper apprentices working in remote water mills; industry had moved to the coalfields where factory operatives had settled in numbers large enough to take action on their own behalf. They purported to be chiefly concerned with excessive working hours at a period when even the law permitted children to labour for 12 hours a day, exclusive of meals, and in practice employers incurred no punishment for disregarding the limitation. Operatives in many industrial towns formed short-time committees exerting themselves under Oastler's guidance to obtain a reduction of the children's working day to ten hours. The movement's parliamentary spokesman, Michael Sadler, introduced a ten hours' bill into the House of Commons and became chairman of a committee to enquire into its merits.

Sadler was an astute parliamentarian who realized that the unreformed Parliament had not long to live. He suggested to his fellow members that evidence in favour of the bill be taken first. Spokesmen sent by short-time committees all over the country voiced at Westminster the opinion that industry had everything to gain from limiting the children's working day to ten hours. When Parliament dissolved, all committees automatically shared its fate. Not having completed its task, Sadler's committee could render no report. But Sadler argued in favour of utilizing at least the evidence already collected and enlisted his fellow members' support to its publication. They little realized that, as parliamentary committees normally published evidence only in conjunction with reports, the evidence given by one side to a dispute and unrebutted by the other would be universally mistaken for a report. Manufacturers raised an outcry against such sharp practice. One of the first tasks awaiting the reformed Parliament of 1833 was this problem of factory legislation which it entrusted urgently to a Royal Commission.

An unenviable task faced the commissioners. Both sides of industry laboured under a grievance: manufacturers because they had never even been heard, workers because no action had followed Sadler's committee. The appointment of the commission confirmed their suspicion that the government wanted to shelve the question. Anxious to avoid the trap into which their predecessors had fallen, the commissioners decided to examine conditions on the spot instead of hearing witnesses in London. More than ever convinced that the dice were loaded against them, the workers boycotted the commissioners during their tour of factory areas. Nevertheless, the commissioners knew that they were expected to uncover abuses and recommend action; without doing so, they could not preserve industrial peace. Manufacturers stressed that production constituted an integrated process: limit any of the workers involved to ten hours a day, and material in the course of production would accumulate at certain points, owing to the absence of hands needed to perform the next operation and send it on its way. Thus ten hours for juvenile workers really signified ten hours for the whole factory; commissioners concurred with the manufacturers' view that such a drastic limitation would ruin British industry. Between the Scylla of workers' wrath and the Charybdis of manufacturers' forebodings they steered a narrow course which led to the Children and Young Persons' Act of 1833.

Sadler had lost his seat in the election to the reformed Parliament. Deprived of their spokesman, workers approached Lord Ashley, better known by his subsequent title as the seventh Earl of Shaftesbury, a Dorset landowner as yet without experience of industrial problems. But Lord Shaftesbury (as we will for convenience's sake call him), inspired by a profound sense of duty born of religious fervour, lost no time in acquainting himself with factory conditions; his long connection with their reform dated from the measure of 1833.

The Act created two categories of juvenile workers: children from nine to 13 years of age (those under nine were not to work in regulated establishments at all) and young persons between 13 and 18. It applied to textile factories in which power-driven machinery operated, excluding lace mills. Children received effective protection by the limitation of their working day to nine hours; in addition they had to attend school for two hours on every working day. Far less effective protection applied to young persons: they were neither to do nightwork nor be employed for more than 12 hours a day. What really put teeth into the Act, thus distinguishing it from all its predecessors, was the appointment of four full-time inspectors charged with enforcing its provisions.

Both sides of industry expressed their dissatisfaction with the 1833 Act, workers because it did not limit hours for all juveniles to ten a day, manufacturers because it saddled them with visits to their factories by men whom they chose to regard as industrial spies. Yet only four inspectors had been appointed for the whole of the United Kingdom. What neither side could foresee was the astonishing ability and efficiency of these factory inspectors—model civil servants before the civil service in its modern form had come into existence. They fought battles over admission to manufacturing premises, both for themselves and for the assistants they had to appoint to help them cover their immense areas; they standardized forms to create unambiguous records of time-keeping; wherever they met with resistance, they tried to carry the day by tact or persuasion, only in the last resort having recourse to prosecution before the local magistrates. Realizing that only a consistent policy could make industrial practice uniform throughout the kingdom, they met twice a year to exchange information on action taken and to concert future proceedings; they embodied their deliberations in reports to the Home Secretary which were printed as a public record of the policy pursued. Very soon no draft legislation on working conditions was submitted to Parliament until the Home Secretary had obtained the factory inspectors' advice on what could and should be achieved.

Coal mines were not factories in any legal sense; no legislation regulated employment in an industry seething with bad labour relations, largely hidden from the rest of the community owing to the geographical isolation of mining villages. By contemporary standards miners were well paid, all the more as they usually had to be their families' only wage earners; mining villages afforded little opportunity of employment to their womenfolk. Miners' grievances, at least in the Durham-Northumberland coalfield, centred on the terms rather than the wages of their employment: the fact that once a year they were assembled to have their contract of employment for the next 12 months read to them; they probably could not even hear, let alone understand, the terms drawn up by some lawyer to regulate their working lives for the year to come. In practice they found that, though they had to present themselves for work on each working day, the masters were under no equally stringent obligation to provide them with employment; they were remunerated by measure, not by weight, of coal won, and suffered deductions for non-combustible 'dirt' which they had sent to the surface. Neither ventilation nor safety devices were adequate, rendering the occupation a highly dangerous one, with an unenviable accident rate; nor could improvements be easily devised for an industry whose geographical conditions and terms of employment varied not only from coalfield to coalfield, but even from pit to pit. If miners were indignant and embittered, mineowners matched their truculent and obstinate mood; owning the land as well as the coal beneath it, they resorted to evictions of strikers and even of shopkeepers who granted credit to miners in disputes with their employers, and circulated among themselves black-lists of miners who had incurred their hostility.

Having achieved a measure of success in factory legislation, Lord Shaftesbury turned to conditions in coal mines. Parliament granted him a Royal Commission on the subject in 1840 which made a most painstaking investigation on the spot, commissioners or their assistants descending mines in the various coalfields. So urgent did they consider the reforms of some of the practices discovered that in 1841 they rendered an interim report before even completing the main enquiry. It told of children as young as eight sitting in complete darkness underground for as many hours as the pit operated, in order to pull strings which opened doors, normally closed for ventilation, whenever a truck of coal passed, of boys of ten responsible without supervision for the winding mechanism operating the cages by which miners ascended and descended, of 'the repugnant mode of conveying coals on the backs of ladies' still prevalent in the Fife and South Yorkshire coalfields. Worst of all from the point of view of Victorian morality was the employment underground of women and girls to pull or push coal trucks; like the men among whom they worked, they were stripped to the waist because of the heat. The moral rather than the safety hazards shocked Parliament into an immediate Act forbidding the employment underground of women and appointing a mining inspector to enforce this regulation. The tightening up of safety regulations had to await some tragic mining disasters in the 1850s.

When workers first campaigned for the limitation of the children's working day, their solicitude concerned less the welfare of juveniles than their own employment opportunities. Manufacturers, rather than employ a category of workers whose presence subjected the factory to inspection and regulations, might dismiss all juveniles in favour of adult labour, thus creating more work and better payment for the latter. This happened to a considerable extent as the result of the 1833 Act. When employers substituted female for child labour, the operatives extended their campaign to include the limitation of women workers' hours and gained part of their objective in 1844 when all women workers obtained the degree of protection granted to young persons. This fell short of a ten hours' standard day, an aim which Shaftesbury continued to pursue and almost carried to a successful conclusion in 1847; at the last minute, another political question caused his temporary resignation from Parliament, and the Ten Hours' Act was carried in his absence. It proclaimed the limitation of the working day for all protected persons (children, young persons and women) to ten hours.

The Ten Hours' Act had passed comparatively easily at a time of depression, when none of the manufacturers affected had orders enough to keep his factory running for ten hours a day. Once business picked up, the restriction proved irksome, and factory owners tried to circumvent it by the ingenious device of the 'false relay system'. The Act prohibited protected persons working for more than ten hours a day, but, argued employers, it did not stipulate that such work had to be continuous. They could require their services for, say seven hours, then keep them on the premises in order to make up the remaining three hours whenever it suited the manufacturers best. Such a system deprived protected persons of the benefits which the Act had been designed to secure. Factory inspectors prosecuted, but magistrates often did not convict, so a test case was taken to the Court of Appeal in 1850. In a judgment which even contemporary opinion condemned as bad law, that court found that the Act of 1847, being restrictive of the liberty of the subject (the subject being the factory owner), had itself to be restrictively interpreted, hence that the false relay system did not contravene it. To override the effect of this decision required an amending Act which Shaftesbury obtained, but he had to sacrifice half an hour's working time to purchase government support; the standard day for protected workers now became ten-and-a-half hours. Not until 1874 did protected persons achieve a statutory ten hours' day.

A book on economic history cannot pursue in detail the course of factory legislation after the middle nineteenth century. The principle of interposition between employer and worker was of fundamental importance; its details depended on technical and scientific progress on the one hand, medical knowledge on the other. Early factory legislation had concentrated on overstrain as the most urgent problem of its day, concerning itself with limitation of hours. Reduction of accidents required environmental improvements which gradually came to be pursued for their own sake. As the nineteenth century passed, workers' personal welfare assumed greater importance; it was recognized that, while women worked in factories, there ought to be women factory inspectors to pay attention to their special needs. Industrial nursing as a separate branch of the nursing profession developed in the twentieth century which saw the move from preventive to positive measures; instead of merely shielding factory workers from harm, they provided amenities, most of which—such as works canteens, rest rooms, infant crèches, a medical and dental service, superannuation and other staff welfare schemes—owe their existence to two world wars. In periods of full employment manufacturers vied with each other for labour; what was introduced by the best of them to tempt workers into their service became in the course of time the standard for industry in general.

Where workpeople sustained injury through accidents, employers' liability had always given rise to disputes. Originally lawyers took the view that a man entered employment with his eyes open to the risks it entailed. Even after an Act of 1880 had conceded the employer's liability to a workman injured through somebody's negligence, the principle remained limited by the doctrine of 'common employment' which exempted the employer from claims founded on anything done by the injured person's fellow workmen. As long as negligence had to be proved by the worker, he found it almost impossible to obtain compensation. At least for certain employments the burden was shifted in 1897. An Act in 1906 not only greatly extended the range of compensation, but included a schedule of industrial diseases; it now became the rule for a workman to obtain compensation unless his own causative or contributory negligence could be established.

Apart from the elaboration of regulations, factory legislation since the middle nineteenth century has progressed by extension —extension to persons, to establishments and to processes. During most of the nineteenth century, legislation had applied to protected persons. Where an establishment employed them side by side with other workers, the whole labour force benefited from the attention of the law and the factory inspectors. Manufacturers however could still keep the inspector out by employing only adult male workers; not until 1895 did these come within the scope of factory legislation in their own right. Extension to establishments originally operated by statutory definition, each new law enumerating the types of factories to which it applied. In 1867 Parliament initiated an unsuccessful experiment defining factories as industrial establishments employing 50 or more persons and subjecting them to strict regulation controlled by the factory inspectorate, while meting out far more lenient treatment, supervised merely by local authority personnel, to workshops, places employing less than 50 people on industrial work. Such a dichotomy tempted establishments giving work to approximately 50 persons to dismiss a number sufficient to qualify for less burdensome regulation as workshops; moreover, in industry it is the small man, short of capital and hard driven to make ends meet, who cannot afford good facilities for his workers, whereas large manufacturers, mainly concerned to avoid interruption in production through labour disputes, do not grudge pennies or even pounds spent on staff welfare. The Act therefore reversed priorities, quite apart from entrusting the supervision of workshops to a body of officials experienced in the suppression of nuisances, but not in the problems of industrial working conditions. In practice these defects manifested themselves so clearly that the failure of the measure led to its repeal after 11 years, all supervision of industrial establishments reverting to the factory inspectorate.

Bringing further occupations and processes under regulation was the most far-reaching of the extensions by which factory legislation pervaded industrial life. The early Factory Acts had applied to the textile industry, defining the establishments covered in terms of end products. The dangers against which they protected workers lay however not in the end products, but in the processes involved in manufacture. This was first recognized in 1845–6 by subjecting to factory legislation print, bleach and dye works, irrespective of the articles printed, bleached or dyed; in due course further extension took place along those lines. Shop assistants in 1892 obtained limitation of hours for protected persons, though shops could hardly be said to be 'factories' in any sense. A problem which defied solution for a long time concerned workers labouring in their own homes. The law of the country raised obstacles to the invasion of a private residence, thus hampering the protection of workers pursuing their employments in a domestic setting, as most trades had done in the earlier eighteenth century. Of the difficulties created by this conflict London factory inspectors had a demonstration when in 1884 they undertook a house-to-house visitation of 1,478 tailoring establishments in the East End, only to find that over one half they possessed no jurisdiction at all, whereas for another quarter they had no power to require improvements in sanitation. Tailoring of this type provided a good example of the most intractable problem connected with out-workers, that of the sweated trades. What the period defined as sweated trades were industries still carried on under the putting-out system—proof, if any were needed, that the Industrial Revolution had brought far more good than evil in its wake. Sweated workers usually laboured in their own homes, out of contact with one another, under separate contracts, knowing neither whether the rate for the job was what their fellow workers received nor whether employment would continue beyond the job in hand. A House of Lords committee discussed sweated trades from 1888 to 1890, but the Act which embodied its conclusions in the following year obliged employers only to keep lists of out-workers for the factory inspectors' scrutiny and to furnish out-workers with particulars of wage rates in writing. Not until the *Daily News* in 1906 sponsored a public exhibition showing products of sweated trades side by side with remuneration received by the workers making them was public opinion really aroused and a National Anti-Sweating League formed to seek an effective remedy. This took the form of the Trade Boards Act of 1909, importing independent arbitrators and statutory power into the fixing of wage rates in trades where no adequate collective bargaining machinery existed.

The Beginning of Workers' Organizations

In early modern times, a young man entered industry by being bound apprentice to a master in some craft. Having served his apprenticeship and learnt the trade, he would become a journeyman for a few years, working for wages in order to accumulate sufficient capital to acquire the necessary tools and set up shop on his own. Unless unusually incapable or extraordinarily unlucky, he could expect to spend the best part of his working life as an *entrepreneur*, independent at least in name, if not in economic reality. This picture oversimplifies the situation even in the sixteenth century, when some people never had an opportunity of acquiring skill in a craft and had to be content with a subordinate position in industry, becoming jacks-of-all-trades rather than masters of any. Development of costlier equipment and fewer opportunities for independent enterprise differentiated more and more trades from the crafts in which the older order fought a rearguard action, at least up to the onset of mechanization, in some instances even beyond it. Where the possession of a factory equipped with machinery alone enabled a man to compete in industry, apprenticeship served no longer as a starting point for those who wanted to climb the higher rungs of a career in manufacturing. Once an industrialist had to be a factory owner, very few people could expect to become industrialists. While still entering industry at the bottom, the vast majority no longer rose to the top; after or even without apprenticeship they reached the stage of journeymen, wage earners working for an employer, and remained in that status throughout their lives. However free in law, a man offering his services in return for wages was in a vulnerable position; at most times, workers needed employment far more urgently than employers needed hands. Man to man, the worker could not match his employer's bargaining power; his only hope lay in combining with his fellow workers. This formed the basis of trade unionism.

Geographical shifts attendant upon the Industrial Revolution favoured the growth of trade clubs. While uneducated men, unused to written communications, had worked scattered in villages throughout the countryside, they had had no opportunity even to find out whether they had common grievances, far less to make common cause. Mechanized production drew them to the factories; they occupied smoke-darkened little houses forming the unending streets of industrial towns; the same knocker-up roused them from their sleep at an early hour to answer the summons of the same factory whistle; in the evening they sought solace in the same public houses from their mean surroundings and drab hard lives. Over a glass of beer, talk would soon turn to wages, living and working conditions; somebody might suggest collecting a fund, entrusted to the publican as treasurer, to insure contributors against sickness, unemployment or burial expenses—this would turn them into a friendly society; or jointly asking employers to increase wages—this would constitute a trade club. Having chanced their hand, they would not normally pursue the matter further; early trade clubs were impermanent organizations.

Men in Britain had always been permitted to associate together for any lawful purpose. Up to the eighteenth century the law had contained nothing whatsoever prohibiting men from combining to make demands upon employers in respect of wages or working conditions. But in the eighteenth century, lawyers and economists became convinced of the desirability of establishing freedom of trade: no contract between any two parties to be limited or influenced by any outsider. They turned their faces against 'restraint of trade' in the form of influence that anybody exercised on agreements to which he was not a party. Restraint, not freedom, had been the dominant influence on trade throughout recorded history. To lend respectability to the new departure, lawyers resorted to the fiction of contending that common law had always prohibited restraint of trade. This enabled them to declare illegal any combination of workmen attempting to dictate or limit terms of employment.

Against restraint of trade employers could by means of a civil action obtain an injunction calling upon the men to desist. To have them punished, they had to prove a criminal offence, using for this purpose the laws against conspiracy. As it was not always easy to prove conspiracy, employers resorted to Parliament to pass special Acts. Such laws called upon a particular group of workers to desist from combining against their employers, fixing penalties for disobedience. When London millwrights in 1799 petitioned Parliament for a law of this kind in respect of their refractory journeymen, Parliament decided to pass instead a once-for-all measure prohibiting trade combinations for the purpose of fixing wages and working conditions. Though the statute outlawed employers' as much as workers' associations, it fixed penalties only for workers' infringements. The Act of 1799 and an amending measure in the following year were known as the Combination Laws.

Why did a Parliament dominated by landowners indifferent to the problems of urban industry make so determined a stand against the weak attempts of workers to protect themselves? The ruthlessness of the Combination Laws becomes intelligible only in the context of their day. Britain had been at war with France for six years; from this side of the Channel the French Revolution seemed a mass mutiny of French workers against their employers. Any organized working class resistance to employers in Britain therefore assumed the appearance of a fifth column, an enemy force undermining the home front from within. Britain's position in the 1790s was gloomy, at times critical; she was fighting for her life. So she brought all the weapons of war to bear upon the enemy within the gates. Troops stopped demonstration marches, however peaceful; magistrates read the Riot Act to disperse assemblies; home security agents—the rude language of the time called them spies—insinuated themselves into meetings and plots which they denounced, usually much exaggerated, to the Home Office. From being opponents of the employers, trade clubs had become public enemies.

Though peace in 1815 ended the threat of enemy action, trade depression caused much labour unrest in the post-war years, rendered more serious by widespread displacement of craftsmen by machinery. Not until 1824 did the Combination Laws come under substantial attack. A very remarkable man, Francis Place, engineered their repeal in collaboration with a Radical member of Parliament, Joseph Hume. Place and Hume believed that wages, like prices of other services and goods, followed the law of supply and demand and could not be changed by trade clubs. The workers did not share this view. Trade was good in 1824; no sooner had combination ceased to be illegal than workers used their new freedom most vigorously to obtain higher wages in many trades. Employers bitterly blamed Parliament which reviewed the repeal in the following year. It did not put the clock back to the extent of outlawing combination, but tolerated peaceful bargaining, to the exclusion of obstruction, molestation and the fomenting of strikes. By failing to define these offences, the law created a twilight in which trade clubs and unions existed for the next half century.

Trade clubs up to the middle nineteenth century were colourful, but unimportant. Small, scattered, representing an insignificant fraction of the total labour force, they gained temporary and local successes at times of good trade, but achieved no permanently higher wage levels. Nor was this their main objective. They represented a far more general dissatisfaction than could have been assuaged by higher pay alone. Fuel was added to the flames of discontent by theories of social revolution formulated by the early socialists, above all by Robert Owen, according to which capitalist society deprived workers of part of the value of their product; their rightful deserts could be restored to them only by overthrowing and re-building society on a cooperative, instead of a competitive, basis. Not every member of every trade club consciously adopted this theory; many anyhow would have found it beyond their comprehension. Its revolutionary implications caused governments however to maintain a hostile attitude and serve intermittent notices upon the movement—of which the deportation of the Tolpuddle Martyrs in 1834 was the most spectacular—

that they would tolerate no attempt to destroy the structure of society. It would have been ludicrous to treat as a serious threat the action of six farm labourers in one of the remotest villages in England, but many working class leaders had plans of national coordination in order to develop and assert the trade clubs' power; Robert Owen's Grand National Consolidated Trades Union was only one of a number of attempts to weld the many small fragments into an effective national movement. When it reached a membership of 500,000, the government took fright; had it succeeded, it might have become an instrument of the social revolution which Owen considered necessary. The Grand National Consolidated Trades Union spent most of its funds and energies on the defence of the Tolpuddle Martyrs and the support of their families; it broke apart less than 12 months after their transportation. Such experiments in the organization of workers' movements remained doomed to failure: clubs had not the strength to weather early nineteenth century slumps, and communications were too undeveloped to allow organizations to function on a national scale. That is why the real history of trade unionism does not begin before 1850.

Not that local trade clubs disappeared at one blow in the second half of the century. Being an underdeveloped form of trade unionism, they persisted in areas of underdeveloped industry as long as artisans in under-mechanized workshops engaged in an ever more hopeless competition with the more fortunate operatives of industrially advanced areas. They formed the last refuge of displaced craftsmen in their desperate straits. It was a member of one of these trade clubs at Sheffield who murdered a non-unionist razor grinder in 1866, true to a tradition of violence which by this time had been abandoned by the main stream of the trade union movement.

Trade Unions in the Nineteenth Century

By 1850, communications made national organization possible; though sadly under-privileged in regard to education, the working class had thrown up a number of self-taught leaders with new ideas regarding the type of organization which would further the workers' cause. It would not spend its strength in futile revolts against the capitalist framework of society, but make of the law of supply and demand an instrument as serviceable to workers as to employers. Demand for workers always implied demand for goods and services which they produced. Empirically trade unionists had always known this; no strike ever achieved its end unless demand was brisk enough to make it worth the employer's while to pay higher wages rather than submit to interruption of production. Both workers and employers prospered in proportion as their goods and services were wanted. Hence both sides of industry shared a common cause; only unenlightened people thought that their interests diverged. Common interest based on demand found tangible expression in a sliding scale proportioning wage rates to the state of demand by raising and lowering them in conformity with the selling price of the product; this became a feature of collective agreements, general in coal mining, widespread in the iron and steel industry. Workers who thus shared in the prosperity of their industries could not expect to remain untouched by their depressions; at a time when the State provided no unemployment benefits, trade unions in the pursuit of this policy had to assist their members by unemployment insurance.

The real strength of unions rested on their power to furnish or withhold supplies of certain skills; of these they held a monopoly, always provided they could induce all craftsmen in a particular trade to join their ranks. As their efficacy stood in direct proportion to the degree of monopoly achieved, they tried from the outset to force every man possessed of the relevant skill to join the organization, to establish a 'closed shop'; nobody endangered their power more than the outsider who, not belonging to the union, offered to perform equal work at a lower rate. This explains their long-standing hostility to women workers (except in textile unions where women predominated) on whom they looked as predestined blacklegs, and to apprentices, if introduced in excessive numbers, because this reduced apprenticeship to a mere smokescreen for dilution; it also accounts for the prevalence of demarcation disputes in industries where changes of technique caused members of one union to encroach upon operations traditionally performed by those of another.

Unions sought monopoly power in order to restrict the supply of a particular skill; by rendering it scarcer, they hoped to raise its price. The simplest method consisted of diminishing the number of men offering their services; all these unions made financial contributions towards the one-way tickets of emigrants among their members. But labour supply can be reduced by a diminution of hours as well as of men. Systematic overtime had become a habit in many industries, especially in engineering; the unions conducted campaigns against it. By associating themselves with factory reform, they helped the ten hours' movement to success and gradually introduced the Saturday half-day; a very belated milestone was erected by Parliament on this road when in 1908 it limited the underground coalminers' working day to eight hours. Not quite as clear-cut as resistance to excessive working time was the unions' dislike of piece-work; though many felt that payment in proportion to output merely tricked workers into supplying services in excess of those spontaneously rendered, piece rates were too firmly embedded in the wage structure of some industries, especially cotton textiles, to be dislodged, and the more perspicacious trade unionists realized that, even if a worker were paid by the hour, he would not retain employment long if his output remained noticeably below the standard prevalent in the industry.

To pay adequate benefits to members afflicted with sickness or unemployment and to accumulate a substantial reserve for labour disputes, unions had to levy high dues which only skilled men in comparatively well-paid occupations could afford. This coincided with the policy of restricting organization to workers in whose skill a monopoly could be established. The first union formed on this basis originated in the amalgamation of various engineering trade clubs into the Amalgamated Society of Engineers in 1851. Within ten years it had accumulated £73,000 —the report sent a shiver down the spines of newspaper readers, few of whom performed the arithmetical exercise of dividing the sum by the number of the Society's members in order to ascertain its adequacy in the event of a total stoppage of work. So successful was the Amalgamated Society of Engineers and so widely imitated by other unions that it earned the name of the 'new model' union; indeed, the trade unions predominant from the 1850s to the end of the 1880s are usually described as new model, craft or amalgamated unions. Even among skilled workers, the urge to combine was stronger in some trades than in others. Nearly two-thirds of all unionists were employed in building, coal mining, engineering, general metal working (including shipbuilding) and cotton. There also remained skilled occupations in which workers continued to organize on a local trade club basis instead of adopting the new model: examples occurred in boot and shoe manufacture and tailoring, except where the latter trade concentrated in the biggest towns.

Amalgamated unions covered large areas—often a county, sometimes the whole country. Clubs or lodges at local level now turned into branches, subject to central control over funds and policy. Union organization needed full-time attention, coupled with the ability to invest and administer considerable funds, correspond with, and concert the policy of, a large number of branches, even at times to conduct negotiations with employers or their organizations. No longer could these tasks be performed by the man who spent his working day at the bench or in the yard, devoting his spare time to union service. Administrative ability was very different from the skill required from members working at the trade; unions had to appoint full-time paid officials to handle their affairs. By virtue of their knowledge of union business, such officers were predestined to become the leaders of the union movement as a whole. This became clear in 1860 when five general secretaries of large trade unions with headquarters in London had occasion to foregather at meetings of the London Trades Council, the coordinating committee which unions formed in towns for the discussion of local problems. They were typical representatives of new model unionism: self-educated, shrewd, forceful and moderate. Without any official mandate or position other than their individual secretary-ships, these men in the next decade established their ascendancy over the trade union movement. In their own day, they were spoken of as 'the clique', but are now better known as 'the junta', the name bestowed upon them by the Webbs. They gave the movement a leadership which it had hitherto lacked.

Not that all unionists wanted to follow whither the junta led. Engineers, shipbuilders, carpenters and joiners, craftsmen plying their trades alongside large numbers of unskilled men, were constantly concerned lest employers attempted to transfer some of their work to the labourers at a much lower rate of remuneration. In the iron and steel industry, a small number of highly skilled workers acted as sub-contractors, becoming them-selves employers of the great mass of labour. Neither in cotton nor in mining did craftsmen fear encroachment on the part of the unskilled to the same extent. Differences in working conditions made for differences, not only in the manner in which societies were organized, but even in the policy pursued. Nor was this all. In some trades, unionists eschewed centralization altogether. In cotton, local organizations occasionally federated for a common cause, but otherwise pursued their efforts separately; though miners found it necessary to undertake joint agitation for legislation in their interest, they were too severely rent by internal differences over policy to allow a single union to represent them all. Even in the heyday of new model unionism, union organization exhibited a variety of patterns.

Unionists, especially in the North, not only adopted their own patterns of organization, but also disagreed with the junta over policy. Antagonism between employer and employed assumed harsher forms in the North; lockouts of workers by employers, organized in local trade associations in order to counter union pressure, occurred more frequently. Northern operatives hankered after a more militant policy than the junta pursued. In 1868 the Manchester and Salford Trades Council called a conference of all trade societies to discuss common problems; the mere fact of the meeting taking place at Manchester served notice on the junta that the game would not be played on their home ground. The junta retaliated by ignoring the summons; the Manchester meeting represented only a part of the British trade unionists. It resolved to make conferences of trade unions an annual event, giving them the name by which they are still known today: the Trades Union Congress. Not until 1871, impelled by the threat of legislation dangerous to trade unions, did the junta decide to close the ranks of the movement by lending its support to the Trades Union Congress. The Congress throughout its existence remained what it had been in 1868: a voluntary organization which individual unions could join or leave at will. It acted as a forum for discussion, deliberation, even recommendations, but never acquired the power to order any trade union to act contrary to its own wishes. As it assembled only for five days in every year, but in the interval had to preserve continuity and to safeguard its interests, it elected every year from 1871 onwards a Parliamentary Committee to watch legislation concerning trade unions, but also to report on the progress of the movement and guide Congress debates.

TABLE F

	EMPLOYED POPULATION IN GREAT BRITAIN (000)	WORKERS REPRESENTED AT TRADES UNION CONGRESS (000)
1871	12,117	289
1881	12,739	464
1891	14,500	1,303

In the third quarter of the nineteenth century, with Britain happily ensconced as the workshop of the world, the junta's policy scored considerable successes. In an expanding economy, larger slices of the national product for one sector do not imply smaller ones for another; workers obtained a better share, not at the expense of, but at the same time as, employers. In such circumstances, it made sense to hold that employers and workers had identical interests, that conflicts between them were artificial and unenlightened and that their differences could be resolved round a conference table. The policy which the junta pursued limited unionism to skilled men. They alone could afford high contributions, nor could unions ever have established a monopoly of unskilled labourers' services; if their labour were withheld, others could easily replace them. Moreover, union opinion questioned their capacity for 'scientific unionism', their willingness to submit to union discipline. The junta leaders deliberately avoided permanent political commitment; at each election, trade unions presented their demands to both parties and exhorted such of their members as had votes to use them for the side which made the most satisfactory response. In this manner they obtained many piecemeal advances in public health, factory legislation and education without any exertion greater than the use of the ballot box.

The industrial system at most times placed employers in a stronger bargaining position than those who depended on them for employment. In order to compensate for their weakness when individually confronting individual employers, workers had sought collective strength by combination. Employers had naturally resisted the desire on the part of their operatives for greater control over their remuneration and working conditions. Trade unions, in order to improve the terms of their members' employment, had to take the offensive; employers, merely wishing to retain their erstwhile economic superiority, fought a rearguard action. It consisted mostly of refusing to recognize trade unions, of insisting on individual bargaining; sometimes it went to the length of exacting from their workers a pledge that they would not join unions. Usually employers felt strong enough to give battle single-handed, but where workers in combination had been successful in gaining concessions, employers sometimes took to heart the lesson of greater strength derived from collective organization. Here and there, the employers of a trade in a town or district would combine into an association for the purpose of resisting the inroads made by trade unions. Coal owners in Durham and Northumberland, master builders in London showed the way. Only in a few industries did such trade associations cover larger areas, notably in iron and building; the most comprehensive mustered textile employers in Lancashire, Yorkshire, Derbyshire and Cheshire. By the 1870s, when trade unions had formed a Congress and urban workers had votes which compelled Parliament to listen to their demands, employers endeavoured to counter their influence by the establishment of the National Federation of Associated Employers of Labour. But even that body lasted only a few years. The vast majority of industrialists still trusted to their ability to dictate the terms on which they would engage their employees.

When a Sheffield razor grinder was murdered by a trade club member exploding a powder keg in his house, the press laid the crime at the door of the trade union movement as a whole, little realizing how far it had left behind the clubs whose members had believed in murder as a weapon in industrial disputes. The following year (1867) saw a Court of Queen's Bench case of crucial importance to the trade union movement, the Bradford Boilermakers' decision. The secretary of the Bradford branch of the boilermakers' union had absconded with its funds; the union sued for recovery. Going back to the repeal of the combination laws, the court found that, though union membership was not punishable, unions were associations in restraint of trade, hence illegal. It followed that they could not be persons at law, hence could not stand possessed of funds nor sue for their recovery. Unions suffered a rude shock on discovering that their funds, unlike those of friendly societies, did not enjoy protection; in order to safeguard them, the law had to be changed. To achieve this as well as to correct the erroneous image which the press campaign had created in the public mind, the junta suggested a Royal Commission on Trade Unions which was duly convened. Evidence given on behalf of the unions before that commission represented the junta at its best. It made much of the services which unions rendered to their members by insuring them against ill-health and unemployment; men formerly driven to desperate expedients in emergencies now willingly acquiesced in peaceful bargaining and abided by union decisions. Far from stirring up industrial strife, unions made an important contribution to social stability. This view commended itself to the Royal Commission; though not unanimous in all respects, its recommendations took account of most of the junta's wishes. Legislation in the 1870s granted trade unions legal personality, freed them from the threat of conspiracy for doing collectively anything which was lawful, if done by a single person, and repealed a number of Acts, known as the master and servant legislation, which had prejudiced workers in litigation with employers. Though molestation, obstruction, intimidation and persistent following remained forbidden, peaceful picketing was legalized.

To British industrial supremacy, the junta's policy had been well adapted. When in the last quarter of the nineteenth century one industry after another felt the impact of foreign competition, the limitations of new model unionism became apparent. A sliding scale of wages varying with selling prices had benefited workers exceedingly over a period of two-and-a-half decades of stable or rising prices; the downward trend after 1875 made workers for the first time conscious of its grievous impact in a depression. When production slowed down, even skilled men found themselves out of work. This greatly embittered demarcation disputes; unions fought more obstinately for what they considered their members' prerogatives if the latter faced the alternative of unemployment. Demarcation disputes strained the trade union movement's ability to speak and act as a whole. By insisting on maintenance of wage rates, it benefited those among its members who succeeded in remaining in their jobs, but did nothing for those who became unemployed. Dissatisfaction with the unions became rampant; among others John Burns and Thomas Mann, out-of-work members of the Amalgamated Society of Engineers, after 1884 combined their search for employment with speeches up and down the country demanding a new union policy. These demands found backing from the new and revolutionary doctrines of the day: that of land nationalization put forward by Henry George, and the various brands of socialism—preached in its true Marxist purity by Henry Hyndman, in a more reformist version by the Fabian Society.

That experienced trade unionists had lost their employment and found time and opportunity to interest themselves in the organization of workers as yet without any representation at all, was a blessing in disguise to unskilled labourers. By their complete neglect of the unskilled, trade unions had created a dichotomy in the working class of which its members were only too well aware. A crisis caused suffering among skilled unionists, but hit unorganized labourers far harder. As long as they remained inarticulate and leaderless, they had little chance of improving their lot. An attempt in the early 1870s to organize agricultural labourers had borne only temporary fruit. Not until the late 1880s did the unskilled workers achieve permanent organization. The first group to strike, women making matches in the East End of London, owed its success in 1888 to little more than accident: a journalist, Annie Besant, enlisted public sympathy and financial help by a description of their working conditions. A larger section, gas stokers, reduced their working day from 12 to eight hours by a surprise announcement of collective action in London, though in the provinces more than a mere threat was required. But the decisive breakthrough came with the great London dock strike of 1889. In the docks unskilled workers laboured alongside skilled and unionized stevedores and lightermen; trade union history was made when the latter supported a dockworkers' strike by withdrawal of their own labour. Again much depended on public sympathy and contributions, as dockworkers were far too poor to withhold employment for any length of time out of their own resources. Shepherded by strong and determined leaders, dockworkers proved themselves as capable of scientific unionism as their skilled colleagues and secured an almost complete concession of all their demands.

It was dockers, gas workers, farm labourers, firemen, merchant sailors and a host of others classed as unskilled workers who formed the 'new unions' making their mark in the 1890s and entering on a phase of vigorous and sustained growth around 1910—people on the margin of existence, unable to pay high contributions, hence expecting from their unions very low friendly benefits or none at all. Possessing no irreplaceable skill, they pursued no policy based on monopoly, nor did they jealously guard their jobs from intrusion; not who did the job, but that the rate for the job should be paid, was their main concern. An interest in the prosperity of their industry they willingly left to their employers, being far more preoccupied with their own livelihood. That industry should pay them a living wage, formed the main principle of new unionism; where it negotiated sliding scales of wages, they were based, not on the selling price of the product, but on the cost of living. If an industry could not afford to pay a living wage, then it was parasitic: it took out of its workers more than it put back into them; if it had to close down or move away, new unions felt no compunction.

Forcing industry to concede a certain wage level, whether it could afford it or not, was a policy which could never command the employers' assent. New unionists were well aware of this and did not expect to obtain any advances in collaboration with employers, nor did they ever believe that workers' and employers' interests could be identical. On the contrary, they acted on the conviction that interests conflicted sharply and that attack all along the line and incessant harrying of employers alone would secure their aims. One of the weapons they needed in this fight was political power. They found in Parliament two parties, in both of which employers played a large part. New unionists did not trust any party representing employers to do justice to workers; only a party dedicated to the working class interest would satisfy their demands. It was at their insistence that an Independent Labour Party established itself in 1893 with a near-socialist programme, a party independent of Conservatives and Liberals, entirely devoted to the promotion of the workers' cause. In order to increase the number of its supporters and the chance of its parliamentary candidates, the Independent Labour

Party in 1900 combined with the Social Democratic Federation (Hyndman's Marxist organization), the Fabian Society and the trade union movement in a Labour Representation Committee. After its success in the general election of 1906, the Labour Representation Committee changed its name to Labour Party. Only at the end of the first world war did it abandon its policy of championing the workers' cause exclusively and realign its aims so as to appeal to a wider electorate.

Over tactics, new unions clashed with their predecessors. Absence of demarcation disputes made inter-union collaboration among new unions easier. Not possessing the bargaining strength or experience of the older organizations, new unions campaigned for State enforcement of measures which amalgamated unions preferred to achieve through collective agreements. Such conflicts put a strain on union solidarity, the more so since new unions could outnumber the old at Trades Union Congresses for a short period. New unions for the first time organized women on a large scale, and craftsmen in the long run had no option but to offer women membership of whichever union covered their trade. Unskilled workers were more volatile than skilled: membership of new unions fell off sharply in the bad years of the middle 1890s, compared with the solid support enjoyed by new model unions in fat years and in lean.

Trade Unions in the Twentieth Century

TABLE G

	EMPLOYED POPULATION IN GREAT BRITAIN (000)	MEMBERSHIP OF TRADE UNIONS (000)
1901	16,312	2,025
1911	18,351	3,139
1921	19,369	6,624
1931	21,074	4,611

Employers reacted to this greatly increased threat to their authority—some mildly by schemes of co-partnership and profit-sharing designed to establish a bond between workers and the firm which employed them; such projects had a vogue in the early 1890s. Many reacted more sharply, by long lockouts in the cotton and coal mining industries, by dismissing all union members, as did the London and North Western Railway Company, or by creating registers or even mobile reserves of non-union labour. But the time when industrialists could call the whole principle of collective representation into question had passed. Though individual employers, sometimes whole trades, fought rearguard actions, only the least perspicacious could doubt by the end of the nineteenth century that trade unionism had come to stay. So much had it become part of the accepted and necessary pattern of the industrial scene that the Trade Boards Act of 1909 empowered the government to render statutory assistance to workers in fixing wages for trades where unions were either non-existent or too weak to play an effective part in bargaining. As soon as workers had organized themselves sufficiently to conduct collective negotiations successfully, the trade board could be dissolved, leaving wages to be determined by the two sides of industry unaided. The threat to trade unions in the twentieth century did not come from employers, but from the law. Created in a period of individualist thought, the law had not easily adapted itself to associations, least of all to those threatening compulsion. If it could not suppress them, it tended at least to circumscribe their powers. This may have accorded ill with twentieth century realities, but it was not—as has so often been contended—the fault of bad or biased judgments. Lawyers had always regarded themselves as guardians of individual liberty; they continued to play their traditional part. It was unfortunate that, as the century progressed, trade unions had less and less use or respect for individual liberty.

The three collisions marking the conflict of law and trade unions all took place in the railway industry—one of the trades withholding recognition of workers' organizations longest—but only one of them involved employers. This was the Taff Vale case. In 1901 the Taff Vale Railway Company sued the Amalgamated Society of Railway Servants for, among other things, compensation in respect of damage caused to the company by a strike organized by the society's officers. Since the 1870s trade unions had enjoyed legal personality; the House of Lords held them, like any other person at law, responsible for the actions of representatives performed on their behalf: it awarded the company not only £23,000 damages, but also the costs of the case, thus almost doubling the union's pecuniary loss. However logical, the award completely jeopardized trade unionism. Though a strike may not be undertaken solely to cause employers damage, no strike is likely to succeed in its objective unless employers suffer damage in its course. If unions have to compensate employers for such losses, they are deprived of the right to strike, the only ultimate sanction at their disposal. Nothing rallied trade unionists to the Labour Representation Committee more effectively than the Taff Vale decision: if this was the law, they required political power to change it. And change it Parliament in 1906 did, as soon as it assembled: an Act freed unions from the doctrine of 'representative action', as applied to legal persons, and put them into the exceptional position of being able to sue, but not to be sued at law for anything done by their servants or agents in furtheranceof a trade dispute.

A railway man named Osborne, who was secretary of his branch of the Amalgamated Society of Railway Servants, but whose political allegiance belonged to the Liberal party, observed with disapproval that the union contributed to Labour party funds. He thereupon sued the society for a declaration that it had no right to use any part of his own contribution for political purposes. The House of Lords, seized with the case in 1909, scrutinized legal definitions of trade unions from the repeal of the Combination Laws onwards. These described them as associations for industrial purposes. On this basis, the court declared that it was *ultra vires* for trade unions to engage in political activities. Such a rule, if maintained in force, would have crippled and eventually starved out of existence the young Labour party, the great bulk of whose funds came in the form of trade union affiliation fees; its members in Parliament, men without private means, lived on salaries paid by trade unions which treated attendance in the House of Commons as a service rendered to the movement as a whole. Here again only a legislative cure could redress the balance; first aid came in the form of payment for members of Parliament from public funds in 1911; a more comprehensive statute two years later legalized political activities by trade unions on three conditions: a majority of members had to vote in favour; unions had to keep general and political funds separate, and each individual member had to have an opportunity to contract out of the political contribution.

This last rule was the opening blow in a ding-dong battle to shift the onus of form filling. Up to 1927 a member wishing to contract out had to take the initiative, but legislation after the general strike of 1926 substituted contracting in, with bad effects on Labour party funds; the man wishing to pay the political contribution now had to inform the union accordingly. One of the first acts of the Labour government in 1946 consisted of the re-introduction of contracting out.

One of the members contracting out of the political fund, Arthur Birch, was in 1946 elected chairman of his branch of the National Union of Railwaymen. This position implied control or management of the branch's political fund; when the union declared him ineligible for the chairmanship by virtue of his contracting out, he contested the validity of this action in the Court of Chancery. Judgment in 1950 found fault neither with his capacity for holding office nor with the union's reaction, but with the latter's rules. In order to enable men contracting out of the political levy to hold any offices to which their fellow members might elect them, unions had to provide for separate administration of political funds. This prevented unions from using their rules to put at a disadvantage non-contributors to political funds —a principle already laid down in the 1913 Act.

The first world war weakened trade unions. Outwardly, on the contrary, they gained in stature: the government, in the interests of national unity, sought their advice and cooperation in adapting industrial conditions to the war. Precisely because they did not fail the nation in its hour of danger, because they agreed to accept for the duration normally unpalatable measures such as dilution of labour, compulsory arbitration and a degree of wage restraint, they found themselves at a disadvantage *vis-à-vis* employers on the one hand and their own members on the other. Who could and who could not be spared for the war effort, was a decision which only employers could make; it gave them an opportunity of having troublemakers conscripted, while declaring as indispensable key workers those whom they favoured. Inflation eroded the real value of wage packets; by their undertakings unions bound themselves not to enforce wage increases by means of strikes. These obligations, entered into by unions and honoured by their officers, gave unofficial leaders an opportunity of diverting workers' loyalties. They usually sprang from the ranks of shop stewards.

A shop or collecting steward had originally been a lowly functionary in the union hierarchy who at workshop level collected members' contributions and gave out membership cards and notices. The war cast him in a new rôle. Hitherto workers in any one establishment had usually belonged to a single union; if they wanted to communicate collectively with employers, the district secretary of their union was their natural representative. Dilution brought into war industries members of many unions as well as non-unionists; no longer were officers of any one union entitled to speak in the name of a workshop force. Yet negotiation there had to be, at a time when avoidance of industrial conflict was practically a military necessity, when factories and workshops faced extraordinary problems born of the national emergency, which could be settled only in the light of conditions in the individual establishment. What could be more natural than that each workshop or factory department should elect its own shop steward, some one familiar with local conditions, known personally to the workers, always on the spot and better able to judge the circumstances of each dispute than the trade union official responsible for the district? Backed by the allegiance of the workers who had elected them, shop stewards could put forward demands more effectively than officials at higher levels in the union hierarchy, bound by national agreements, preoccupied with the national interest and burdened with responsibility for a large number of establishments in their district.

Not that all shop stewards were irresponsible firebrands; on the contrary, the majority consisted of men conscientiously performing a laborious and difficult job of mediation in a situation fraught with stress. Nor did they represent a new departure in workers' organization; had not the earliest union leaders been workers at their respective trades, organizing their fellows in their spare time? However valuable the services rendered by a large number of shop stewards in many establishments working for the war effort, the limelight inevitably played on a minority of extremists who saw in the war mainly an opportunity for wresting concessions from the nation while it was involved in a struggle for survival. The government had to act circumspectly, even in the face of 'illegal' demands; on one occasion a whole committee of shop stewards was deported from Scotland and released in the Midlands without any charges being preferred. Employers who detested them did their best to foster the impression that all shop stewards conformed to this pattern. Trade unions themselves were no more enamoured than employers of a cog which threatened to throw the whole machinery out of gear.

Employers and trade unions therefore looked to the end of the war to consign shop stewards to the limbo whence they had come. Their survival owed nothing to their success in endearing themselves to either of these groups. There was only one person in industry who wanted the shop steward, upheld him, refused to do without him: the ordinary worker. Increasingly after the war, as units of production became larger and more powerful, trade unions in their turn had to grow to comparable size, either by amalgamation or by vigorous recruiting, in order to hold their own. In the early 1920s, fusion of labourers' unions brought about the two largest workers' organizations yet known, the Transport and General Workers' Union and the National Union of General and Municipal Workers whose membership ran into six figures and operated in some 200 industries. This increase in union size was in the interests of the workers themselves, but entailed problems of industrial democracy inseparable from mammoth organizations. Their local unit was the branch, a geographical sub-division which had lost its meaning, instead of the workshop, the significance of which workers recognized. Union officers became more and more remote, unable to feel the pulse of the rank and file; the ordinary unionist knew his general secretary as well as he knew the Minister of Labour—not to speak of the fact that soon after the outbreak of the second world war the general secretary of the Transport and General Workers' Union became Minister of Labour! In theory, union officials remained not only accountable to, but removable by, the whole membership. In practice, the business of these giant organizations had to be conducted by men with a reasonable assurance of continuity of office; their annual re-election was a mere formality.

Estranged from their union hierarchy, subject to union decisions in the making of which their share had grown infinitesimal, workers saw in the shop steward their ideal of a union official: a man accessible at any time, who would listen to their grievances and suggestions on the spot and take them up without the need of a lengthy enquiry to acquaint himself with workshop conditions. If he refused to act, nothing prevented an aggrieved party from calling a workshop meeting that very day, getting the shop steward deposed and another elected in his place. Thus shop stewards fulfilled a deeply felt need of industrial workers; gradually, though grudgingly, employers and trade unions had to accept and integrate them into the industrial pattern. This did not happen without friction, but two functions a shop steward could fulfil better than anybody else: he could act as spokesman of an individual shop labour force and as expert assessor regarding the application of national agreements to local conditions. When afforded an opportunity of appearing in these rôles, he could make a positive contribution to industrial peace.

The exigencies of war required a higher degree of organization from many groups in the community. Employers of labour had never before succeeded in maintaining for any length of time an effective association unless it were confined to a single industry. In 1916 they founded the Federation of British Industries, a new and successful organization representing manufacturers generally. However, the Federation soon found itself fully occupied with representing the industrialists' point of view to Parliament; within two years of its foundation it abandoned the industrial relations part of its work to a newly established body, the National Confederation of Employers' Organizations (subsequently the British Employers' Confederation). This signified that employers as well as workers were now equipped to bargain on a nation-wide scale, if desired.

Reappraisal of the movement's structure after the first world war caused the Trades Union Congress in 1921 to replace its Parliamentary Committee by a General Council, a kind of general staff to provide intelligence and guidance. The actual congress was a mere annual event; for 51 weeks of every year, the General Council had to represent the movement. Considerable regrouping was in progress among the forces ranged behind it. Though the differences between craft and general labourers' unions, so important before the war, had not been obliterated, their significance was reduced by the tendency to form newer unions on the basis of the industry in which men worked rather than the operations they performed: the National Union of Railwaymen accepted into membership anybody who drew a remuneration from a railway company, whether working on the permanent way, driving a locomotive, setting signals or issuing tickets, but alongside this industrial union two organizations continued to cater on craft lines for locomotive engineers and firemen on the one hand and for clerical staffs on the other. Threatened by the increasing size and bargaining power of organizations catering for the less skilled, craft unions in the interwar years adopted a noticeably more aggressive attitude to employers; they refused to acquiesce in the diminution of 'established differentials', the proportion by which their wage rates had always exceeded those of unskilled men. This had been an issue in the first world war when every flat-rate increase or cost-of-living bonus narrowed the gap; it became a far more serious and intractable problem in and after the second, because full employment and the need for the greatest possible utilization of every pair of hands put a premium even on men who in conditions of lower pressure would have been considered redundant or even unemployable. Another group whose weight in the trade union movement had not been seriously felt before the first world war were the white-collar workers: clerks, shop assistants, teachers, musicians and others. They introduced a conscious middle class element into a movement whose higher ranks had anyhow long ceased to belong in any significant sense to the working class. Yet the 20 years between the two wars were full of frustrated ambitions for the trade union movement, on account of the chronic depression and the unemployment endemic in British industry.

On the labour front the government approached the second world war in fear and trembling. It knew the measures necessary for successful prosecution of the war: prohibition of strikes and lockouts, wage control, industrial conscription. It knew equally well that the trade union movement would not agree to them and that any politician would pay by loss of office for his temerity in advocating them in public. Every government department dropped responsibility for industrial labour like a potato too hot to touch; instead of a policy, there was a series of compromises. Yet without cooperation from the workers the war would be lost. Only by entrusting responsibility for the Ministry of Labour to the most prominent personality among trade union leaders, Ernest Bevin, could such cooperation be obtained; once in office, Bevin had no hesitation in demanding sacrifices from the workers which in his capacity as their representative he would have been the first to denounce. As in the first world war, strikes and lockouts were outlawed, though not thereby prevented; wages underwent a degree of control which kept them below the rise in the cost of living up to 1942, but lost much of its hold thereafter; the nearest approach to industrial conscription consisted of a certain amount of direction of labour, though this did not prevent poaching of workers among industries all desperately short of manpower. In return for pledging cooperation in the war effort, the trade union movement acquired seats in all the highest councils of State and a right to be heard on all questions of importance.

If the war had lifted unions into the saddle, full employment after the war confirmed them in power. Not only did Labour governments rule the country from 1945 to 1951, but labour in a sellers' market dictated its own terms, especially once war emergency legislation had been withdrawn. Whether it be higher wages, shorter hours, the 'closed shop' or fringe benefits, employers resisted union demands at the risk of finding themselves deprived of labour in a world clamouring for their goods. Why should a worker try to satisfy his employer, if any one losing his job had the choice of at least two vacancies awaiting him? Even where the labour-saving effects of automation might have threatened the ability of workers to impose their own conditions, a policy of reducing the working week correspondingly countered this danger. In these circumstances, labour turnover assumed alarming proportions. Nothing short of a period of less full employment could have diminished the workers' supremacy. But the major political parties had committed themselves to full employment, remembering the nightmare of interwar unemployment, and workers knew that their voting strength would unseat any government which contemplated going back on this pledge.

The opportunities for abuse which this pinnacle of power afforded worried the best trade union leaders a good deal. They knew better than most that those who sought to undermine the British economy for their own ends looked upon the trade union movement as the handiest Trojan horse through which to introduce disruptive elements into leading positions. Shop stewards

TABLE H

EMPLOYED POPULATION IN THE UNITED KINGDOM (000)		MEMBERSHIP OF TRADE UNIONS (000)
1950	32,532	9,288
1955	32,085	9,719
1958	31,178	9,616

formed the most vulnerable sector of the union movement; the penetration of certain shop stewards and their organizations by communists became household knowledge, almost obliterating the efforts of the great majority of shop stewards to continue discharging their duties without ulterior political motive. But owing to the fact that a majority of trade unionists did not bother to attend branch meetings or exercise voting rights, a minority of militant communists succeeded in capturing leading posts in the hierarchy of a few trade unions whose whole weight was then thrown into the scale of disruption, all on the pretence of securing to the worker a fair share of the product of industry. Success remained more limited in other unions, where a dangerous rift opened between top leaders, alive to the difficulties of keeping the British economy on an even keel, pledging their cooperation in improving productivity and safeguarding industrial peace, and rank and file members grimly muttering defiance in the background. Whenever a trade union leader accepted managerial office in one of the nationalized industries, there were those in the movement who treated such a change of post as a betrayal, who urged unionists to decline all responsibility so as to keep themselves free to put forward irresponsible demands. The cleavage in the trade union movement between those demanding power without responsibility and those who, because of a responsible attitude, constantly risked losing command of the movement, boded ill for Britain's industrial future in the 1960s.

The Settlement of Industrial Disputes

Unions do more than maintain and improve their members' wages or even working conditions. In addition to collective bargaining, they cooperate in the amendment and extension of factory legislation, suggest, and in many instances run, welfare schemes or institutions for workers and their families, and provide—sometimes directly, sometimes in collaboration with universities, the Cooperative Movement or local authorities—educational facilities for their members. But the fight for higher wages has always occupied the centre of trade union activities. Where disagreement about the appropriate level of remuneration divided employers and workers, both sides had to resort to industrial action or find ways of settling their dispute.

A difference between employers and workers must either lead to industrial action (a lockout or strike), or both sides must sit round a table and resolve it peaceably. This can be done in one of two ways: they can be brought to agree, or a solution can be imposed. In the second case, an impartial outsider is indispensable because he must formulate the decision; this form of settlement is called arbitration. But even where agreement between the parties is the aim, it can usually be reached more easily and quickly if an outsider, not personally involved and known to favour neither employers nor workers, discusses the issues with both parties—if tempers are frayed, he may at the outset not even be able to seat them at the same table, but may have to keep them in separate rooms, acting as go-between until he has established a basis for negotiations—and suggests how they may be resolved. Settlement in this manner is known as conciliation. British practice has always applied two principles to both conciliation and arbitration: a voluntary settlement, adopted by the parties of their own free will, is preferable to a compulsory one which has to be imposed upon them; autonomous machinery, which any industry has established for the settlement of its disputes, takes precedence over statutory machinery made available by the government; the latter is only a second-best.

Arbitration in the nineteenth century had a long and on the whole unsuccessful history, owing to the State's desire to introduce it on its own terms. These included the appointment of arbitrators by magistrates; workers rightly or wrongly suspected magistrates of sympathy for employers, therefore did not trust arbitrators whom they had nominated; indeed, workers would not agree to arbitration at all, unless informed beforehand who was going to arbitrate. They would not brook the State's reluctance to recognize trade unions and their collective bargaining, its restriction of arbitration to individual wage bargains. Finally, the State wanted to enforce by law arbitration awards, but this suited neither side of industry; workers and employers, having heard the award, demanded the right to decide whether or not to accept it. In the circumstances, various laws on arbitration up to 1896 remained dead letters. This does not mean that arbitration did not occur; wherever both sides of industry voluntarily agreed upon it, industrial disputes were settled by arbitration.

Conciliation, after informal beginnings in the earlier nineteenth century, made a real start in the 1860s. At the suggestion of a large and influential employer, A. J. Mundella, the hosiery trade of Nottingham established what became a model conciliation board, consisting of employers and workers in equal numbers and dealing with disputes either as a full board or through committees drawn from its membership. Voluntary joint boards in other districts and in other industries copied the successful example, all composed on the principle of equal representation of both sides, the workers usually nominated by the trade unions concerned. When arbitration occurred, it was through voluntary joint boards being requested in particular instances to act as arbitrating, instead of merely conciliating, bodies.

By 1886, when A. J. Mundella had become President of the Board of Trade, he added to his ministry's organization a Department of Labour Statistics. Officially it concerned itself with the collection and publication of information on labour matters and the conduct of enquiries into questions of industrial interest. The latter function opened a door to its officials to lend assistance in conciliation proceedings in their capacity as independent parties; ample experience in the settlement of labour disputes turned them into a cadre of expert conciliation officers. Official recognition of this development in 1893 changed the department's name to Labour Department. Its chief conciliation officer, Sir George (later Lord) Askwith, more than any other man contributed to the restoration of industrial peace in the turbulent years preceding the first world war.

Up to the end of the nineteenth century, conciliation remained local. Voluntary joint boards had been welcomed and recommended by the Trades Union Congress and enlightened employers in a number of industries. That conciliation after 1900 was undertaken on a country-wide scale, during and after the first world war even on a national basis, resulted mainly from the piece of legislation which set on it the seal of official approval and laid down its framework for the future, the Conciliation Act of 1896. This authorized the Board of Trade to enquire into the causes and circumstances of any industrial dispute; even on the application of a single party it could start conciliation proceedings, whereas it required the consent of both to set on foot arbitration. This preserved the general principle that either party could be made to come and sit at a table, but that neither could be coerced into accepting any decision against its will. Sufficient recourse was had to arbitration procedure to justify the President of the Board of Trade in appointing permanent arbitration courts in 1908. They consisted of three panels, recruited from representatives of organized employers, trade unions and independent parties, whether Labour department officials or outsiders; the last was known as the chairmen's panel. If parties to an industrial dispute agreed to arbitration, they applied to the Board of Trade either for a single arbitrator (who would be drawn from the chairmen's panel) or for an arbitration court which assured parity of workers' and employers' representation. In most industrial disputes, employers and workers can be relied on to vote on opposite sides, acting in practice as assessors, the actual decision having to be made by the chairman.

Industrial peace, desirable at all times, became a vital necessity during the first world war. Protracted negotiations with both sides of industry enabled the government for the duration of the war to replace voluntary by compulsory arbitration and make its awards binding, not only on both parties, but in the munition industry even on all establishments engaged in the same production. So voluminous and important, among the Board of Trade's duties, did labour relations become that they were hived off in the middle of the war (1916) when a separate Ministry of Labour was established.

The spirit of collaboration born of the national emergency justified hopes that the wartime necessity of settling industrial disputes without violence might become a post-war virtue. A select committee of the House of Commons under the chairmanship of Mr. Speaker Whitley in 1917 sought means of continuing joint consultation, perhaps even arbitration, once emergency legislation had been repealed. It recommended joint councils at three levels, national, district and works, to be established voluntarily by employers' associations and trade unions in every industry to discuss problems of mutual relations entrusted to them by both sides. Whitley councils came into existence in the post-war years, but proved a disappointment. Many major industries never set them up at all; in others, trade unions and employers' associations refused to surrender the right to negotiate on wages or other questions of importance on which they could bring their strong bargaining power to bear, leaving to Whitley councils only minor matters and condemning them to insignificance. Whitley councils prospered however in public employment where they had the success envisaged by their authors. Sometimes large general unions with small groups of specialized workers, whose employment needed separate conditions or safeguards, entrusted Whitley councils with negotiations concerning such terms, thus opening to the councils a new field of activities. In and after the second world war, Whitley councils took on a new lease of life in the guise of joint productivity councils appointed in an endeavour to enlist the cooperation of both sides in improving productivity in their respective industries.

Most major industries in the interwar years had or established machinery for wage negotiations and the solution of disputes. To assist a host of minor trades unable or unwilling to do so, the government in 1919 set up the Industrial Court. Like all arbitration bodies, it consisted of an equal number of employers' and workers' representatives with an independent chairman. A labour dispute could reach the Industrial Court only if the Minister of Labour, once the conciliation or arbitration machinery within the industry had been exhausted, referred it to the court; to do so, he required the consent of both parties, implemented in practice by the continuation or resumption of work pending the court's decision. The number of cases heard by the Industrial Court in its first year of existence—539—testified both to its importance and to the willingness of trades to resort to it.

This procedure of settling industrial disputes ministered to expediency—many would argue that there could be no higher virtue about the solution of conflicts which know no right or wrong. Any award served, provided it proved acceptable to the parties; arbitration knew no policy and admitted of no principles, except to settle at any price. Industrial peace was the apotheosis of the whole mechanism interposed between the two sides of industry. Yet in practice it soon became apparent that the public interest suffered. Arbitrators were expected to behave like judges and disregard anything not pleaded before them. In any dispute, skilled and experienced spokesmen presented the case for both sides, but nobody played the part of *amicus curiae* to inform the tribunal of the public interest. In the nineteenth century, it had been reasonable to argue that the public interest was not involved; not so in the twentieth, when every wage award provoked consequential claims in a number of related industries, until a change of wage rates had worked its way through the whole industrial system, affecting in the process the general price level and the distribution of the national income. Employers and workers were free to arrive, or not to arrive, at a settlement, according to the degree of obstinacy and self-confidence prevailing among their ranks, even though industrial action, if taken close to the point of consumption, could inflict on the public much greater inconvenience, even suffering, than on the opposing party. This found at least partial recognition in the Emergency Powers Act of 1920: where industrial action threatened to withhold the essentials of life, defined as food, water, fuel, light or the means of locomotion, a royal proclamation could empower the government, neither to conscript nor to punish lockers-out or strikers, but to organize services for the population so threatened. Only twice before 1945 was it used: in the coal strike of 1921 and in the general strike five years later.

Settlement of industrial disputes after the second world war was bedevilled by the desire to preserve two conflicting freedoms, both part of the national tradition not to be lightly sacrificed. Freedom of employment safeguarded the right of workers to choose what trade they wished to pursue, and freedom of employers whom and how many they would engage. These freedoms were reconciled with the needs of industry by the price mechanism: an overmanned industry became unprofitable and had in the process of cutting costs to lower its wages, thus losing some workers who could earn more elsewhere, whereas an understaffed industry could not produce all the output demanded of it and had to raise wages in an endeavour to attract additional labour. Freedom of collective bargaining on the other hand implied the right of workers' and employers' organizations to reap the full benefit of the terms which their bargaining strength could wring from the other side. Such bargaining strength put out of action the regulatory price mechanism: a strong union, especially if it operated a closed shop, could extort higher wages even on behalf of a labour force already vastly in excess of requirements, while a monopolistic industry, however inefficient and overstaffed, made ends meet by holding helpless consumers to ransom. These opportunities had existed before 1939, but remained latent as long as neither side was strong enough to push the conflict to extremes, especially in view of the reservoir of unused capacity, both of equipment and manpower, available at most times.

The apparatus for settling industrial disputes failed to provide for the most dangerous contingency of all: a conflict in which, machinery within the industry having been exhausted and agreement to submit it to arbitration not forthcoming, one side objected to reference to the Industrial Court. To avoid what could in these circumstances degenerate only into a trial of strength subversive of democracy and reminiscent of the law of the jungle, the Minister of Labour in 1918 had been given the power to call a Court of Enquiry. Staffed like the Industrial Court, a Court of Enquiry enquired into, and reported to the Minister on, the conditions leading to the dispute. If it thought fit, it added to its report recommendations which might facilitate a solution. The court had no powers beyond those enforcing the attendance of witnesses. The Minister of Labour published the report; this ended the functions of the court, but was designed to enlist in favour of its recommendations the moral force of public opinion. Courts of Enquiry were rarely called; as befitted a weapon of last resort, it was unsheathed only sparingly. However, the disputes on which they reported occurred mostly in industries of national importance and involved all the basic issues of industrial relations. Up to 1939, this last bastion defended industrial peace with surprising success; parties accepted reports by Court of Enquiry without any show of force. During the second world war, acquiescence in compulsory arbitration formed once again one of the sacrifices made by both sides of industry for the war effort. In the full employment atmosphere of the 1950s, on the other hand, workers could not always be persuaded to bow to the recommendations of a Court of Enquiry. If they failed to do so, complete stalemate ensued; no other weapon remained in the armoury to protect industrial peace. Until this gap could be filled, industrial relations were bound to form the chief danger point of British domestic policy.

VI | TRANSPORT

The Inheritance of the Past

As activities multiply, more people and goods have to move longer distances; rarely can they be used to best advantage unless they are available in the right place at the right time. Transport is among a country's most important economic activities; upon its ease or difficulty depends not only the quantity, but also the variety of supplies available as well as the willingness of men to serve where they are wanted. Goods can always be shifted more economically by water than by land; hence the importance for trade of coastal shipping and navigable rivers. The cost of moving cheap and bulky goods a mere 25 miles across country may well double their original price, putting them beyond the purse of distant purchasers; where otherwise they might be exported, the added expense of transport may price them out of the market. Thus can transport make or mar a country's success in international trade.

Britain has been well endowed by Nature: an elongated island of moderate distances in which no place is more than 100 miles from the sea, inland water transport provided by a number of rivers, no dense forests or impassable mountain barriers. Compared to the Continent of Europe, Britain enjoyed easy communications. Nor had Man neglected the opportunities provided by Nature. Wherever the Romans had conquered a country, they had constructed a network of roads; Britain formed no exception. But that had been well over 1,000 years ago. No systematic civilian road building had taken place since Roman days, though feet and hooves had worn tracks into paths through constant usage. Whether constructed or merely trodden, roads need upkeep. In the sixteenth century Parliament had entrusted this duty to the parishes.

Parishes enlisted all inhabitants in the work of road maintenance. Each parish elected annually or every other year a surveyor of highways. His was an honorary office; not that it constituted an honour—all parishioners in better circumstances either had or procured exemption from serving—merely that it remained unpaid. Under the surveyor's direction everybody had to contribute to the repair of the roads according to his means: large landowners by furnishing road-mending materials, more affluent farmers by providing horses and carts, the least wealthy their own labour aided by their own tools. As supervisory authority and court of appeal for parties aggrieved, there remained in the background the justices of the peace.

Organization for road repair thus existed, but did it work? It had two decisive weaknesses. The first was the unit of administration. Parishes were unsuitable for the task, both on account of their small size and because they had no interest in speeding the passing traveller on his way by maintaining through-roads in good condition. Yet who else could have undertaken the job? The government had neither the money nor the machinery to do it.

The other weakness was lack of expert knowledge. To enrol all citizens as road menders may be democratic, but brings no skill to bear on the job. Nobody attained proficiency in a task in which he engaged for eight hours on a mere six days of every year. Unskilful work was performed under inexpert supervision. Mostly farmers, the surveyors of highways were preoccupied with earning a living rather than with repairing the parish roads. Their qualification for the office at best was honesty; at worst, merely their inability to escape election. Nobody knew or cared how roads ought to be mended. Ploughing them up, smoothing over the surfaces, putting sand, gravel or pebbles on top, constituted the maximum of maintenance achieved. Roads suffered from the ignorance—and even more from the indifference—of the people charged with their upkeep.

Payment of rates has never been popular, least of all in the days when it took the form of labour services. Some people indeed converted them into money payments by engaging substitutes to perform their labour for them. In the early nineteenth century parishes hit upon the idea of making road repair work a condition of granting relief to able-bodied paupers, thus lightening the burden on parish ratepayers. Whether a general citizen, his substitute—technically known as 'the King's Highwayman', but colloquially as 'the King's Loiterer'—or a recipient of poor relief, the road mender performed a minimum of work; his exertions may have been good for his soul, but hardly for the roads.

'From London to Land's End, or even to Exeter, Plymouth or Falmouth, you have such roads as the lazy Italians have fruit, namely, what God left them after the flood!' lamented a foreign visitor around 1750. He voiced only one of a spate of complaints which filled the century just past. During this period roads had been subjected to a form of travel for which their makers had never intended them. Built for horse and pedestrian traffic, they had consisted of causeways, two to four feet wide, surfaced with stones. When coaches and carts of various types came into use, the wheels carved deep ruts into the soft ground on either side of the causeway, ruts which froze in winter and filled with slush at other seasons. Greater trade and activity multiplied the number of wheeled vehicles; roads gave way under their weight, so that subsequent travellers preferred to encroach upon surrounding fields. Such was the state of communications that fragile goods could not be transported overland, other merchandise only slowly at great expense, and hardy was the traveller who trusted his comfort and safety to a coach. Even the rider faced the danger of his horse losing its foothold in the mire into which many roads had degenerated.

Roads and Waterways

Parliament, its ears ringing with laments about the hazards of travel, filled the seventeenth century statute book with laws designed to adapt road users to the roads: limitations on the number of draught animals, methods of harnessing, weight to be carried, narrowness and height of wheels: one bill would even have forbidden wheels altogether and insisted on solid rollers, thus turning every passing vehicle into an engine for road repair. Salvation did not lie that way; Acts of this type could not be enforced. Even had they been obeyed, they might at best have prevented further deterioration; they could not improve bad roads. If the State was incapable of undertaking responsibility for the roads, only private enterprise could do so—the solution which the eighteenth century adopted. Groups of local gentlemen, whether from a spirit of public obligation or merely for gain, took over control of stretches of road; Parliament gave them power to erect toll gates, charge fees to users (except pedestrians) and on the security of these revenues raise loans to repair and maintain these highways. Large numbers of such bodies, known as turnpike trusts, obtained Acts of incorporation from the 1720s onwards.

Turnpike trusts encountered some public opposition, justified in instances where trusts proved more zealous in collecting tolls than in bettering the conditions of their roads. On most turnpiked roads mounted and wheeled traffic obtained from the improvements benefits well worth paying for. Sure of their revenues, turnpike trusts could afford to employ skilled services. Not only did they engage full-time paid workmen as road builders and menders, but architects and engineers for the first time turned their attention to problems of road foundation and shape, surface composition, gradients and other technical details. So famous became the men who devoted their lives to the construction of better highways that some of their names entered into the terminology of civil engineering: whether or not a 'macadamized' road represents perfection, it recalls one of the first civil engineers to work brilliantly along new lines. Thomas Telford and John Metcalf were as famous as John Loudon McAdam for the roads —the two former also for the bridges—they built. Between them, civil engineers and turnpike trusts ushered in the industrial revolution of the British road system.

Private enterprise however provided only a partial solution. Enterprise was required; if any particular locality lacked it, no turnpike trusts were formed. It had to be remunerated by the user in transit, interrupting his journey by a multiplicity of toll gates and turnpikes where he had to pay his fee in cash—an irritating manner of collecting his contribution. Above all, private enterprise demanded prospects of reasonable profit; where roads remained insufficiently frequented or could easily be avoided, nobody hazarded capital on their improvement. Hence turnpike roads did not become a network, but a patchwork, dense around important centres of commerce, fairly regular along the main channels of trade, but thinly distributed or absent in the interstices. Turnpike trusts represented essentially local interests; only military authorities looked at highways from a national point of view. Moreover, the smoke which rose along the Stockton and Darlington Railway in 1825 wrote in the sky the doom of turnpike trusts. Well might they for some little time enjoy an Indian summer of feeding traffic to the new iron road; as fast as railways could be built, highways were superseded as lines of long-distance communication and transport. For lack of tolls, turnpike trusts languished and faded. Wherever they gave up the ghost, just as where they had never existed, highway maintenance was back where it had been at the end of the Middle Ages: the honorary surveyor elected by the parish meeting supervising ineffective work by reluctant parishioners or their substitutes.

Places situated along navigable rivers enjoyed considerable transport advantages and were far more likely to develop into trading centres than localities cut off from water transport. River navigation could often be extended by strengthening banks, widening and dredging beds or even eliminating meanders by a shortcut. Builders of roads and bridges also acquired experience in hydro-engineering: between 1650 and 1750 they doubled the mileage of British rivers available for navigation. The workmen whom they employed on this and subsequent construction work of a similar type came to be known as inland navigators—'navvies' for short. Such improvement helped riverside dwellers, but did nothing for the others. For Man to make a river where Nature had failed to provide one was only one more logical step—yet so bold a step as to need disguising in order not to frighten away potential backers. The first canal built in Britain, from St. Helens to the Mersey in the middle 1750s, masqueraded as the Sankey Navigation, a scheme to render navigable the Sankey river; in fact, the Sankey was a completely inadequate little brook, the Navigation nothing less than the first canal. Not until James Brindley built a canal from the Duke of Bridgewater's coal mines at Worsley to Manchester was the name 'canal' openly given to such new constructions.

The first canals were brilliant commercial successes. The need to unite Lancashire coal and Cheshire salt by easy water transport had led Liverpool and St. Helens business men to finance the Sankey Navigation; the Bridgewater Canal cut the price of the Duke's coal in Manchester by one half. The latter part of the eighteenth and the first quarter of the nineteenth centuries form the canal age of British transport. Industrialists all over the country, but particularly in the North of England, penetrated new markets which canals opened to their output. Small wonder that Josiah Wedgwood became chairman of the Grand Trunk Canal Company: goods as fragile as pottery were doomed to purely local sales until a safe and comparatively cheap means of transport carried them to consumers all over the country and even abroad. He was only one of a large number of manufacturers who backed canal ventures not only for the profits to be earned, but also for the scope offered to the products of their industries.

Like turnpike trusts, canals were the outcome of private enterprise backing the ingenuity of engineers with capital raised chiefly from local sources. Not all engineers were as sound as Brindley, nor all capitalists as shrewd as Wedgwood or the Duke of Bridgewater. Of the 2,300 miles of canal constructed in Britain, a number should never have been built; much capital sunk in canals was lost or at least remained inadequately remunerated. In the middle 1790s there was a canal mania—a wave of speculation in canal building beyond all reasonable proportions. Thus British canal companies showed widely differing results: some were highly successful, some paid for themselves, others forever hovered on the edge of bankruptcy. As they varied commercially, so physically: there was no single standard of depth or width; each canal was a law unto itself.

Parliament, as a condition of incorporating canal companies by Acts, had attempted to check abuses, mainly by limiting the rates of dividend which a company could distribute before lowering canal dues. Most canal companies found ways round the law and abused the monopoly which was theirs by virtue of their unique capacity for carrying heavy and bulky goods. Users had no alternative, though they resented the unwillingness of canals to forward through-traffic: an industrialist sending a barge on a journey over three canals not only had to ensure that its draught and width cleared three navigation channels, but had to bargain for user fees with three separate companies. Nor did canals accept all traffic offered to them; they could pick and choose. Contemporaries benefited greatly from canals, at the same time as they smarted under their tyranny. No wonder that they gladly abandoned them as soon as yet a newer means of transport appeared on the scene and that canals quickly became superseded by railways. Canal transport was limited geographically by the difficulties and the capital outlay entailed in adding to the canal system. Nor could it be speedy, but it was cheap. Over level country it could haul bulky goods conveniently and without undue effort for long distances in large quantities, particularly once steam tugs came into their own. The distribution of coal, grain, ore and building materials would have benefited, had not canals been doomed to a century of stagnation and neglect.

Railways

Of all the innovations of the Industrial Revolution, railways conformed most closely to the economists' model. They embodied new techniques: smooth wheels running on smooth rails, steam power harnessed to propulsion, with subsidiary inventions relating to braking, coupling, shunting, signalling and the myriad of other activities which go to ensure safe operation. Not only in the engineering, but also in the financial field were new devices required; for the size of railways surpassed anything hitherto attempted. There had been few individuals able, like the Duke of Bridgewater, to risk £250,000 on a single enterprise; there was none who could finance the construction of a whole railway unaided. Methods had to be devised to attract capital from a multitude of medium-sized, even small investors, to beguile their funds out of the safety of landed property and gilt-edged loans into industrial enterprise. Not all the devices were reputable or even successful, but at least they were new.

Conveyances known as rail ways or tram ways had existed for about a century—wheeled wagons propelled over wooden platforms or metal plates by gravity or drawn by horses. Some had been used for public transport of goods; most existed inside collieries where they shifted the mineral. The Stockton-Darlington Railway project did not mark a conscious departure from precedent: it was to carry to the sea and markets beyond coal from some of the less accessible parts of the Durham coalfield. When shortly before its opening in 1825 some people expressed a desire to ride on the inaugural train, it took the promoters by surprise; they had not thought of their railway as a means of passenger transport. However, they had a few wagons adapted for the carriage of cattle; they had no objection to freighting them for the occasion with a human load. Nor had they made up their minds in favour of any one mode of locomotion; steam engines were tried as alternatives to horses. The decision came four years later when a much more important railway was projected, designed to link Liverpool and Manchester. Uncertain about the best method of propulsion, the promoters of this railway laid down a long straight stretch of track at Rainhill near Liverpool and called a kind of race meeting at which everybody propounding a suitable means of traction could enter his runner, the reward being not only a prize, but the contract for moving the trains on the new line. It was here that George Stephenson's 'Rocket' won not only the day, but virtually the coming century for the technique of steam propulsion by locomotive.

Like canals, railways swept all before them. Their first promoters, coal owners of Durham and cotton traders of Liverpool, were as much concerned with shifting their goods quickly and efficiently as with drawing dividends from the capital ventured in the new mode of transport; seeing their goods swiftly borne past the gates of their establishments did as much to convince them of the value of the new conveyance as the profits which the railway earned. Both were a potent argument in its favour. Men who imported cotton via Liverpool, sent it eastward into the manufacturing areas of Lancashire and then re-exported the cotton cloth through the same port, found not only plenty of employment for the local railway; they also accumulated more capital than could at all times profitably be used in the cotton trade. Only too gladly therefore did they venture such surplus in railways elsewhere, once their shrewd business judgment had pronounced a railway project sound and promising. That is why from the 1830s onwards among the railway investors up and down the country there appears so often a 'Liverpool party', a group of backers referred to as 'the men from Lancashire', men who knew a good railway when they studied its prospectus.

Not all railway investors were as skilled or as cautious. Sound railways looked too temptingly like easy money for investors to remember that not all railways were sound. Putting their funds into railways appeared to open brighter vistas than lending them to the government; if the latter was safe, the former dazzled by their prospects. Promoters who needed substantial capital backing from private sources to turn schemes into railways had no reason to underestimate future profits. How probable the yields forecast in invitations to subscribe to a new railway company, only a knowledgeable business man could judge; not all those who hoped to jump on the new steam wagon to prosperity were even business men, let alone knowledgeable. They included the customary contingent of widows and orphans, dependent on invested savings to yield them a living, torn between the imperative demands for security and the lures of unprecedented yields; they were joined by small capitalists from every walk of life who believed that railways could perform the miracle of turning their modest nest-eggs into vast fortunes. Waves of such confidence, not substantiated by economic reasoning, swept over the country in the form of speculative manias; railways caused three of them, the first of moderate proportions in 1825–26, another in the middle 1830s, the largest one a decade later.

Schemes of the size of railway projects could rock the whole market from which they sought their funds. When prospects appeared good, an atmosphere of expectancy and buoyancy pervaded financial circles. Everybody was anxious to share in the opportunities which seemed to open on all sides. At such moments the country's capacity for making capital available within a short time was vastly overestimated. At the height of the third railway mania it was proposed to sink £132 million in railway construction during 1846 ; on the last day on which they could be deposited in Parliament for consideration in the 1846 session, 1,263 railway bills struggled for submission.

Manias entailed considerable dangers; at some time the rosy dreams of speculators had to be interrupted by the sharp impact of reality, and then the dreamers were hurt—widows, orphans, small clerks, country parsons, briefless barristers, even the shrewd business men were drawn into the vortex. Not only did they suffer a rude awakening from dreams of unparalleled riches; the capital they had ventured was at best condemned to a long period of sterility, more often lost when railway projects were abandoned in a sudden general panic. Loss of confidence affected sound schemes hardly less than hazardous ones; pessimism, once engendered, was as excessive as had been the optimism of the boom. Not only railway projects suffered; completed railways satisfactorily operating saw their shares carried below par on the wave of mistrust. Depression spread beyond railways to the wider investment market; there would be a year or two of slump when nobody could raise capital in London for any project; investors had burnt their fingers and fought shy of risks. Those would be bad years for trade and industry, years of unemployment both of men and resources. Railways under construction however were better placed. Once commenced, a railway line earns nothing until it is in operation over a definite stretch of country, whether or not this is the full extent of its concession. Only by running can it obtain revenue. Promoters therefore strove to complete any railways they had begun, whether times be good or bad; even in the depth of a slump they did their best to provide sufficient capital to put their railways into running order.

Those who had raised excessive hopes may have been over-confident of their own chances of success. Not all promoters were even honest. If railways constituted a temptation to gullible investors, their appeal to those who preyed on them was even more irresistible. Whether railways were built or not, companies could be formed, capital collected, shares issued. In the process, fees accrued to lawyers and directors; promoters granted themselves loans from the funds accumulating in their hands and manipulated stock exchange prices. Even a company which never cut a sod of ground earnt 'birth and burial fees' for the lawyers who pleaded its case for an Act before Parliament, established and subsequently dissolved it. There were many reasons for founding railway companies; to build a railway was the best, but not the only one.

Railways met with much opposition. Landowners were convinced that their lands would suffer in value from having railways close by. Even when they did not subscribe to the more exaggerated fears of milk turning sour inside the cows or birds falling dead from the sky when a train passed, they did not want railways within earshot of their property. This was serious for promoters: not only did their opponents own the land over which they had to run, but they dominated the Houses of Parliament which had to grant them Acts of incorporation. Either railways gave up the attempt of reaching the destination of their choice— a company trying to push its line to the centre of one of the older university towns was defeated by the objection that 'this project would be as displeasing to Almighty God as to the Vice-Chancellor of the University of Cambridge'—or they had to purchase acquiescence at almost any price. Similar, though less powerful, resistance came from farmers near large towns. Hitherto they had had what amounted to a monopoly of perishable food supplied to these towns; the coming of railways enabled consumers to draw on a much wider area.

If such opposition could be bought off or pacified by participation, rival transport interests considered railways a mortal threat. Neither turnpike trusts nor canals could in the long run withstand railways, the former because road vehicles remained technically backward, the latter because they had left it too long before putting their house in order. When at last they awoke to the threat, the public had no confidence in their last-minute rate reductions, their attempts to speed up services and improve navigation. The railways bought them out and in that way laid for a hundred years the ghost of competition. But the greatest threat to new railways came from existing railways. If there was anything more to gladden a lawyer's heart than to be briefed to argue the case of a new railway scheme for an Act of incorporation, it was the prospect, once successful, of being briefed to fight against newer schemes potentially encroaching upon a line now in operation. Large sums were spent by railway companies defending before parliamentary committees their own place in the sun and denying it to rivals.

Opponents were not alone in costing the railways money. That their promoters and legal advisers required remuneration, has already been mentioned. So did engineers and contractors, the men who formed the plans, surveyed and prepared the track, laid the rails and erected the installations. To begin with, nobody had any experience of such work. Where tunnels had to be blasted through rock, Cornish miners, used to explosive, were employed; East Anglians accustomed to drainage work dug cuttings and embankments. Those who undertook the tasks of construction were small men—builders, bricklayers, excavators, anybody who had experience in similar jobs. Men of small means, they only undertook a short stretch at a time; a railway line would be contracted for in separate sections. When a contractor had completed his section and received payment, he could tackle another section further along the line, leap-frogging over the in-between sections under construction. Small contractors did well enough as long as the going was reasonably good. Unusual difficulties, such as marshy or shifting ground or impenetrable rock, often proved beyond their powers altogether or at least held them up unduly; in any event the completion of the railway was delayed. Companies therefore smarted under the necessity of having to employ a multitude of small men and yearned for the day when contractors would be large enough to undertake the completion of a whole line by an agreed date, each day ahead of schedule securing for the contractor a premium, each day of delay costing him a fine.

Inevitably contractors grew to this stature; small men could not permanently keep their footing in railway building. Thomas Brassey, Samuel Peto and others assembled a large labour force—Irish immigrants, displaced Scottish Highlanders, the surplus agricultural labourers picked up in the South and East of England when building railways there—and a vast array of implements designed for the job. Thus equipped, they could construct railways more cheaply than their rivals. The development had its dangers: the large apparatus had to be maintained and paid for; once dispersed, it was difficult to reassemble. To prevent disintegration, it needed to be continuously employed. Once upon a time contractors had been called in by engineers to build a railway; now contractors, faced with a dearth of work, would call in engineers to find them a railway to build. Whether such railways would ultimately constitute paying propositions for the subscribers of the capital was not the contractor's first concern.

Nor were contractors the only ones to prey on railways. Landowners soon had their eyes opened to the boost which the coming of rail transport gave to land values. Where farming did not pay on ancestral acres and nobody looked like establishing a town, what better way of turning them to profit than by making them carry a railway? Landowners still held power in Parliament; far from keeping them away, they now used it to block the bills of railways which did not pass right through their grounds, purchasing the land required at a substantial price. Nor was the sale of land their only reward. When a railway bisected their grounds, this caused inconvenience technically known as 'severance' which called for compensation. Moreover, they could insist that the company built eight bridges across the railway line to enable easy passage everywhere along their grounds. No sooner had the ink dried on the clause embodying this obligation than the landowner offered to renounce his right to seven of the eight bridges—at a substantial consideration per bridge!

With friends to reward, opponents to pacify and ransom to pay, British railways were not cheap to build. Nor could they be; with no precedent to guide them, their constructors had to be pioneers, try all new methods once and write off those which failed. Theirs was not a virgin country where land was to be had for the grabbing or at least on the cheap; in a settled and developed community land has its price which needed to be paid in full. Parliamentary procedure for private Acts had been devised to safeguard established rights; much was exacted from a claimant wishing to cut across them, as did railways when asking for powers to purchase land compulsorily in the last resort. Heavy initial capital investment went to the establishment of British railways; they would have to earn large revenues to remunerate investors adequately ever after.

Of this need railway companies were well aware. Having started, they felt, with all hands raised against them, they saw no reason to spare their customers once they had them at their mercy. For that is how the relationship developed. Parliament rarely authorized more than one concession over any line so that a company, once it had obtained its Act, expected to be the only transport contractor in its area, withering road and canal operators into oblivion. It was free to charge 'what the traffic could bear'. But what would the traffic bear? At the outset it could not be known; it had to be tried. Railway companies experimented with rate fixing, endeavouring by constant adjustment upwards and downwards to maximize their profits. Users never knew what their journey or that of their goods would cost next. Pressure was exercised also in other ways. First-class passengers paid more than others; railways discouraged the latter by contriving to render their journeys uncomfortable, inconvenient and slow. Having earned a public welcome in their crusade against the monopoly attitude of canals, railways themselves acquired obnoxious habits. They bought out branch and feeder lines which might have diverted traffic to other railways; a plausible plan for the construction of such a branch line often sufficed to elicit a takeover bid from an existing railway anxious to ward off the threat. Once the initial expense of a railway had been incurred,

no price was too high to maintain its earning capacity undiminished.

Transport monopoly was a danger which Parliament had
foreseen and tried to forestall. Railways could not come into
existence without an Act which incorporated them as joint-stock
companies and conferred powers of compulsory purchase.
Parliament, when petitioned, could attach conditions to its grant.
In scrutinizing railway schemes, parliamentary committees
looked at individual merits. They never attempted to fit lines
into an overall plan; a national railway network did not enter
into their consideration. Their aim was the prevention of ruinous
competition which would ensue from any two railways running
close to each other. They exacted the price of such protection
by curbing the railways' rapacity: Acts prevented companies
from distributing dividends higher than ten per cent without
applying excess profit equally to the benefit of shareholders and
users by reducing the charges to the latter. Companies could not
disregard this stipulation, but many circumvented it. Stronger
measures were required: when at the Board of Trade, Gladstone
in 1844 piloted through Parliament an Act which because of its
concern with passengers became known as 'the Poor Traveller's
Charter'. Every company was to run on every weekday over
every part of its system at least one train which would stop at
every station and charge no more than a penny a mile for third-
class accommodation—the famous parliamentary train. Railways
affected to believe that this would ruin them; in practice, the
resulting increase in railway travel led to all third-class fares
being scaled down to this basis which persisted until 1914. But
the Act did more. It conferred on the State power to buy out any
future railway company which had been in operation for 21 years.
Discussions in Parliament made it clear that the measure was
intended as a check on railway companies tempted to abuse their
powers by charging excessive rates. Not for more than a century
did the State take such action, but this measure for the first time
introduced British industry to the prospect of nationalization.

Railway construction needed all manner of supplies from
every kind of industry, though pre-eminently iron, steel and
engineering products. The British economy in the middle of the
nineteenth century expanded at a rate not experienced before,
largely because of the railways' enormous appetite for locomotives,

for coaches, for rails, for stations, for springs, sleepers, buffers, windows and a myriad of other requirements. Sometimes railways rescued from extinction what seemed a doomed trade: they made stage-coach builders embark on the production of railway carriages and trucks on a scale they would never have reached in the days of road vehicles; new industries were called into existence to minister to needs unknown before, particularly locomotive building; eventually whole new towns were established to supply a large railway system with rolling stock and equipment. Never had a single industry exercised so potent a multiplier effect on the whole of the economy.

Not only their construction, but also their operation made railways the fulfilment of an economist's dream. They enabled people, goods and ideas to travel faster and farther than before. They widened markets: wherever railways operated, speedy and above all reliable transport came to be taken for granted. Commercial life benefited. No longer did wholesalers and retailers keep large stocks; a message to manufacturers anywhere in the country would quickly replenish their inventories; their capital was released for other purposes. A larger circle of customers, some at a greater distance, could expect prompt and punctual delivery of goods and more frequent visits from commercial travellers whose rounds had become less strenuous.

Most inventions had seen the light accompanied by riots from those who feared displacement and unemployment. Railways were spared such disapproval. Men looked upon them as machines which increased rather than limited their range of freedom, their usefulness and enjoyment. The earliest promoters planned railways as a means of goods transport; the ordinary citizen knew better. Railways as a whole before 1850 drew more revenue from fares than from freight; people were determined to travel by the new method. Division of passenger accommodation into three classes indicates that all classes of the community used the railways. Nor did they limit themselves to timetable travel. As early as 1841 Thomas Cook discovered the possibility of chartering trains for organized excursions—a discovery which opened up vistas of holiday trains, seaside trains, trains for sporting events or exhibitions, the whole range of 'specials' run for the occasion.

Britain had been a national community long before railways

were invented. Yet railways made that community more meaningful by linking the different areas speedily and firmly. When introduced around 1840, the penny post had been based on stage-coaches; the swelling volume of letters would quickly have exceeded their carrying capacity, had not the railways relieved them of the burden. On the day in 1843 when a newspaper was sold at Gateshead within 12 hours of rolling off the printing press in London, the national daily press had been truly born. For the first time a national trade union in the 1840s maintained its existence over six years because easy communication could link headquarters and branches. Fixtures were kept by amateur sportsmen at the weekend, men who had to be back at work on Monday morning. When the Great Exhibition took place in Hyde Park in 1851, railways ran excursion trains from all over the country at cheap fares. Those who travelled in them to London could not help reflecting, as they looked around them, that once the railway had come, the face of Britain could never be the same again.

Development up to the First World War

The revolution which the railways achieved in inland transport came to the high seas by the steamship, but while railways spread in industrial countries at great speed, steamships established themselves much more slowly. To begin with, they were neither faster nor cheaper than sailing ships which had provided ocean transport since the Middle Ages. A well-built clipper might outrace the early steamboat whose boilers were not only dangerous, but greedy; propulsion by steam required so much bunker coal that little cargo space was left. Steamships made their appearance on rivers and canals; not until the 1830s did they venture out into the open sea. Usually at first there was merely an auxiliary engine in a sailing ship which relied on the wind when it blew, but did not remain becalmed when it dropped.

The clipper might get there first. Yet on the other hand she might not. Regularity rather than speed commended steamships to those concerned with scheduled arrivals. Not that early steamships were very regular, but at least their record was better than that of sailing ships whose length of journey varied by 40 per cent according to wind and weather. For a long time steam and sailing ships competed side by side, the sailing ship retaining the bulky commodities which were in no hurry; she required a smaller crew and did not pay for her propellant power, thus compensating for her rival's growing speed and capacity. The opening of the Suez Canal (1869) which sailing ships could not navigate weighted the scales decisively in the steamship's favour. Yet even at the end of the century sailing ships carried a sizable proportion of the world's bulk cargoes.

Ocean shipping in its nature serves international trade. Steam propulsion at sea was not a British invention. International competition existed in this mode of transport from the early days. However, in the 1860s and 1870s Britain established her superiority and kept it unchallenged until the first world war. Partly she owed it to two British inventions, that of the compound marine engine by John Elder and that of the steam turbine by Sir Charles Parsons, even more she owed it to her wealth of good-quality bunkering coal by which the steam was raised. When all ships were built of timber, the Atlantic seaboard of the American Continent had enjoyed advantages over Britain; extensive woods close to the coast had made it an ideal location for shipbuilding yards. But once steamships were constructed of iron, the Tyne, the Wear and the Clyde came into their own; iron ore deposits in combination with coal supplies near the sea now determined the location of shipyards. For the United States it was particularly unfortunate that the Civil War crippled her shipbuilding activities; by the time peace had been re-established, she had been outdistanced in that industry.

Not that British shipbuilders ever enjoyed easy prosperity. Techniques and equipment changed too rapidly to afford the industry a period of rest. A quarter of a century after turning from wood to iron for the construction of hulls, shipbuilders abandoned iron and took to steel instead. Engines followed each other in quick succession: reciprocating, triple and quadruple expansion engines, each furnishing more thrust and power for a smaller quantity of coal. Cargo ships themselves changed; from being all-purpose carriers, they specialized in the transport of particular cargoes, such as wheat or bananas; refrigerated ships brought meat, dairy produce and eggs, while oil came in tankers.

Competition from other countries always existed. Showing the flag on the high seas was a matter of national prestige. Anxious to secure representation, foreign governments stimulated their fleets by subsidies, at the building stage for vessels which, though merchant ships, would convert easily into troop carriers in case of war, at the operating stage by straightforward payments per mile travelled, favourable mail and other government contracts, treaty clauses reserving sea transport to their own ships, and exemptions from port and other dues exacted from foreign-owned vessels. In spite of many worries British ship-builders were highly successful. In the period from 1892 to 1894, of all merchant tonnage launched in the world 80 per cent came from British yards. The proportion had dropped by 1914, but was still substantial.

International trade had existed, even flourished, for centuries before a steamship took the sea. Steamships could ease, intensify and cheapen it; by themselves they could not change its nature. That they did so nonetheless is due to their interaction with their great landward counterpart, railways. Up to the later nineteenth century, international trade had been an exchange of goods primarily between seaboards. Ports had drawn on their immediate hinterland for materials to dispatch abroad and as a market for imports. Only to a very limited extent could inland areas share in international trade; unless exceptionally accessible, they had remained excluded from all but commodities of high value in proportion to their bulk and transportability. But the combination of railways and steamships broke this isolation: even the bulkiest goods could now be shifted easily and cheaply on land as well as at sea. Though international trade was not new, far larger populations benefited from it, more so in foreign lands, but even in Britain.

Like many public utilities, railways soon discovered the benefit which flowed from operating on the largest possible scale. This stimulated the expansion of their activities, the elimination of potential competitors. Having nothing more to fear from road and canal operators, railway companies swallowed each other. Once the larger ones remained alone in the field, their thoughts turned to amalgamation. But here Parliament resisted. It refused to countenance any moves likely to increase the monopoly powers of concerns which anyhow threatened to take undue advantage. Railway companies, Parliament pointed out, had to remain within the terms of the Acts which established them. Such Acts authorized them to operate railways, not to amalgamate with other railway companies. To obtain power to do that, they would have to seek new Acts from Parliament; they were unlikely to obtain them. Parliament went further: in the Railway and Canal Traffic Act of 1854 it turned railways into 'common carriers', imposing upon them an obligation to carry any traffic offered to them; it also prohibited the exercise of 'undue discrimination' which meant that—unlike traders in general—railways were precluded from offering more favourable terms to large than to small consumers of their services, at least in the field of goods transport. The government established fairly detailed control over the railways' pricing policy, first compelling them to publish their rates, subsequently even imposing upper limits on freight and passenger charges.

However, before the century was out, Parliament had to modify the vigour of its anti-monopolist attitude, in view of accumulating evidence that railways, far from making excessive profits, in many cases could not avoid operating at a loss. 1914 still saw 124 separate railway companies in Britain, some prosperous, many merely subsisting, a few threatened with commercial extinction; but quite a number had disappeared through end-on amalgamation, a procedure which did not excite unfavourable public comment because it did not eliminate any competition which had hitherto existed.

If railways after 1850 proved less prosperous than had been expected, this absence of monopoly profits owed nothing to road competition. As carriers of through-traffic, roads in the second half of the nineteenth century were of no account; legislation handed their care to the local authorities—clear evidence that they were considered of purely local concern. A national grant of funds to improve the Holyhead road remained entirely exceptional. Moreover, Parliament reverted at times to its seventeenth century habit of trying to adapt road users to the road. In 1861 it empowered the government to banish from the roads any particular type of locomotive traction engine if it caused excessive wear and tear; four years later it repealed that particular measure in favour of the law ordering a man holding a red flag to walk in front of every road vehicle mechanically propelled, the famous 'man-and-flag' Act so beloved by Victorian cartoonists. Yet perhaps a glimpse of the shape of things to come was discernible when the State for the first time offered highway authorities a 25 per cent grant towards the upkeep of main roads: recognition that some roads were of more than local importance.

By weight of numbers cyclists took precedence over motorists as road users in the 1880s; their frail vehicles and imperfect tyres suffered much damage from bad surfaces. Early cycling clubs formed themselves into pressure groups to stimulate highway authorities to road improvements not hitherto deemed necessary. To lobby effectively was difficult while responsibility for roads remained diffused among 132 counties or county boroughs, 279 non-county or metropolitan boroughs, 812 urban and 661 rural districts—1,884 different highway authorities. To create some kind of national body, the government in 1910 established a Road Board and financed it from tax and licence revenues to construct new and improve existing roads; but it was ineffective. In the long run, motorists were far to outweigh cyclists as road users, though the private motor-car was till something of a rarity up to 1914, and motor-driven trucks, lorries and cycles things of the future. Long-distance road transport was only just awakening from three-quarters of a century of slumber.

For very short distances, especially in towns, railways had never displaced roads to the same extent. Traffic in the few largest urban areas might justify purely local lines, whether above or under ground, but the bulk of all transport within a town necessarily used its streets. Traffic of this type was growing fast in the second half of the nineteenth century, as a necessary corollary to increasing urbanization: the more people lived in towns, the greater the volume of commodities required to keep them supplied. Shorter working days and higher incomes enabled the more prosperous town-dwellers to move to the suburbs where the premium on space was lower and life more pleasant; they travelled to and from work daily. Road improvements in the later nineteenth century continued to be practised chiefly on city streets subjected to heavy and ever-increasing wear by a throng of pedestrians, messengers, porters with barrows and horses pulling carts. Tramways, first horse-drawn and subsequently propelled by electricity, added to the congestion as well as to the furniture of streets, and in the last ten years before the first world war the motor-bus made its appearance.

Surface Transport in the Twentieth Century

Her position as an island determined certain of Britain's strategies: she put her main effort militarily into the maintenance of sea power, legally into rules of war which limited the destruction of merchant shipping. To keep the sea lanes open was a question of life and death for a country which depended on imports of food. Though not technically part of the armed forces, merchant shipping caught much of the limelight during both world wars; shipping space circumscribed import programmes, thus curtailing productive activities based on overseas raw materials. U-boat warfare from 1914 to 1918, limited at first, but soon restricted by no rules whatsoever, aimed at sinking the maximum number of merchant ships engaged in the commerce of Britain. Not all these ships sailed under the British flag, but British vessels predominated among them. In absolute tonnage space (though not as a proportion of her total sea-carrying capacity) Britain suffered more than any other nation during the first world war: the enemy sent to the bottom of the sea almost eight million tons, representing 37 per cent of her pre-war tonnage, in addition to a million tons lost through marine risks, offset by only five million tons of new construction or enemy vessels captured and rendered serviceable.

It goes without saying that British shipyards worked to the limit of their power to repair merchant vessels damaged and to replace losses. Nor did the period of overfull employment terminate with the end of the war; it took several years to fill the gaps left by enemy action, especially as post-war orders poured in from foreign as well as British sources. But in 1921 the replacement boom came to an end. Not only British, but world merchant tonnage had been restored to its pre-war capacity; it had even overshot this target. Instead of adding to depleted merchant fleets, shipyards were now reduced to making good normal peacetime wastage. This alone accounted for a severe contraction in orders. In fact conditions were worse. International trade had not recovered in the same proportion as shipping capacity: the world's larger merchant navies found fewer goods and passengers to carry. Not only were no new ships wanted; existing ships lacked employment. The complaint affected all shipbuilding nations, but Britain worst of all. When her bunkering coal had been unobtainable during the war, many of her former customers had built oil-burning ships, acquiring experience in a technique which in Britain developed more slowly. More and more shipping changed over to this new form of propulsion after the war, being constructed elsewhere. Countries with few ships to replace, but shipbuilders to employ, gave their home industries preference; British shipyards, accustomed to a large quota of foreign commissions, suffered more than most.

The impact of these changes brought to the Tyne and the Wear the worst depression which this area had ever known. At its height between 1930 and 1932, shipbuilders combined to buy up and close one shipyard in three so as to eliminate redundant capacity; no other policy seemed possible at the time, but it engendered an atmosphere of hopelessness, misery and long-term unemployment on an unprecedented scale for the large number of shipyard workers who made up almost the entire working population of certain North East coast towns and could find no alternative employment anywhere in the area. Depression over-hung the whole country, though in no other industry was unemployment equally severe; the government, hard-pressed on all sides, could give only limited assistance to any one industry. It backed the closing of redundant shipyards, subsidized tramp shipping and shipowners who scrapped old vessels and replaced them by up-to-date ones; it came forward with a special grant for the *Queen Mary* when the Cunard Line had suspended construction—the employment provided made it worth the government's while to ensure its progress. 1932 marked the nadir of the industry's fortune, but decisive improvement came only in the late 1930s when international trade recovered and the shadow of another war fell on the sea.

For merchant shipping the second world war repeated many of the features of the first. But losses reached their peak halfway through, not near the end of, the second war; from the middle of 1943 onwards shipping space ceased to be the most serious of the shortages with which Britain had to contend. Again shipyard capacity was overstrained and had to be augmented by the prefabrication of certain types of vessels at inland factories. Once more the post-war period experienced a replacement boom, but this time it tapered rather than fell off to a peacetime level of employment. There was no repetition of the disastrous slump of shipbuilding and shipping in the late 1920s and early 1930s.

Technical changes there were, setting disquieting problems to those responsible for commissioning and building ships: the day of the giant passenger liner had passed; the 'blue riband' of the Atlantic had become an extravagance; instead, the trade called for medium single-class vessels capable of being switched to carrying travellers to wherever sun and blue skies could be found at the particular season of the year. Outward freights of coal giving way on the home journey to grain and raw materials, the profitable basis of pre-war shipping, no longer predominated; one-way voyages in ballast had become the rule. This made for higher costs and reduced the cargo-carrying fleet, especially tramps—the ships on which Britain relies for her food and essential supplies. Though by marine engineering considerations alone the largest tanker is the most economical, it could load only one type of oil when smaller quantities of assorted oils might have to be shifted, nor could it berth at any but the largest terminals; it might not be able to negotiate the Suez Canal physically, not to speak of the dues levied and the political obstacles encountered. More than its foreign competitors was the British shipbuilding industry hamstrung by labour strife; whether it centred on differences between employers and workers or on demarcation disputes between rival unions, the outcome never varied: ships on order came off the slips after more delay and at a higher cost than expected. This may go some ways towards explaining why United Kingdom ownership of shipping, amounting to over half the world's total before the first world war, after the second fell to one-fifth. Well might the shipowner's head ache before he ever raised his eyes to behold a new competitor in the sky.

At the outbreak of war in 1914 there were available to the whole British army 807 lorries or tractors, 20 cars and vans, 15 motor-cycles and not a single motorized ambulance. Nothing illustrates more clearly the general ignorance of the contribution which the internal combustion engine was destined to make to transport. By the end of hostilities, the sum total in the service of the army of vehicles mentioned above exceeded 100,000, not to speak of the tank, a British invention put into combat in 1917. The motor vehicle had at last arrived. Released from war service, it began its conquest of the roads.

These could hardly yet accommodate motor vehicles in large

numbers. Traffic censuses had been begun by the Road Board, but the use of roads during the war provided little indication of post-war requirements. Between 1920 and 1923 roads were for the first time classified, though the classification remained crude. Existing roads were widened and the building of arterial roads began in the 1920s—a hopeful programme halted by the great depression which befell the country at the end of the decade. The most significant development in the 1930s was the concept of trunk roads, arterial roads of national importance for which the Minister of Transport himself took full responsibility. At last the way ahead seemed clear, wide and reasonably straight for motor vehicles. But in commending themselves to more and more people and goods, they inevitably came into conflict with the railways.

Under legislation prepared in advance, the British government immediately upon the outbreak of war in 1914 took over the undertakings of the railway companies and ran them for the duration of the war as a single unified enterprise: British railways. The change was greater in law than in reality; the same physical assets, organized and operated under the control of the same men, worked for, and at the expense of, the State, which paid the companies a fee for their use. With increased need for transport created by troop and civilian population movements, employment of workers at a distance from their homes, arrivals of imports at unfamiliar and remote ports, longer hauls of scarce goods previously supplied from local stocks, the railway system during the war was fully used; the government had no difficulty in paying companies in respect of railway operation a generous remuneration, while retaining a very satisfactory revenue. However, like most productive capital, railway equipment during the war suffered excessive wear; little replacement could be undertaken, and at the end of the war the government handed the railways back in bad shape. It did not however return them to their pre-war owners. This would have been exceedingly difficult, given that joint use of equipment and the construction of joint facilities had completely blurred separate financial responsibility and participation, nor did the companies wish for it. To face the post-war world they preferred to combine into four large concerns: the Great Western, the London Midland and Scottish, the Southern and the London and North Eastern

Railway Companies. As regards rail transport, they held regional monopolies. At the boundaries they might overlap; a Londoner had his choice of travelling to Reading or even as far as Exeter either by Southern or Great Western Railway; similarly the L.N.E.R. and the L.M.S. vied for the honour of conveying him to Leeds or Bradford. They did not vie very hard. Fares were the same, whichever company quoted for the journey; he had to study his timetable minutely to discover whether the quality of services differed.

This organization may have met the railways' requirements, but could not ensure their success. Still bent on the prevention of profiteering, the government placed a ceiling on each company's annual earnings and subjected rates and fares to approval by a Railway Rates Tribunal. It need not have bothered; no company in any interwar year ever reached the maximum permitted revenue. Railways had a monopoly of their particular type of transport; from this they could not be ousted. But they now suffered the consequences of the erosion, during the inflation of the world war, of the capital reserves they had accumulated for investment in modernization schemes. Only the Southern Railway undertook large-scale conversion from steam to electric traction; so far as other companies had similar plans, shortage of capital caused their abandonment or at least indefinite postponement. They may have made such technical advances as resources at their disposal rendered possible, but this did not endear them to a public unversed in the intricacies of the economics of transport. This public was withdrawing its patronage from the railways which now tasted some of the bitter medicine which they had inflicted on their road and canal competitors 100 years earlier. For a century they had enjoyed a virtual transport monopoly; now a vigorous and growing competitor had arisen, the motor vehicle. It had not been compelled to become a 'common carrier'; road operators accepted business if offered in a convenient form and at remunerative rates, leaving awkward loads and unprofitable traffic to the railways. Flexible by nature, motor vehicles picked up human or inanimate cargoes at the point of departure and set them down at the exact destination—a service with which railways, tied to their permanent way, could not compete.

Railways however constituted more than one means of transport among several; they were a public service. No fully developed country in the modern world can do without a railway system, nor would those responsible for national safety contemplate population movements, such as the mobilization of the forces or the evacuation of certain groups of civilians in the event of war, without railways. It was incumbent upon the government to temper the gusts of transport competition to the shorn lambs operating railways; in 1919 a Ministry of Transport came into existence, ostensibly to coordinate transport development. Throughout the interwar years road hauliers were restricted in their freedom whether and where to operate and what to carry, whereas railways were progressively authorized to discriminate in favour of large-scale users and to employ road vehicles of their own in order to collect and deliver goods beyond rail heads. In fact, railway companies jointly acquired and operated the two largest road parcel carriers in the country.

This policy kept railways alive; it made no contribution to the rationalization of the country's transport system. On the contrary, competitive efforts by railways and hauliers concealed and distorted ever more effectively the real costs of transport to the country as a whole, as distinct from what users paid. Only an integrated system, using road or rail as alternatives so as to minimize the total effort and manpower involved, could have achieved this, but not even the pressure of another war brought it about. Railways once again operated under the government as a single entity, whereas road haulage under its separate managements attained a limited degree of cooperation. Railway engineering in the second world war performed near-miracles; though suffering heavy punishment as obvious targets for enemy bombs, railways never remained for long out of action. War proved that railways had become neither unnecessary nor obsolete; used to maximum capacity, they rendered excellent service and earned good revenue. After the war a Labour government cut the Gordian knot by nationalizing both rail and road transport, adding the waterways for good measure; under single ownership alone could an integrated national transport system be achieved.

The Labour government did not endure, nor did a transport system in the nation's hands. Political changes returned to private ownership much road haulage, though neither railways nor canals. In the absence of integrated management of all means of transport, none could develop as a public service, because all had to follow policies dictated by considerations of competition. Outright competition impels participants towards efficiency; it does not induce rivals to concentrate on traffic most suitable for their medium, abandoning what others can carry at lower cost. Motor hauliers, though once again owning and operating vehicles, had to look to the government to repair the war-worn highways and build up-to-date through-roads. To an island with a limited surface, multi-lane highways are a luxury afforded only at the expense of competing land uses; the government however felt compelled to provide them in response to the clamant solicitations of road haulage interests joined by private motorists, an ever-increasing section of the population. Railways meanwhile engaged in the largest and costliest scheme of modernization ever undertaken in order to replace out-of-date steam traction by electric or diesel propulsion. Perhaps the greatest revolution was the least conspicuous of all, exciting hardly any public comment: the re-discovery of canals. So bad had been their condition that they had furnished little assistance during the war when transport had proved one of the bottlenecks to the war effort. Now that railways no longer feared them as competitors, hydraulic engineers improved their capacity for carrying cheaply and efficiently bulky loads which should not impede the many people hurrying across the bustling streets and thronging the railways of a highly developed country.

Air Transport

To Colonel W. N. Pilkington, of the famous St. Helens firm, belongs the credit of having chartered the first aircraft for an overseas business trip from this country. The date was July 1919. As in so many other fields, the first world war had stimulated fresh thought on aviation. Though the aeroplane's contribution to military activities had remained limited, it had taught men to fly; the sensational exploits of a few pre-war pioneers had become a recognized technique of aircraft piloting. Flying, however, meant more than a technique or even a method of travel; it was a way of life. Those who had grown wings were unwilling to abandon them for humdrum terrestrial pursuits. Was there no civilian future in flying? Many believed there was, among them G. H. Thomas who at the height of the war registered an international air transport company 'to enter into contract for the carriage of mails, passengers, goods and cattle'. Here was faith abundant in the new medium. Yet of the four British companies undertaking cross-channel flights in 1919, three had given up 15 months later; the fourth was limping along on charter flights alone.

As a means of transport, the aeroplane was new and untried, as a piece of engineering an intricate and very expensive product. Crew and fuel occupied much of its space, as in early steamships, leaving little room for payload; methods of propulsion and safety requirements imposed upon it an immensely costly mode of operation. Making its *début* in the international field, it encountered foreign competition from the outset; two French and a Dutch company were providing cross-channel services in 1919. Passengers and cargo, even mail, required much persuasion to entrust themselves to the unfamiliar element. The government saw that the infant, however promising, would survive only if nursed over a prolonged period. Civil aviation could not get off the ground without a substantial public subsidy.

When converted to this necessity, the government adopted a novel policy. Hitherto it had always conceived its function as the fostering of competition, even where public services were provided. Times had changed; competition now came from the foreigner. If British civil aviation was to hold its own, it had to concentrate all its resources on a united effort. This is why Imperial Airways was born, the 'chosen instrument' of government aid, an amalgamation of all British civil aviation firms then in existence, with the chairman and one director appointed by the government. From 1924 to 1931 it was the only British air line, pushing beyond Europe in 1926 and starting domestic air services in the 1930s. In 1934/35 it declared its first dividend.

Yet civil aviation in the interwar years remained a hothouse plant, manured and watered by a government which sheltered it from the chilly winds of competition; like many an impatient gardener, it would every now and then dig up and inspect the roots to see how firmly and well its *protégé* was established. No regular British service had been started across the North Atlantic, though one had reached the planning stage by the time the second world war broke out. It was that war which brought aviation to maturity—civil no less than military, since much ferrying home of aircraft manufactured overseas, carrying of politicians and diplomatists on foreign journeys and collection of essential cargoes formed part of the war effort. Military flying of thousands of missions left the country in possession of a wealth of highly skilled and experienced pilots when peace came once again. Many of them, schoolboys before the war, had learnt no other trade.

That the future of international movement of passengers and mail lay in the air, became clear soon after the war. What had been the luxury of a few wealthy and intrepid travellers became a fever spreading to larger and larger numbers of the population, symbolized by the progressive introduction of reduced air fares—second-class, tourist, economy. Travel agencies before the war had chartered whole liners and trains for group holidays; now they chartered aeroplanes. Alongside the government-owned 'chosen instruments'—two or three in the post-war world, operating scheduled services to different sectors of the globe—a number of private companies earned their living almost exclusively from charter flying. Progress in cargo was slower. Wartime governments had fostered public relations with allies by having British newspapers flown to Paris for sale on the morning of publication. Other occasions occurred where speed of delivery was essential, but size and weight of cargo had to be small to make the expense of transport worth while. Gold, precious stones and live animals filled transit sheds of airports more frequently than humdrum commercial cargoes. However, as turbine succeeded combustion engine and jet liners replaced turboprops, aircraft became not only faster, but larger and more powerful, rendering size and weight of loads carried less of a handicap. So far as future potentiality of air transport is concerned, nothing can be more certain than that the sky alone is the limit.

VII | TRADE

Overseas Trade to the Middle Nineteenth Century

The discovery of America at the end of the fifteenth century had established the commercial importance of countries bordering the Atlantic whence ships could most easily reach the New World. Britain was the latest and slowest of the Atlantic seaboard nations of Europe to make full use of these opportunities, owing to the scarcity of commodities suitable for exchange. As long as sea voyages involved much time and risk, ocean transport was expensive; countries had to offer their wares at a very low price to overcome the handicap of heavy freight charges. In such conditions, no country contributed to the international market more than one or two commodities on a really large scale. Britain had traditionally supplied woollen cloth; though small quantities of corn, herrings and minerals figured among her exports, woollens formed the staple and backbone for more than two centuries. In the trade with her American colonies she faced a quandary: the northern colonies, with their temperate climate, appreciated woollen cloth, but had no goods to send to Britain in return; the produce of their agriculture pursued on lines similar to, though less developed than, that of the home country would merely have competed ineffectually with the output of British farms. Not so the southern colonies situated in the tropical zone, whose sugar and tobacco Britain welcomed: their hot climate precluded the use of woollen cloth; though they bought from Britain a variety of industrial products, above all iron goods, they offered no outlet to her chief export.

A similar difficulty confronted Britain in the Mediterranean countries which produced a variety of goods highly prized by British consumers: port, sherry, silk and all kinds of Mediterranean fruit. But even in winter the prevailing temperature did not justify the woollens of the kind Britain traditionally manufactured. British industry had however adapted itself to this desirable market by fashioning its wool into lighter and more colourful cloths acceptable to Mediterranean customers: the 'new draperies' owed their success chiefly to their suitability as exports to an area in which Britain wished to buy. Attempts to sell woollens or any other goods of British manufacture in the Far East were futile. The Emperor Ch'ien Lung did not overstate the position in his message to George III:

> The Celestial Empire possesses all things in prolific abundance and lacks no product within its borders. There is therefore no need to import the manufactures of outside barbarians in exchange for our own products.

His claim related to China, but rang true likewise of India, where however Britain, through the East India Company, wielded more influence. Britain traditionally imported from the Far East spices and tea; in the eighteenth century Indian cotton fabrics became the fashion in Englishwomen's wear, creating a market to which Lancashire manufacturers eventually succeeded. This justified British anxiety to do business with the Far East, but made available no goods acceptable to Far Eastern countries in exchange for their exports. Payment in gold and silver caused strains on the British balance of payments which gave rise to much unfavourable comment.

To pay her way in markets unwilling to absorb her manufactures, Britain developed two devices: invisible exports and trade in commodities produced by others. As 'invisible' we describe trade which a customs officer cannot see, consisting of services instead of goods. The services rendered by British traders in the eighteenth century took the form of shipping. Foreign merchants freighted British vessels for journeys, not only between Britain and their own countries, but also from one foreign port to another. Typical of this form of export was the 'country trade' of India. East Indiamen, the East India Company's large ships, could make only one round trip a year between England and India, owing to dependence on prevailing winds which kept them in India for several months. They did not spend the time idle in port, but carried cargoes between Indian and Chinese towns all along the coast, earning freights which helped to finance the British import surplus from India.

Many countries which had no use for Britain's manufactures were pleased to buy the produce of her colonies. American tobacco and West Indian sugar found ready markets throughout Europe; Newfoundland cod was described as equivalent to gold because it enjoyed a never-flagging demand. Britain could sell abroad all the tea and cotton goods from India which she did not want to consume at home. The British entrepôt trade, which imported merchandise from one country in order to re-export it to another, flourished and doubled in the first half of the eighteenth century. Product diversification took notorious shape in the slave trade which formed one leg of a triangular transaction. English ships set out from Bristol or Liverpool, carrying to the Gold or Ivory Coast of Africa manufactures, mainly metal goods made in the Midlands. These they bartered for slaves whom they carried to the southern American colonies or Caribbean islands on the infamous 'middle passage'—a transaction rendered extremely speculative by the high value of the human freight, offset by its excessive mortality rate, owing to the inadequacy of provisions, the hardships suffered in transit and the casualties through attempts at escape. In return for slaves sold, ships on the homeward journey carried cargoes of tobacco, sugar, molasses or rum.

By these different routes, long before she achieved pre-eminence in the manufacturing field, Britain had become a great trading nation. She did not attain this position without rivals. The high seas were open to all seafaring nations; up to the middle eighteenth century, Britain could not compare with the Dutch, unchallenged masters of the sea for a century and a half, whether in building or using transport or fishing craft. Both in the Far East and in the New World, the Dutch colonial empire had been larger, richer and mightier than the English. What enabled Britain to outstrip Holland in this field was chiefly population. Far-flung colonies needed settlers and administrators; if settlements were attacked by indigenous people or European rivals, forces had to be sent to their defence. Only a large and populous country could spare the men necessary for such tasks.

By using her colonial possessions to buttress and expand her overseas trading position, Britain put into operation a theory of empire. Colonies were overseas territories, sometimes settled by emigrants from the British isles, sometimes merely used as trading areas in which British merchants maintained warehouses and shipping facilities at convenient focal points. Occasionally the British crown, more often some great British trading company, provided personnel to rule the territory and keep the peace. Against external aggression, colonies enjoyed the protection of the British navy. Their function, according to this theory, consisted of supplying the mother country with commodities which she could not produce herself, either to obviate buying from foreigners for gold or to enable her to re-sell to other countries against precious metals. Colonies thus complemented Britain's own activities and improved the balance of trade for the Empire as a whole. The theory postulated colonies where climatic and mineral endowment differed significantly from Britain, so that their produce did not compete with her own output. To describe the temperate colonies on the American seaboard as New England was anything but a compliment; it indicated their economic similarity to old England, hence their unsuitability and unprofitability as a colonial territory.

Britain's more highly developed economy furnished to her colonies not only cadres of administration and protection, but also supplies for their needs and outlets for their produce. Britain looked upon them as limbs of a powerful and well-organized imperial body, but not as economic units trading on their own account with the outside world or even with one another. Ireland exporting corn or cattle, New England colonies pursuing iron manufacture beyond the smelting stage, exporting wool and trading foodstuffs directly against the sugar and molasses of the West Indies,—such activities incurred prohibition as incompatible with the imperial pattern. The more important colonial produce could be shipped only to England in the first place. In the opposite direction, colonies had to buy their imports from England under a system which compensated colonial consumers for tariff charges imposed on the goods during their passage through England.

In return for services rendered, Britain expected her colonies to conduct through her all relations with foreign countries and with each other, to yield to her the first-fruits of all trade. The system favoured her commercial community, as the navigation laws protected her merchant navy. Colonial goods had to be carried in English or colonial ships; most commodities from foreign countries could be brought to Britain only in British ships or those of the country of origin. Though such legislation barred from British shores trade which might otherwise have reached them in foreign bottoms, it ensured employment for the British merchant marine, the nursery and training ground of British sailors on which the Royal Navy relied in case of war. The whole system hinged on naval power. Because of her command of the seas Britain could enforce it on colonies and foreign countries alike.

Colonies struggling to subsist were grateful for the protection afforded by this system, the outlets for their produce provided by English traders, the inflow of goods from a more highly developed economy. Not until a colony had left the subsistence stage behind and wanted to industrialize or establish its own position in international trade, did it find the system irksome, the more so as colonists had no voice in the rules made, and the laws voted, at Westminster. Typical of the impatience of vigorous adolescents with the restrictive hand of an imperious mother was the revolt of the 13 American colonies, up to 1763 dependent on the British navy for protection from the French, but after the end of the Seven Years' War concerned to carve out a future of their own design.

From the late seventeenth century onwards, statistics of goods passing the national frontier had been kept in Britain. Though suffering from imperfections, these records of overseas trade provided direct evidence of changes in volume and direction. Home trade expanded in at least a similar proportion, dominated by foodstuffs and coal; as late as the 1820s, the coastwise coal trade surpassed in value the whole of the country's overseas trade. Mostly, however, internal commerce left only indirect proof reaching us through a myriad of small and uncoordinated channels: the pamphlets of the period, the chorus of complaints about inconvenience and delay of transport, expansion of coastal shipping, demand for instruments of payment and credit, surviving business records. They contribute to the composite picture of an ever-increasing number of transactions which go to make up the sum total of internal trade.

British overseas trade at the end of the eighteenth century received an unprecedented stimulus from the new discoveries and inventions in industry. The development of cotton manufacture seemed a direct response to limitations on the sale of woollens abroad: at last here was a textile material light enough to prove acceptable to dwellers in hot climates and cheap enough for masses of potential customers in countries with low purchasing power. Metal goods, reduced in price by mechanization, enjoyed similar advantages. From having been preoccupied with the fear of glutting overseas markets, British exporters now could not obtain supplies fast enough to fulfil all the demands made upon them. Increasing population and the transfer of productive resources from agriculture to industry prompted the country to buy more foodstuffs and raw materials from overseas, thus stimulating imports as well as exports.

The French wars administered a temporary setback to this expansion of overseas trade. In the long run, non-intercourse caused more damage to countries like France and Germany, cut off from Britain's industrial know-how, or to Holland, backing the loser in the contest, than to Britain. In the short run, trade was impeded by Napoleon's Berlin and Milan decrees, countered by the British orders-in-council, measures by which each party declared the other in a state of blockade. But Britain, possessing command of the seas, continued trading with the colonies, whereas Napoleon could at the most cut her off from intercourse with the remainder of Europe. Nor did even this commerce cease altogether; Britain supplied continental countries via neutral entrepôts such as Heligoland, Gothenburg or the Azores. It was during these wars that London constructed the first of her large docks to store safely vast quantities of colonial produce which Napoleon could prevent her neither from importing nor from re-exporting to some of his reluctant allies. Overseas trade was inconvenienced by the war, even more by the non-intercourse laws of the United States culminating in the British-American war of 1812–14. But it could not be stopped.

Paradoxically it was not the war, but the peace which hit overseas trade hard. Most European countries during hostilities had had to obtain their colonial goods from Britain; now that they could once again buy direct from extra-European territories, the British entrepôt trade contracted painfully. In the depression which followed the peace, the commercial community sought means of softening the blow. In a petition to the government in 1820, London merchants mooted the idea of repealing tariffs not required for revenue purposes. Controversy over import duties filled the first half of the nineteenth century.

The commodity which occupied most space on British-bound ships and paid the largest amount of import duties in the 1820s was timber. Of industrial raw materials, cotton also played a large part, followed by wool, silk and hemp. West Indies sugar bulked largest among the tropical foodstuffs, one third passing through Britain on its way to ultimate consumers elsewhere. This article still accounted for one third of the country's total customs revenue in 1841. Spirits, tea and coffee were minor items in this category. Corn and flour came in every year, often only in negligible quantities, depending much on the adequacy of British harvests; in a heavy year like 1827, they accounted for £1 million worth of import duties. Practically no manufactures were imported, whereas British exports consisted primarily of manufactures and the re-exports of colonial produce. Cotton cloths and yarns had pride of place, but woollens, hardware and cutlery all figured on the list, with a new item, industrial machinery, representing future trends.

When he wrote *The Wealth of Nations* in 1776, Adam Smith had drawn attention to the ill-effects of tariffs which denied consumers the benefits of international division of labour arising where each country supplies the goods it is best placed to produce. To this economic argument, Radicals in the early nineteenth century added a political: duties levied in proportion to the consumption of goods burdened poor people more heavily than rich, because the purchase of necessities absorbed a far larger percentage of the total means of the former than of the latter. Both from economic and political points of view, direct taxation of income was preferable, affording consumers a higher measure of satisfaction and different income groups a greater degree of justice. But these were theoretical arguments. The petition of 1820 ranged parliamentary voters on the side of freer trade.

Tariffs serve to protect struggling industries, especially if recently established, against their more successful foreign rivals. Most industries everywhere had grown up under the umbrella of double protection which import duties and the cost of transportation from foreign countries afforded. The petition of 1820 represented the opinion of merchants, men anxious to increase the exchange of goods, but before modifying tariffs, Parliament received addresses from manufacturers whose products would be affected. They customarily pleaded for continuation of protection, sometimes even for increases in tariffs considered inadequate. By the early nineteenth century several British industries had reached maturity. Far from requiring help against foreign rivals, they hoped to penetrate their opponents' markets. Protection in Britain provoked retaliatory measures abroad; if Britain freed trade, there was at least a chance that other countries might follow suit. Nor could British manufacturers expect large sales to foreign countries, unless these could earn the sterling wherewith to buy British exports.

While important sectors of British industry had grown to the point of dispensing with protection and taking their chances in free international competition, many trades, especially those not yet transformed by any changes, maintained the traditional outlook. Nor could the government afford to act rapidly. Quite apart from protecting industry, tariffs contributed to public revenue; before they could be abolished, the Exchequer had to secure an alternative source of income. Immediately after a major war which has inflamed national passions, the atmosphere rarely favours a reduction in import duties which can be represented as a concession to foreigners, especially if the mood in other countries offers little hope of reciprocity. Thus William Huskisson, member of Parliament for Liverpool, a constituency which earned its living by overseas trade, and President of the Board of Trade in the middle 1820s, had only limited scope for tariff reforms. He found a tariff complicated to the point of incomprehensibility; he left it thoroughly spring-cleaned. He abolished embargoes (import prohibitions), prohibitive import duties and export bounties, all of which yielded no revenue to the State. He reduced the rates levied on the raw materials of industry, except timber, to an almost nominal figure, thus hoping to cheapen British manufacturers' costs. For all other goods, he aimed at a tariff ceiling of 30 per cent, partly to reduce the profitability of smuggling, partly because he did not believe any industry which required higher protection could survive in the long run. Where reciprocal concessions could be obtained, Huskisson was prepared to take the risk of sacrificing government revenue; in other cases a reduction of duty might be expected to lead to greater consumption, compensating the government by the increase in the volume of imports for the fall in the rate of duty. Over a wide range of commodities, Huskisson upheld or even created imperial preference; but too wide a difference between the rates paid by colonial and foreign goods encouraged smuggling, as when timber was sent all the way from the Baltic to Nova Scotia, thence back to Britain, in order to enter at the lower rate applicable to colonial produce. A reduction in the duty on the foreign article could only cheapen costs all round.

The tariff, as reformed by Huskisson, was a less irrational, but hardly a less potent instrument of protection. British trade could be freed more effectively only after the defeat of powerful vested interests in protection as well as the opening up of a new source of public revenue. The former, as exemplified in the repeal of the corn laws, has already been described. Landowners were the most prominent, but not the only defenders of protective measures; three years after the loss of the parliamentary battle over corn duties, ship builders and owners suffered a similar defeat when the navigation laws were repealed, allowing goods to be brought into the country on equal terms by ships of whatever nationality. The measure which enabled the government increasingly to dispense with tariff revenue was income-tax. Taxation of incomes as an emergency method of raising funds for the French wars had been repealed when peace was restored in 1815. Sir Robert Peel re-imposed it in 1842 as a purely temporary measure to stop a run of budget deficits; three decades had to elapse for politicians and taxpayers to realize that income-tax had come to stay. It enabled the country to set out by the middle of the nineteenth century on the road to free trade—a road which it followed to its destination and did not abandon until the outbreak of the first world war.

The Era of Free Trade, 1846–1914

Taking visible trade alone, Britain had probably had a surplus of imports over exports ever since 1815. Her largest industry had to purchase abroad the whole of its raw material, cotton. Though the woollen industry had grown up in Britain because of the abundance of sheep and the high quality of their fleeces, increasing industrialization and more intensive land use narrowed down the area devoted to sheep runs; woollen and worsted manufacturers more and more imported their wool, above all from Australia. Trades using timber, especially the building industry, or iron ore had to rely largely on foreign supplies. Beyond raw materials for production, Britain continued the tradition of importing tropical foodstuffs. Besides, she bought increasing quantities of cereals, especially after the repeal of the corn laws. Among exports, textiles retained pride of place, constituting 60 per cent of home-produced goods sold abroad in the early 1850s. Iron goods, especially rails and other material for railway use, assumed great importance in the third quarter of the nineteenth century when countries adopting rail transport looked to Britain for their equipment—sometimes also for constructional labour. Though still a minor item on the export side, coal made a contribution valuable in terms of shipping space utilization as well as of currency earned: most British imports, being raw materials or food, were bulkier than the manufactured goods exported. But for coal filling some of the space, ships would have had to travel outward in ballast to a greater extent, thus adding to freight costs. While these export items could not equal in value, any more than in volume, the import total, invisible earnings turned the deficit on visible account into a surplus. Shipping, banking, insurance and capital investment gave rise to an income sufficient not only to cover the excess of visible imports, but even to leave a substantial margin for lending abroad.

Free trade does not denote complete absence of tariffs. It is compatible with dues levied on imports to raise revenue, provided corresponding excise duties are paid by the same commodities, if produced at home. Free trade balances the scale equally between articles of foreign and domestic origin. Britain in 1846 had taken only the first steps on this road; she was not even yet certain whether she wanted to travel its whole length. Where reduction of tariffs increased consumption sufficiently to swell Exchequer receipts on balance through the larger volume of goods paying duty, the State had every reason to seek freer trade for the sake of public revenue, but complete repeal rather than reduction of duties offered no such obvious rewards. Chancellors of the Exchequer were tempted to scale down duties merely to the point where they maximized their revenue.

In going well beyond this stage, chiefly by Gladstone's tariff reforms of 1853 and 1860, Britain in the third quarter of the nineteenth century paid tribute to the superiority of her own industry and to the prevailing mood in the world. British industry wanted protection neither for itself nor for its competitors, but equal opportunities for all; nor was it unaware that at this juncture equal opportunities secured for it the lion's share of orders. Only 15 important revenue earners remained to the British customs after 1860, none of them manufactures, but even for foodstuffs the slogan of the 'free breakfast table' exerted a powerful appeal. Nine tenths of the tariff revenue by the end of the century came from four commodities, spirits, wine, tea and tobacco.

Though free trade brought Britain substantial advantages, she was not alone in promoting it at this period. Though her treaty with France sparked off the new policy in Europe, a similar agreement had been concluded six years earlier between the United States and Canada, two nations whose gain from reducing protection was far less obvious. While the world has never seen a period of free trade, it experienced in the three decades after the middle of the nineteenth century freer trade than ever before or subsequently. Though embodied in bilateral treaties between the countries concerned, the movement was not co-ordinated and affected some earlier than others; in the United States the tariff represented a bone of contention between Southern free-traders and Northern protectionists, being lowered up to the eve of the Civil War and raised during and after it. In the area later to become Germany, Prussia had formed a customs union and maintained a low level of duties in order to keep out her rival for German hegemony, the Habsburg Empire, which could not afford to scale her tariff down to the common standard. Napoleon III yearned to play the liberal ruler, but did not sit safely enough in the saddle to afford this luxury; having to maintain an authoritarian régime internally, he at least followed a liberal policy in overseas trade, hoping at the same time to earn the applause of his British neighbours. Even Austria-Hungary and Russia lowered their tariff walls in the 1860s and 1870s. This scaling down of duties was often accompanied by stipulations for 'national treatment' and most-favoured-nation clauses. National treatment concerned traders rather than trade, assuring to foreigners equal treatment with nationals regarding freedom of residence, movement, making contracts, owning property and access to courts of justice. To treat another State as a most favoured nation meant extending to it any concessions granted to a third party and reduced tariffs between two countries simply by virtue of one of them having conceded a lower duty to an outsider. By 1914 Britain was a party to 80 such bilateral treaties. The movement towards freer trade formed a natural corollary to the shrinking of distances separating countries in the wake of improvements in communication such as the electric telegraph, the steamship and the Suez Canal.

Every step along this road increased the volume of international trade, none more than that of Britain, the country which had gone farthest in her reliance upon imported foodstuffs for which she paid by manufactures. In addition to increasing in volume, it changed its character. Once news of the quantity and quality of a distant harvest could travel faster than the crop itself, merchants could buy it unseen for later delivery. Markets in 'futures' grew up, in which men bought and sold produce yet to come. This enabled the manufacturer to cover his requirements of raw materials for a period ahead at a firm price which he could embody in his cost calculations. Nor was it on the purchase side alone that he gained from the new means of communication. For sales in foreign territories he had hitherto relied on exporters, firms without whose intimate knowledge of business habits and markets of some particular country he could not have gained a foothold in foreign parts. The exporter bought from the home manufacturer for prompt payment and re-sold to the foreign customer, often on extended credit, or at least acted as agent, negotiating the sale against a commission. Cables, subsequently even more the telephone, made direct communication between maker and consumer possible and easy; no longer did they need an intermediary. As regards payment, a bill drawn on the foreign customer and accepted by him left in the manufacturer's hand a negotiable instrument which he could turn into cash at once, whereas the customer did not have to pay until it fell due.

In the third quarter of the nineteenth century, Britain's foreign markets expanded faster than those of her colonies. The bulk of exports to the latter still went under the consignment system, goods being consigned for sale to agents or banks acting as commission houses in the colonies for British manufacturers or exporters. The colonial recipient as the weaker financial party could not be expected to pay for goods except when, and in proportion as, they were sold; financial risk rested on the supplier. Colonial exporters to Britain also consigned goods to their agents in London, Liverpool, Glasgow or Bristol, where they were sold at the owners' risk, often at auctions; not being able to finance the transaction, suppliers simultaneously drew bills on their British correspondents for the amount they hoped the sale would realize. Only the India trade followed a different pattern: a few very wealthy and powerful merchant houses, with establishments in both countries, carried it on by means of transactions within their firms, settled by payments which might amount to £10,000 for a single deal.

The speed with which British exports penetrated foreign countries raised doubts in some minds as to the necessity of possessing colonies. Not that economists could have queried the value of an Empire with which one quarter of the United Kingdom's overseas trade took place. The mother country drew from India alone an average annual income of £3 to £4 million on account of administrative services. Yet politicians were less enthusiastic. James Mill described the Empire as 'a vast system of outdoor relief for the upper classes'; though Queen Victoria valued her ability to translate to a colonial bishopric any canon of Windsor whose wife had become obnoxious to her, Disraeli in his salad days wrote to Lord Malmesbury that 'colonies hang like millstones round the neck of the mother country'. A party of Little Englanders even suggested the negotiation of voluntary agreements between Britain and her colonial territories severing political while maintaining and extending economic links. This atmosphere of greater relaxation contributed to the passage of the British North America Act of 1867, which conferred upon Canada Dominion status—power of self-government within the British Empire.

The world movement towards freer trade was reversed in and after the late 1870s, except in the United States where the change had taken place just before the Civil War. Different political reasons caused gear to be reversed in different countries: France, traditionally a protectionist nation not overmuch concerned with foreign trade, had never liked Napoleon III's policy; after his overthrow, she only waited for the trade treaty with Britain to expire. A bad attack of phylloxera, ravaging her vineyards in 1875 and casting her in the unaccustomed rôle of an importer of wine, strengthened her determination to protect her home produce. Bismarck in 1879 for reasons of German domestic policy suddenly switched from support by national-liberal merchants to an alliance with conservative industrialists and *junkers*, purchasing their backing by a tariff—moderate enough at first, but subsequently increased. Higher duties invited retaliation until among the large nations Britain alone remained a free trade country. Doubts were voiced even in Britain whether in a world of tariff barriers a free trade area could survive. Industries suffering from foreign competition campaigned for a 'fair trade' policy which would have armed the government with powers to retaliate by tariffs against countries which used this weapon towards Britain. Germany in the 1880s and 1890s and a little later the United States incurred particular wrath because they made the most damaging inroads on the industrial market; some organs of public opinion conducted a campaign against the trademark *made in Germany*. Public clamour tended to overlook that Germany between 1895 and 1914 was Britain's best overseas customer and that Britain constituted Germany's largest foreign market. Rivalry and mutual dependency had grown up together. British opinion as a whole remained sceptical of the value of protection, even if the cake were covered by a seductive icing of imperial preference. Joseph Chamberlain, fighting in the general election of 1906 on that platform, lost it handsomely.

The era of freer world trade, though past, had left its mark. 'National treatment' remained, along with many most-favoured-nation clauses. Tariffs had returned as protective rather than prohibitive measures; governments could draw revenue from customs duties only to the extent to which they did not keep imports out altogether. Many countries operated double-decker tariffs: one rate of duty to all comers, a lower rate to those which offered reciprocal concessions. Allowing imports into the country free of duty, Britain stood to benefit from such reduced rates. International trade did not increase as rapidly as it had done up to the 1870s (estimated to have been eightfold between 1830 and 1878), but it still grew at an impressive rate (three-fold between 1878 and 1914); Britain did not do as much of it as she had done at the earlier date (19.6 per cent in 1876–80), but her share was still considerable (14.1 per cent in 1911–13). Especially of primary produce, of which she had absorbed almost one third of world imports in 1876–80, she still at the outbreak of the first world war accounted for one-fifth. Within this category of primary products, the share of foodstuffs had climbed to equality with industrial raw materials. Though Britain's part in the world's exchange of food and raw materials gradually grew larger than in manufactures, she had begun importing considerable quantities of the latter; else alarm at German and American competition would have fallen on deaf ears. Altogether, especially between 1875 and the end of the century, the growth of her imports continued unabated while her exports did not make so successful a showing, though the picture was distorted by substantial price changes. Industrialized countries made for themselves the less complex manufactures, especially textiles, which Britain had traditionally supplied, though remaining customers for British engineering products. Manufactured goods still predominated among British exports, owing partly to the success of British transport equipment, partly to the discovery of new and more distant markets for the output of the British cotton industry. Meanwhile Britain was casting herself more and more for the unfamiliar rôle of a raw material supplier by expanding her exports of coal.

TABLE I

INCREASE OF THE BRITISH EMPIRE IN THE LATE NINETEENTH CENTURY

	Surface Area (million square miles)	Population (millions)
1860	2·5	145
1880	7·7	268
1900	13·0	370

Greater difficulty in meeting the demands of highly industrialized markets and greater attention paid to undeveloped territories engendered a more imperialist attitude towards over-seas possessions. The Empire grew; so did its importance as an exclusive or at least preferential source of raw materials and as a market for United Kingdom manufactures. The same Disraeli who had once rashly spoken of millstones fastened one of these ornaments more securely round the neck of his sovereign when he crowned Queen Victoria Empress of India in 1875. When in the same year the khedive of Egypt, afflicted with one of his periodical bankruptcies, sold his shares in the Suez Canal, Disraeli scooped them up for the British government, combining a brilliant stroke of business with a consolidation of Britain's command over access to India and Burma. A Colonial Institute had been established seven years earlier to pursue research into the needs and resources of British overseas territories. These resources, especially the produce of tropical climates which Britain could not obtain elsewhere, had become an indispensable part of the pattern of trade; neither politicians nor merchants could reconcile themselves to envisaging their loss. Sufficient headway was made in the 1870s in diagnosing and combating tropical diseases to enable white men to spend prolonged tours of duty in the colonies without permanent injury to their health. The professor of modern history at Cambridge, J. R. Seeley, wrote a coruscating justification of Britain's colonizing mission, *The Expansion of England*, in 1883, and the uncrowned poet laureate of imperialism, Rudyard Kipling, coined the expression of the 'white man's burden' and in the last decade of the century lent the wings of poetry to the new policy:

> Never was isle so little, never was sea so lone,
> But over the scud and the palm trees, an English flag was flown.

In the carving up of Africa by the European powers during the last 20 years of the nineteenth century, Britain suffered greater losses and carried away more glittering prizes than any of the other participants.

The Balance of Trade since 1918

The 1914–18 war caused Britain to deviate for the first time from her free trade policy. The McKenna duties of 1915, intro-duced to save shipping space, fell chiefly on 'luxuries': motor cars and cycles, clocks and watches, musical instruments and cinema film. An element of imperial preference was added in 1919. Imposed for ten years in the first instance, they were renewed in 1925. Meanwhile a new category, that of 'key industries', had been created which could be protected by tariffs. An Act of 1921 defined them, but left actual enumeration to the Board of Trade, which applied it to precision instruments, certain chemicals, wireless valves and ignition magnetos. Some more duties in subsequent years served either purposes of revenue or the absorption of unemployed labour into the industries protected. Thus while Britain in the 1920s had not turned her back on free trade in principle, she admitted exceptions where she discerned a national, as distinct from a sectional, interest in protection.

In spite of such exceptions, Britain's retained imports continued to increase. This set her apart from other countries which went to considerable lengths to achieve a greater measure of self-sufficiency. She could afford free admission of commodities because invisible exports still paid for a large share of her import bill and because the terms of trade (the rate at which British exports exchanged for imports) had moved considerably in her favour. Her main imports consisted of raw materials and foodstuffs; scientific and technical progress as well as over-expansion during the war had increased their production in primary producing countries which, in order to sell at all, had to let their output go at very low prices.

However, primary producing countries were not only Britain's suppliers of agricultural commodities, but also customers for her manufactured goods. If their produce sold at lower prices, their purchasing power suffered; they reduced their orders for British exports. Geese that lay golden eggs should not be starved. British industry relying on foreign demand for its output benefited only temporarily from the elimination of two competitors, Germany and Russia. The weight of reparation obligations alone imposed on the former made her return to the international market as quickly as possible—return, moreover, with the most up-to-date equipment which war devastation, runaway inflation and American credits had enabled her to acquire. Poland, heir to Germany's coal mines in Upper Silesia, exploited them on a large scale, keeping British coal out of the European market. This had anyhow been disorganized by a peace settlement which lengthened customs frontiers by 12,500 miles and raised the number of customs units from 20 to 27. However easily Britain bought, her task on the sales side had never been so difficult.

The violent slump which overtook the world in 1929 and lasted till 1933 hit primary producers even worse than manufacturing countries, but did not bypass any nation whose fortune depended on exports. For the first time during peace, international trade not only ceased to grow; it actually shrank. No industrial nation had committed as large a proportion of her resources to overseas trade as Britain who suffered worst. In vain did she try to cling to the tradition which had served her well in the days of her greatness; in a world where every other nation protected producers, a solitary free trade area was bound to become the dumping ground of every desperate producer anywhere in the world who had to earn foreign currency by fair means or foul. Exceptions to free trade had been made hitherto in the national interest; now there was no branch of the economy whose protection would not be in the national interest. In 1931, Britain retraced her steps from the path which for almost a century had led her towards freer and freer trade.

The tariff as introduced in 1931 and elaborated by the Ottawa agreements on imperial preference in the following year, rendered foreign imports liable to a ten per cent duty, unless specifically exempted, while keeping Empire goods free from duty, unless explicitly charged. An Import Duties Advisory Committee recommended to the Board of Trade deviations from the general rule; its policy consisted of levying only light duties on foodstuffs in common consumption, doubling the general rate of tariff on manufactures and trebling it on luxuries and products competing with key industries. Where foreign produce made inroads on the Dominions' market in Britain, the government imposed or increased duties on them, while guaranteeing to the Dominions their preferential position for a number of years.

Duties were supplemented by more direct controls. Outright import quotas limited the physical quantities allowed to be sent to Britain in any one year; for meat and kindred produce, quotas applied to foreign imports in order to preserve a market for Empire goods. A more sophisticated weapon, used for many iron and steel categories, were tariff quotas which admitted at a low rate of duty a fixed volume of imports, subjecting excess quantities to a much heavier rate. Subsidies to producers of miscellaneous domestic commodities, though of modest dimensions, similarly helped to keep imports down, as did the policy of holding the external value of sterling at a low level, thereby raising artificially the cost of imports to the British buyer.

The development of the 1930s showed the outcome of this policy. Up to 1935, the volume of imports remained approximately unchanged from the 1920s; at much reduced prices, this represented a fall in value exceeding one third. Much of them, formerly supplied by foreigners, now came from Empire countries; while the United Kingdom had bought 29 per cent of her imports from the Empire in 1930, she derived 40 per cent from this source in 1938. The movement of the terms of trade in Britain's favour and the use of export earnings to pay for imports rather than to invest overseas enabled her not only to maintain, but even to increase, her import surplus towards the end of the decade. Once military necessity overshadowed all other considerations, this surplus grew beyond all economic reason; neither Britain's exports nor her foreign currency and gold reserves could have paid for her needs during the second world war, had not United States lend-lease legislation and the generosity of certain Dominions postponed the question of payment until after the war.

Abandonment of the gold standard in 1931 slightly eased the position of Britain's exporters; so did her management of sterling parity which made her goods cheap to foreign buyers. This however was a game at which many ministers of finance could play; Britain was neither the first nor the only nation to indulge in competitive devaluation. To foster British exports, more had to be done; governments used imports as a wedge with which to prise open an outlet for exports. A number of countries relied on Britain as their principal market, selling to her far more than they bought from her, for instance the Argentine and the Scandinavian States. A cutting of the trade link would have hurt them far more than Britain; this enabled the latter to apply pressure. Imports were rendered contingent upon an increase in their purchases of British goods (chiefly coal and coke). In spite of these efforts, the volume of British exports continued to decline. As genuine multilateral foreign trade shrank, Britain's share of it grew, but the increase in her proportion could not compensate for the contraction of the total in the earlier 1930s. Once British industries were fully occupied working for the war effort, exports for the time being lost their significance, however desirable it remained during the second, as it had been during the first, world war to continue exporting as far as raw materials, manpower and shipping facilities allowed.

The end of the war brought lend-lease to an abrupt close. Britain, greatly weakened by a military and material effort which nothing short of the struggle for survival could have justified, faced economically the most desperate situation in her national existence. Even after valiant endeavours to increase her agricultural production and a tightening of belts verging on malnutrition, she had to rely on overseas supplies for two thirds of her food. Her manpower had been overstrained in the war effort, labouring for no incentive other than victory, committed to 'blood, sweat, toil and tears': the relaxation of military tension left it limp, monotonously fed, starved of consumer goods, without incentives. The country depended on imports as never before. Not only had they once more to be paid for, but many allies—not all of them voluntary allies—who had accumulated sterling balances during the war through providing, or being coerced into furnishing, goods or services, now expected to dip into these balances to satisfy their own craving for commodities. For almost a decade after the war, the question of protecting home producers against foreign competition did not arise; home producers and overseas rivals alike worked at full stretch to fulfil the plethora of orders pressed upon them. If Britain nevertheless had to cut down imports by licensing methods far more drastic than pre-war tariffs, it was for quite a different reason: the country had not the wherewithal to pay for anything but bare essentials; even much industrial re-equipment, the desirability of which nobody doubted, had to take its place in the queue for scarce foreign currencies. The international community desired relaxation or complete removal of restrictions on the passage of goods across frontiers; national solvency dictated to Britain a far more cautious policy. Accordingly Britain—in common with many other countries—had to maintain a zig-zag course, loosening the safety-valve of import licensing by a turn or two whenever her balance of trade improved and fastening it down again as soon as the import surplus threatened to grow out of hand. For ten years after the end of the war, balance of payment crises followed each other at roughly two-yearly intervals.

In the middle 1950s at last, immediate post-war stringency had been overcome and the strain on exports eased. The government had learnt the lesson that hasty dismantling of controls might even yet provoke a recurrence of crises. Schemes to proceed more gradually were projected on an international basis. Ideally they aimed at a single European group within which duties would be scaled down according to an agreed timetable, but two factions existed in Europe: one for which economic constituted merely a prelude to political integration, the other which sought to keep the two apart and pursued the reduction of economic trade barriers for its own sake. Britain, anxious to preserve her Commonwealth ties and obligations, belonged to the latter group. Her refusal to be hurried into precipitate abandonment of tariffs and other import restrictions drew upon her much harsh criticism from circles which valued some international ideal above Britain's economic solvency. Her import policy remained closely circumscribed by the success of her exports in securing for her the means of payment in international trade.

VIII | BANKING, INVESTMENT AND FISCAL POLICY

The Money Market

Many men, engaged in production without adequate capital, have to borrow it from others. Any economy based on exchange finds opportunities for producers unable to finance their work all the way to the sale of the finished commodity: in the Middle Ages growers have their crops bought and paid for by a dealer before they are harvested, sheepmasters sell, and collect the money for, wool still on the backs of their sheep. Advance payments to sellers constitute short-term loans tiding them over the waiting period before delivery of goods. Provision of finance on this basis represented a private arrangement between buyer and seller, depending on the producer's ability to find a purchaser willing to advance the money; nor would anybody make a loan of this kind, except where he personally knew and trusted the borrower. In other words, though capital could be borrowed, there was no capital market, no impersonal institutional framework enabling a producer to resort to lenders with whom he had enjoyed no previous contact, a capitalist to find a profitable outlet for surplus funds. As the scale of economic activities grew over the centuries, more and more *entrepreneurs* engaged in production well beyond their means and needed outside funds to augment their own resources; good business prospects enabled them to offer attractive rates of interest for capital employed in their production. But often they would not know, far less be known by, people suitably endowed. This established the need for a capital market.

Yet it is wrong to speak of a capital market. Industry requires capital of two types which economists call fixed and circulating capital. Fixed capital consists of equipment of a permanent or at least semi-permanent nature; much of it, in the form of buildings and machinery, is fixed to the ground and immovable, though ships or cranes belong to the same category. Fixed capital renders services to the producer over a long period; it pays for itself over the years, possibly decades; its turnover is slow. The capitalist furnishing fixed capital must be prepared to lend at long term, to remain parted from the principal of the loan over a number of years, during which he will receive only interest. This distinguishes him from the short-term lender who finances circulating capital—capital with a quick turnover, funds with which the producer either buys raw material or pays wages or holds goods already completed, but not yet sold. Such capital 'circulates' in the sense of being spent and replaced quickly, often several times in a single year. Though the short-term lender makes funds available now, he does not want to commit them for more than a limited time and remains free to recall them if necessity arises. There are therefore two capital markets, that for long-term and that for short-term capital, the former usually called the capital or investment, the latter the money market. Both are institutions for the transfer of loanable funds from would-be investors to those who require them for productive purposes; they have little else in common.

Lending of short-term funds has traditionally been undertaken by banks. They inherited this function from goldsmiths with whom customers had left their coins for safe keeping. Originally goldsmiths charged fees for the service of taking custody of people's money and paying out amounts on request, even more if such payments were desired, not to depositors, but to other persons—the early form of drawing a cheque. Goldsmiths soon discovered, however, that all clients never wished to withdraw all their deposits at the same time. Goldsmiths could safely lend out at interest a proportion of customers' funds entrusted to their keeping. Lending added a new and profitable sideline to their activities—so profitable that many gave up their original business and turned into bankers pure and simple, receiving deposits of money from some customers which they used for advances to others. The larger the funds in their hands, the greater the scope of their activities; far from charging service fees, they now offered interest on monies deposited with them, finding their profit in the difference between the rate of interest paid to depositors and that demanded from borrowers. London by the end of the eighteenth century had about 70 banks which had come into existence in this manner.

Goldsmiths plied a trade confined to large towns, chiefly to

London. Banks in the provinces had different origins. Only a handful existed before 1750; yet by 1800 their number had grown to about 400, a clear indication that the need for their services arose in the second half of the eighteenth century. Some stemmed from manufacturers or traders hampered by shortage of funds when they wanted to expand their activities. They had invited members of their families, friends, even employees, to entrust them with any spare money they possessed for use in the business at a good interest. Employing other people's funds successfully, they found the monetary side of their activities more profitable than their original trade, so dropped the latter. The majority of the 'big five' deposit banks of present-day Britain can trace their beginnings to butchers, brewers or other traders to whom banking had initially been an ancillary occupation. Yet others became country bankers because of the excellent opportunities they enjoyed for making payments at a distance. While highwaymen rendered roads unsafe, the remittance of large amounts of money over distances remained hazardous. A trader travelling to sell goods in another part of the country could reduce the risks both for himself and others. To take the best-known example, Welsh cattle-drovers took their livestock to London twice a year. Any Welshman with a debt to settle in the capital would pay its amount to the drover. The money would never leave Wales, but when the drover had made his sales and received the proceeds, he would use them to settle his fellow countryman's account in London and return home with a lighter heart as well as pocket, knowing that he had earned not only the profits of his cattle sale, but also a commission on the payment effected.

At the end of the eighteenth century England possessed a banking system, consisting of London banks on the one hand and country banks (in the sense of provincial banks, not banks confined to rural areas) on the other. London bankers were beginning to specialize, some in currency or credit for one or several overseas markets, others on credit for trade provided in the form of bills of exchange*; yet others became specialists in the purchase and sale of precious metals or the flotation of government loans. All of them enabled Londoners to effect payment by credit transfers between accounts, banks settling

* For bills of exchange, see below, p. 182.

their mutual debts originally by daily exchanges of cash, but after 1773 by means of a clearing house, thus limiting the sums actually changing hands to the uncompensated balances resulting from total daily transfers. Banks in industrial towns were needed chiefly to provide short-term credit to manufacturers hard pressed to finance expanding activities. In rural areas, surplus funds accumulated seasonally—after the harvest until farmers purchased the next season's requirements—or permanently; their owners looked to the bankers to employ the money profitably until it be wanted. Everywhere banks issued notes, promises to pay the holder coin of the realm, which circulated to the extent to which the bank was known and trusted. Nobody could be compelled to accept bank notes if he preferred coin, but most people were glad enough to use them, and it was customary for them to circulate throughout the area served by the issuing bank. In London, Bank of England notes had driven out of circulation those of the other bankers who therefore no longer issued any.

A system which faced banks in industrial areas with constant demands for credit, while their counterparts in rural regions had to find outlets for short-term capital seeking investment, could work only by employing the surplus in one part of the country to meet the deficiency in another. The banks performed this function by means of bills of exchange. A bill of exchange is an instrument of credit. By drawing it the creditor demands, and by accepting it the debtor promises, the payment of a certain sum at a fixed date and place. The creditor can 'discount', that is sell, this promise of future payment to a third person by endorsing it; in writing his own name across the back of the document, he not only relinquishes claim to, but adds his own guarantee of, payment; whoever buys the bill from him, can resell it by observing the same procedure. Bills may therefore change hands a number of times, always 'at a discount', an amount lower than the face value. How much lower, depends on two elements: the length of time which has to elapse before the bill becomes payable, and the confidence felt by the purchaser that on maturity it will be met, either by the original debtor or by any of the endorsers. Close acquaintance with the creditworthiness of signatures enables a dealer in bills to buy at a lower discount, and make a gain on, bills he knows to be safe.

Industrialists needing accommodation to pay wages or buy raw materials obtained bank credit for the amount required, the banker drawing on the industrialist a bill of exchange for the amount lent plus interest and a premium in respect of the risk involved, payable at a date when the industrialist hoped to have earned the value out of the sale of his products. Once the industrialist had accepted the bill, his banker could replenish his own funds by discounting it. Such bills provided welcome investment for holders of short-term capital in rural areas seeking a profitable outlet; by buying them now at a discount, they acquired a claim to the full face value of the bill at maturity. But bankers in industrial areas were not usually in direct touch with their counterparts in agricultural districts. However, all country bankers had London correspondents—London bankers who dealt with their metropolitan business, kept their London accounts and provided them with cash for bills or bills for cash. These acted as intermediaries, purchasing bills of exchange from bankers in industrial, and reselling them to those in agricultural, areas. Bill brokers fulfilled the same function by establishing contact between buyers and sellers for a commission. Thus the banking system created a money market of considerable importance to the British economy; at a time when surplus short-term capital accumulated in certain areas and a stringency of funds arose in others, they overcame the geographical limitation and financed the short-term needs of British industry out of the short-term overflows of British agriculture.

Though a money market was in existence by the early nineteenth century, its pillars, the banks, lacked the strength and stability to perform their functions satisfactorily. Early eighteenth century legislation had granted a joint-stock banking monopoly to the Bank of England: bankers in England could not be organized as joint-stock companies, but had to do business as individuals or partnerships, the law providing that no banking partnership was to exceed six persons. The stability of any bank depends largely on the funds at its disposal; even the pooled resources of six wealthy individuals did not constitute a strong capital basis for a credit institute. Partners enjoyed no more legal than financial security. Their liability for anything done by anybody in the partnership's name remained unlimited. To be responsible with his private as well as his business fortune for anything which any of his partners or employees might do, constituted a risk no man would lightly incur; at the very least he would want to keep an eye on what they did. This militated against establishing branches at a distance which did not allow of continuous personal observation. Banks usually confined their activities to a single locality. This practice during an era when industries were similarly localized rendered a bank dangerously dependent on a single industry, at best on a small number of industries, the prosperity of which played too large a part in the bank's fortunes, especially since just at the moment when the industry felt compelled to lean most heavily on the bank's assistance, the bank found itself least able to provide the needed support. Even more than other business men did bankers suffer from an undue concentration of their eggs in a single basket.

In the circumstances, depositors placed confidence less in the bank's means than in the known reliability of the owner or managing partner—a sound enough basis as long as he lived, but one likely to crumble if he suddenly died without leaving an equally trusted successor. Bankers knew that they could safely lend a proportion of the funds deposited with them, but not how large a proportion; adequate levels of cash reserves and liquidity ratios could be ascertained only by trial and error, processes painful not only to bankers themselves, but also to their clients: every time a bank failed, its bankruptcy devalued its notes, many of them lodged at that moment in the pockets of unsuspecting holders. Nor need the ruin of a bank always betoken insolvency; its assets might exceed its liabilities, but if they were in the form of mortgages or other securities not quickly realized, and if London was too far for a messenger on horseback to take a portfolio of bills of exchange for discount and return with cash on the same day, the throng of customers clamouring for payment at the counter would conclude that the bank had failed and would spread the news, making certain that every single depositor would urgently seek repayment of every penny which the bank held. These risks subjected banks in the early nineteenth century to an unhealthy mortality rate, though they enjoyed greater opportunities of resurrection than ordinary mortals.

Currency management increased instability. Legal tender—money which everybody has to accept in settlement of debts—

in the eighteenth century consisted of gold and silver coins, for the provision of which the Royal Mint was responsible. By the end of the century this institution had overcome the worst quality problems of production: the coins it circulated could no longer be clipped, devalued or counterfeited with excessive ease. It had far less success on the score of quantity: changes in gold and silver value meant that at most times it paid holders to exchange coins of one metal for those of the other, melt down the acquired coins and sell the bullion at the price ruling in the metal market. For most of the eighteenth century, the Mint undervalued silver; this led to a chronic shortage of silver coin required chiefly for small transactions. Search for money tokens of suitable denominations imposed heavy burdens on employers committed to paying wages; manufacturers had to issue token coins backed by their own credit—an illegal practice, yet often unavoidable—or to resort to ludicrous shifts to make up for the shortage of the means of payment. In some areas, bills of exchange for small amounts circulated; bank notes were welcomed as an expedient for filling the gap.

When war broke out with France in 1793 and again when defeat seemed likely in 1797, people uncertain of the future wanted to carry cash in their pockets in order to be forearmed against all eventualities. Such were the withdrawals from banks that they found it difficult to meet all demands; on the second occasion they would have run out of legal tender, had not the government come to their rescue by suspending until further notice convertibility of bank notes (meaning that nobody was entitled to demand coin for these notes). Adopted as an expedient to avert panic, inconvertibility endured for a quarter of a century. Banks freed from the obligation to redeem their notes could issue them to a total limited only by their own discretion. All of them greatly extended their lending activities, thus adding to the country's currency at a time when the total stock of goods and services did not increase in the same proportion; by their conduct they amplified the inflationary impetus anyhow generated by war. In relation to gold, the pound sterling lost considerably in value. This had happened before, but without attracting the same degree of attention. A committee of economists advised re-establishment of the pre-war gold value of the currency once hostilities had ended—a policy which forced the government to reduce substantially by deliberate deflation the amount of purchasing power circulating in relation to goods and services available. Many banks, caught with inflated note issues, fell victim to the stringency of the post-war years. Among other measures, the government prohibited the circulation of bank notes in denominations lower than £5 so as to prevent small and unsound institutions from flooding the country with paper competing with coins. The government took this opportunity of disembarrassing itself of the valuation of sterling in two different metals; the currency, when restored to full convertibility in 1821, was based on gold alone, the standard coins in circulation being sovereigns and half-sovereigns (20s. and 10s.).

Much of the difficulty attendant upon banking business in England arose from privileges secured by the Bank of England in the late seventeenth and early eighteenth centuries as a reward for providing finance for the wars of William III and Anne. Apart from its joint-stock banking monopoly, it kept the government accounts which enabled it to be very selective in what other customers it accepted. Contemporaries contended that 'Bank of England' was a misnomer: as it opened accounts only for chartered trading companies and London merchants, disregarding entirely the growth of industrial life in the remainder of the country, 'Bank of London' would have described its scope more accurately. In spite of its privileges, it considered itself as no different in kind from other banks with which it competed for business.

The Bank of England's monopoly did not apply to Scotland. Freedom to form joint-stock banks developed in that country a sound banking system earlier than in England. Joint-stock companies could be formed in Scotland by private resolution; they lacked corporate personality, but enabled large numbers of stockholders to pool their funds. Private banks in Scotland were therefore absorbed by competitors organized more successfully on joint-stock lines, except for a few old-established houses in Edinburgh. Scottish banks issued notes which enjoyed general confidence, because the public knew the issuers to be carefully managed; failures of joint-stock banks in Scotland were hardly known. Even the smallest man was encouraged to open a banking account; Scottish banks not only paid interest on current account balances, but extended cash credit, even to customers of very limited means, provided they were known and trusted and could find guarantors acceptable to the bank. In this way, Scottish banking reached income groups far lower than those concerned with credit transactions in England and in its smaller geographical area fertilized far more effectively the growth of economic activities.

Improvement of English money market conditions in the nineteenth century had to wait upon a change in outlook on the part of the Bank of England. From being merely a privileged large bank, it had to develop into a national institution, assuming responsibility for the currency as well as functions of lender of last resort to other bankers. This metamorphosis did not take place overnight, nor was it entirely voluntary. Though a number of dynamic governors initiated new policies and created precedents for their successors, pressure by the government played its part in grooming the Bank of England for its rôle as a central bank. The first sign that the Bank attempted to grapple with new responsibilities occurred in 1825, when the money market underwent a crisis causing the collapse of 45 banks. As in every crisis, the currency in circulation proved inadequate to satisfy the desire for liquidity of all those normally prepared to hold part of their capital in the form of claims on others, but at this moment fearing for the safety of such claims and wanting to hold hard cash. The crisis could be resolved only by making additional means of payment available as quickly as possible. In its vaults, the Bank held considerable stocks which could serve this purpose, partly out-of-date gold coins withdrawn (guineas worth 21s.), partly small denomination notes printed, but withheld from issue in compliance with the government's prohibition of notes below £5. By temporarily adding these stocks to circulation, the Bank helped the crisis to abate and eventually to subside.

Nevertheless it did not escape public censure. Many critics attributed the crisis to the weakness of private banks, fettered by the Bank of England's joint-stock privileges, quoting in support the stability of Scottish banking; others blamed the Bank's remoteness from business life in general. Legislation in the following year attempted to remedy both deficiencies. In order to lessen the Bank's concentration upon London, it imposed on it the obligation to open branches in the major provincial centres. At the same time it authorized the establishment of joint-stock banks in England, provided they remained at a distance of 65 miles from London. In 1833 the Bank's privilege suffered further diminution: the 65-mile limit was repealed in favour of joint-stock banks which issued no notes. Though their capital was divided into shares, the law granted no limitation of liability to holders; in that respect their risks were no less than those of partners in private banks.

The Bank of England operated on the legal basis of a charter granted for a number of years and renewed from time to time. As the price of its recommendation to Parliament to renew the charter, the government exacted concessions from the Bank; by this means the government made the Bank conform to the official view of its functions. The most important reform was contained in the Bank Charter Act of 1844. This aimed at preventing crises by putting a stop to the excessive creation of purchasing power in the form of paper money. Bank notes could be issued either by private banks or by the Bank of England. Private banks were easily dealt with by restricting the issuing privilege to banks in existence in 1844 and limiting the volume to the amount in circulation when the Act was passed. Their right to issue notes lapsed if they amalgamated, opened an office in London or went out of existence. The Bank of England could put into circulation an unlimited amount of notes as long as it backed them to their full value by precious metal in its vaults; beyond paper subject to 100 per cent backing it was entitled however to a fiduciary issue initially fixed at £14 million, though augmented by two thirds of the value of any private bank issue which had lapsed. The Act put an end to banknote inflation, but its authors overlooked that the currency could be inflated as easily by a disproportionate increase of credit instruments as of bank notes. It changed therefore the sources of inflation without averting the effects. Moreover, it failed to take account of the excessive demand for means of payment which arises in each panic and must be assuaged, if the crisis is to be overcome.

The danger of confining the currency within a straight-jacket was first demonstrated three years later. Bad harvests in 1845 and 1846 led to food and cotton imports at high prices; the railway mania of the same years suddenly collapsed. A good harvest in 1847 lowered food prices. Those committed to meeting calls on railway shares desperately vied with corn dealers holding in their warehouses food grain imported at high costs for funds to tide themselves over the emergency. The Bank of England's powers to lend were severely circumscribed by the Bank Charter Act; its fiduciary issue was unlikely to satisfy the market's desire for liquid funds in a crisis. The knowledge of this limitation added to general panic. Eventually the Bank advised the government to indemnify it against the legal consequences of over-issuing in defiance of the Act. Promulgation of this letter of indemnity alone sufficed to allay the panic; the Bank did not in fact have to expand the fiduciary issue beyond legal limits. The mere knowledge that it had power to do so brought the acute stage of the crisis to a close.

Ten years later the test was even more severe. On this occasion a crisis had been provoked by excessive speculation on the part of the discount houses—bankers dealing in bills of exchange. Credit based on a bill of exchange can be no sounder than the transaction which has given rise to the bill; if two impecunious firms put themselves in funds by drawing and accepting and then selling a bill to a third party, the prospect of its being met at maturity is doubtful. But even if a bill arises from a genuine sale of goods by the drawer to the acceptor, the latter will be able to settle his debt only if he has meanwhile used and resold the goods at a profit; a bill based on an unsound or unsuccessful commodity transaction offers no better security to the holder than a pure finance bill. Only intimate knowledge of firms involved, close scrutiny of bills and a determination to eschew undue risks could ensure that bills of doubtful ante-cedents did not accumulate in the portfolios of discount houses which usually held them to maturity. To such firms the Bank of England acted as a lender of last resort; in an emergency, they reckoned on rediscounting bills with the Bank, if need be at a loss, thus acquiring cash to meet their obligations. That they had exercised inadequate care and prudence and had over traded, became common knowledge between 1854 and 1857. By way of warning, the Bank of England for short periods limited or stopped rediscounting (refused to buy bills of exchange from discount houses), but they did not heed the signs. They were caught up in a panic which originated in overspeculation in real estate and railroads on the other side of the Atlantic. £80 million worth of American securities were held in British portfolios, many of them in the form of bills of exchange accepted by American debtors; nobody knew whether they would be met. The blow to the money market was devastating: 135 important British firms failed within three months; troops had to be called out to protect from irate depositors the staffs of two Glasgow banks which suspended payment; less than six London discount houses of any size survived the collapse. The government again suspended the Bank Charter Act, but the announcement alone was not enough; for a week the Bank of England had to issue notes in excess of legal limits before the crisis could be brought under control.

The Capital Market

Need for circulating capital had been felt from time immemorial; so short-term credit facilities had developed gradually to supply it. Fixed capital on the other hand played little part in the pre-Industrial Revolution economy; no market at all existed, even in embryonic form, where industrialists could borrow it. That does not mean that no long-term credit could be obtained, only that industrialists had no access to it. The State was always in need of advances, both at short and long term; from being the most capricious and incalculable of debtors, it had after 1689 developed into the safest, able to borrow at the cheapest rate because creditors judged the risk of remaining unpaid to be negligible. Its long-term loans enjoyed the status of trustee securities; the nest-eggs of widows and orphans were safeguarded by putting them into 'the funds'. A capitalist wishing to invest at long term could also buy stock in, or acquire debentures of, joint-stock companies. Joint-stock organization constituted a privilege obtainable only by royal charter or from Parliament and reserved for merchant ventures entailing unusual risks or enterprises considered to possess public utility. Examples of the former were the East India and Hudson's Bay Companies; the Bank of England had qualified under the latter heading because it provided war finance. The majority of public utility undertakings endowed with joint-stock organization by Parliament operated in the field of transport; turnpike trusts were typical, but canal, bridge and later railway construction companies received similar grants. Gas and water suppliers and insurance companies came under the same heading. The advantage of joint-stock organization consisted not only of the division of the capital into transferable shares or stock, but also of legal personality for the company which continued in perpetuity, unaffected by changes in the personnel of its shareholders, could sue and be sued in its own name, and of the limitation of shareholders' liability to the amount subscribed.

A market for long-term capital therefore existed, but ordinary industry was excluded from its use. It dealt in government loans and companies' stocks and shares. Its operators had originally been scriveners, seventeenth century lawyers-cum-estate agents who not only sold land on their clients' behalf, but advised them on profitable investment of the proceeds. Many London scriveners came to specialize in investment, turning into stock and share dealers. At first they transacted business at recognized exchanges, later in coffee houses, eventually acquiring one of they own; when it grew too small in 1801, they built a place of business for themselves which they called the stock exchange. They organized themselves along club lines, being governed by a committee and voluntarily submitting to a code of business rules much stricter than the general law. Two types of dealers combined to form the stock exchange: stockbrokers who acted as commission agents, buying and selling at the orders and on behalf of clients, and stockjobbers, dealing on their own account and deriving their earnings from the margin between the price at which they bought and that at which they sold, the 'jobber's turn'. The latter undertook at all times to quote a price, thus guaranteeing to the public that they could always buy or sell any securities listed by the stock exchange. Not only were quotations supplied, but the public informed what they were; up to 1843 a broker, after that date the stock exchange itself, took responsibility for publishing lists of security prices.

Owing to limitations on the types of enterprise to which Parliament would concede joint-stock organization, only a narrow range of securities was originally dealt in on the stock exchange. To government loans and chartered companies' stocks were added in the early nineteenth century a few insurance companies; loans raised by some of the American States found their way into the market at the same time as stock of a number of companies established to supply London with water. The boom of 1824–25 gave rise to a spate of gas works, bridge building undertakings and South American mines; soon afterwards railway companies invaded the stock exchange in increasing numbers, not only those operating at home, but also those financed by British capital abroad. The stock market therefore expanded impressively in the first half of the nineteenth century, but without as yet admitting enterprises manufacturing cotton, iron or pottery.

How then did the ordinary industrialist obtain finance to set up in business and start manufacture? Luck might have made him a member of a well-to-do family; or personal friends, if not his relatives, might know and trust him well enough to let him have some capital. Men who worshipped every Sunday at the same church or chapel, lived in the same place and knew his circumstances, could form an opinion of his reliability; sections of an industry often owed their initial impetus to members of one denomination, such as a part of cotton spinning to Unitarians or of iron to Quakers. If he had to approach capitalists outside his own circle, a manufacturer might have difficulty in persuading them to lend to industry—a new-fangled pursuit, untried and unfamiliar as yet. But landowners would look with some favour upon a good solid factory building; whatever the merits of industry, they knew the soundness of bricks and mortar and would grant a mortgage on premises even though they mistrusted the activities which went on inside. Similarly landowners sometimes financed extractive industries (mining or quarrying) which took place on their own land, mindful of the enhanced value which these imparted to the estate. A trader rarely had funds to spare for industry; his business required him to finance his commerce by paying his suppliers promptly, while granting credit to his customers. But should his trade be temporarily interrupted by war, he found himself with spare funds until commerce flowed freely again; in such a situation he might keep his capital employed by financing the building up of a promising new industry. Also if his suppliers could not cope with the volume of orders he transmitted to them, if he needed the goods badly and could not obtain them elsewhere, he might unwillingly be drawn into long-term investment even in peacetime, because it enhanced his ability to satisfy his customers.

To an industrialist unable to find a backer by any one of these methods, only two routes remained: to go into partnership or to pull himself up by his own bootstraps. Lawyers had burdened partnerships with a series of handicaps. They had no legal personality: they lacked perpetual succession; the death of a partner terminated the partnership; if the others wished to continue, they had to liquidate the old partnership and form a new one. Nor could a partnership go to law; only all individual partners acting jointly could do so. Anybody suing a partnership had to know and set out accurately the names and addresses of every single partner and take the risk of the suit being abruptly ended by the death of a partner before judgment had been given. Partnerships could place themselves beyond the reach of the law by locating one partner outside its jurisdiction, say in Ireland. Owing to the absence of limited liability, any sleeping partner (who invested, but did not actively work, in the partnership) risked a rude awakening unless he kept at least one eye permanently open. No wonder that few people relished the prospect of either entering upon, or doing business with, a partnership. Thrown back upon his own resources, the eighteenth century industrialist made his way by the exercise of purposeful frugality; he neither hoarded nor spent his earnings, least of all tried to climb socially by the purchase of landed property, but ploughed every penny back into the business. Starting from the smallest beginnings, he financed his expansion step by step out of his proceeds, starving himself into greatness. Many of the pioneers of the Industrial Revolution reached the summit of their ambition the hard way.

As long as no market mechanism existed for the provision of fixed capital, accidents of personal and geographical contact could make or frustrate a captain of industry. Nor, where it was done by patient self-finance, could it happen quickly; however typical of the early days of industrialization, the man ploughing back profits and scorning outside help would have been left behind by rivals with ampler resources at a later stage. Industry required an impersonal apparatus putting long-term capital at the disposal of all who could show prospects of using it to good purpose. In other words, it needed joint-stock organization.

Public opinion drove a reluctant government to concessions: in the 1830s, incorporation of joint-stock companies became possible by letters patent, an administrative action cheaper and less complicated than a private Act of Parliament; companies so incorporated acquired legal personality, but not limited liability, and had to supply a new government office, the registrar of companies, with certain particulars available to public inspection. The concession was more apparent than real: the Board of Trade, entrusted with discretion to grant or withhold letters patent, had confidential instructions to permit incorporation as sparingly as possible.

A select committee of Parliament examined the problem afresh in 1844. Presented with evidence relating to a large number of unsatisfactory joint-stock companies, it traced the evil to three causes: in the nature of their objects some could not possibly have succeeded, some were too badly managed to succeed, others were never even meant to succeed, but merely fraudulent attempts to extract money from gullible investors. The committee attributed these blemishes to insufficient knowledge on the part of the public, whether of objects or actual conduct; by increasing the information generally available, the committee proposed to enable investors to protect themselves. It therefore recommended—and Parliament enacted—that any company could claim joint-stock organization as a right, provided it complied with statutory rules which required disclosure of all relevant particulars to the registrar of companies. Though a step forward, the Act did not achieve much. It merely proved that the real decision still lay ahead; this concerned the grant of limited liability.

Parliamentary committees in 1850 and 1851 enquired into the savings of the middle and working classes and concluded that their better-paid members earned enough to make some provision for their future, but had little incentive to save. If they invested their nest eggs in government securities, they could sleep well, but hardly eat well; so safe was the debtor, so great the amount of money pressed upon him, that the government paid an unattractively low rate of interest. Middle class investors had been spoilt by better yields; until the later 1840s they had found outlets for their surplus capital in railways, rewarded by a rate of return appropriate to industrial risk capital, while protected by limited liability. After 1847 the railways' need for new capital had abated; similarly attractive industrial investment opportunities abounded, but all carrying the hazard of unlimited liability. In the circumstances, men tended to spend rather than save; British industry remained deprived of capital available within the community and anxious to find employment in industry at risks which the owner could face. Nor was this all. The middle and working classes attempted to improve the quality of their surroundings by channelling their savings into a number of institutions devoted to social ameliora-tion. Friendly, building and co-operative societies, penny and trustee savings banks, town improvement companies, all suffered from a system of unlimited liability. The voices advocating limited liability for all comers gained strength year after year. In vain did a Royal Commission composed almost exclusively of lawyers in the middle 1850s advise the government not to tamper with the law. Public opinion could no longer be dis-regarded. By a series of measures limited liability was extended between 1856 and 1861 to enterprises of every kind; an Act of 1862 summarized and consolidated the piecemeal legislation. At last industry had gained admission to the long-term capital market. In the first ten years of the new legislation, 5,000 new joint-stock companies came into existence, though many of them had only a short life and a large number pursued activities out-side industry.

The Further Development of Credit Markets

By the 1860s, therefore, markets for both long and short-term credit had reached conditions of unprecedented perfection. Whether for circulating or fixed capital, an industrialist could obtain funds from a capitalist whom he had never met and who knew of his business only what the registrar of companies disclosed to any interested enquirer. An investor could employ his capital in industry by acquiring shares or debentures quoted on the stock exchange, knowing that even as part owner of an enterprise he was not liable for its debts beyond the amount subscribed—a sleeping partner with his mind at rest. Should he wish to liquidate his holding, he would not inconvenience the industrialist whose activities it sustained: the securities which one holder sold in the stock market, another bought. Even the most inexperienced and ignorant capitalist had at his disposal up-to-date revenue estimates made by the best experts in the form of day-to-day stock exchange quotations to guide his choice of investment. This perfect market operated within the framework of an economy serving as the workshop of the world —a world, moreover, of shrinking distances, lowered tariffs and growing trade, a world which set no bounds to talent and enterprise.

In such a world, it seemed ungracious to remember that not all business interests had favoured the introduction of general limited liability. Critics had described the limited liability law as 'an Act for the better enabling Adventurers to interfere with and ruin Established Traders without risk to themselves', on the grounds that speculators ought at least to venture their own funds, not those of their creditors. Though 5,000 companies had taken advantage of the opportunities of incorporation by 1865, they had not been the manufacturers of Lancashire and Yorkshire whom legislators had in mind; for another two decades they continued to look askance at the man whose last penny and last acre did not pay for his business debts. The time came when even these sturdy advocates of personal responsibility had to admit that business risks might grow beyond the control of individuals, but only prolonged depression in the 1870s and 1880s effected this conversion. In the 1860s the umbrella of limited liability shielded from financial *déluges* delicate denizens of the City of London rather than hardy North country dwellers; credit, finance and banking houses pursued their business in the form of limited companies—business which caused the *Shareholders' Guardian* in 1864 to suggest that a statue be erected to limited liability in the shape of a female figure holding a whitewash brush in her hands. Of the activities which required such protective colouring, investment finance was the most prominent.

A flaw had been detected in the perfect market for long-term credit. An established manufacturer could raise capital by issuing shares or debentures quoted on the stock exchange. But what happened to the *homo novus*, the genius not yet known, the brilliant manufacturing process as yet untried, the epoch-making new idea? If a company were promoted, would anybody subscribe the shares or buy its debentures? Who provided a roof over the head of the financial foundling? The introduction of new enterprises offered great opportunities, matched by the risks incurred. A new type of company came into existence to raise long-term finance for new firms and see them through the initial stages until the market had been prepared to take them over, the investment finance company. It appeared in France and the United States a little earlier than in Britain. Limited liability was indispensable to its mode of operation. It issued shares of low denomination, tempting even small men into subscribing. By making only a low initial call on such shares, it took the chill off the subscriber's first plunge, slily insinuating that, if business developed successfully, perhaps the full amount might never have to be called. This did not provide substantial funds; not even a subsequent issue of debentures could adequately fill the coffers. So the investment finance company set out to attract deposits from the public by acting as a bank. However, genuine banks existed; in order to entice deposits away from them, investment finance companies had to tempt depositors by interest rates at a time when *bona fide* banks no longer paid interest on current accounts. Capital borrowed on debenture was not repayable for a long time, but had merely to be serviced; shareholders expected no refund of principal, only dividends. Depositors on the other hand could at any time withdraw the total or any part of their deposits. These therefore represented money borrowed 'on call', the shortest form of credit possible, taken up to provide fixed capital for new industries. In other words, investment finance companies borrowed short and lent long, risking to be caught one day between the immediate demands of their creditors and the slowly maturing ability of their debtors to repay.

Limited liability was not granted to joint-stock banks until 1858. Investment finance companies were therefore started by discount houses which suffered from no such handicap. Their most prominent, though by no means their only representative was Overend Gurney & Co., a firm which had engaged in the textile trade at Norwich in the eighteenth century, pursuing banking as a by-occupation which gradually became its main business. Establishing itself as a dealer in bills of exchange in London in the early nineteenth century, it had grown into the leading discount house—the 'corner house', as it was known to the discount market for its soundness and reliability—under

Samuel Gurney, a Quaker of exemplary business habits who died almost a millionaire in 1857. His successors believed in shortcuts to wealth. While continuing to discount almost one half of London's bills, they vigorously moved into investment finance and 'covered the sea with their ships, ploughed up the land with their iron roads', as the public prosecutor put it at the directors' trial ten years later. Not only did they spread their resources over two capital markets, but they showed little discrimination. Where long-term investment did not prosper, instead of withdrawing, they helped with further funds, thus throwing good money after bad; rather than foreclose, they would run an industrial venture on their own account. For six years, they continued as a partnership, then in 1864 converted to joint-stock organization. By this time the market had grown nervous; rumours circulated that investment finance companies had undertaken commitments beyond their strength. Little suspicion attached as yet to Overends; though depositors withdrew £4½ million from investment finance houses during ten months in 1865, Overends weathered the storm. Early in 1866 a London firm of a similar name, though unconnected with them, went bankrupt; this was enough to generate mistrust, soon swelling to panic. By May Overends had to close their doors; most of the other investment finance companies followed suit, dragging into ruin a large circle of investors.

Investment finance companies had been unfortunate as well as imprudent. Holding discount houses responsible for the crisis of 1857, the Bank of England had thereafter refused them credit facilities. Not able in an emergency to count on aid from the Bank, discount houses had been compelled to establish their own cash reserves—adequate for a prudent firm in normal times, but insufficient to weather a major storm. The invasion of the long-term capital market in the form of investment finance companies by discount houses, dealers in the money market, sharpened the Bank of England's disapproval. Overends attempted, but failed, to persuade the Bank to change its attitude. When crisis loomed ahead, the Bank raised its rate to ten per cent, thus making credit available to the market, though at a penal price; but even at that price it would not help investment finance companies. Its policy served to eliminate unsound elements from the capital market, but not to avert the crisis which broke with full force; two days after the closure of Overends, the Bank Charter Act suffered its third suspension. Even after the removal of this fetter on the Bank's capacity to lend, Bank rate had to remain at ten per cent for another three months before the crisis subsided.

Though painful, it taught the British financial market a valuable lesson—a lesson brought home to practically all other countries only through the much greater and worldwide crisis of 1929–33. This was that it is too dangerous to borrow short and lend long, hence that it cannot be the function of banks— archetypes of short-term borrowers—to provide fixed capital for industry. Investment financing as such constitutes a valuable service to the community, provided it selects its objects with some care and borrows its capital on terms commensurate with its lending activities. Future investment finance companies raised their funds for periods as long as those of the loans required by their industrial clients.

Nor did the unfortunate initial experience inhibit the further and more widespread use of general limited liability. Business enterprises, as they grew in size in the late nineteenth, even more in the early twentieth century, needed ever larger infusions of capital to sustain the scale of their operations. It became customary for undertakings running into millions of pounds to be owned by a multitude of shareholders whose individual contribution on an average amounted to a mere £2,000–£3,000. Though owners in law, they were in fact no more than recipients of dividends, having invested in the expectation of a comfortable yield and taking little interest in 'their' company, provided dividends satisfied their hopes; indeed, some of them had become owners without enquiring whether the company manufactured cotton, built docks or prospected for oil. Widely diffused and inexpert ownership left responsibility and power in the hands of those concerned with the company's conduct, the managers. They could expect freedom from interference, even from the shareholders' elected representatives, the board of directors, as long as dividends were paid regularly and at a satisfactory level. Men engaged to manage other people's property made policy and exercised control; the real owners, though provided with opportunities by repeated reforms in company law, had neither the expert knowledge required nor even the desire to relieve the managers of this power. Giant business enterprises, with the eyes of the whole country upon them, were far more sensitive to public opinion than to any clamour on the part of their own shareholders; at best they behaved in what their managers considered the public interest rather than that of their owners.

The small investor expected to enjoy limited liability when he put funds into a large venture. But why should not small-scale business, even a one-man shop, benefit from the same advantage? In 1907 the law gave statutory recognition to the private limited company, a device designed to extend the protection of limited liability even to the smallest business and accepted already by case law. A private limited company, though a joint-stock organization in name, did not need to be a company in fact; it could be owned by a single proprietor, provided he transferred one share into the name of another person. Its shares were not bought, sold or quoted at the stock exchange, its disclosures to the registrar of companies less extensive than those of its public counterpart. Though less capital was invested in private than in public companies, far more of the former came into existence; by 1913 four out of every five companies on the register were private.

Non-cooperation with the discount houses, initiated by the Bank of England in 1858 to mark its dissatisfaction with their conduct, had serious drawbacks, as the crisis of 1866 had shown. Before 1857 the Bank had made short-term loans to discount houses, as to its other customers, at the Bank rate—defined as the rate at which the Bank of England discounts first-class bills. This rate governed borrowing from the Bank if an emergency arose, hence all financial houses adjusted their own lending rates to Bank rate. All interest rates in the money market were interdependent, moving up and down with Bank rate. Non-cooperation put an end to daily contact between the Bank and the money market and to this almost automatic adjustment of interest rates; had the Bank not lost this day-to-day touch, it would have realized more quickly the imminence of the 1866 panic and acted with greater promptitude to limit its impact. As it was, the imperfect knowledge which the Bank had of money market movements caused its rate until the 1870s to limp behind changes in other rates. Instead of adjusting itself currently to conditions prevailing in the money market, Bank rate became merely a penal rate for those whom improvidence drove 'into the Bank' as a last resort. If however Bank rate represented the highest cost at which an imprudent business house could save its skin, the Bank could not exact it from its regular customers; so as not to penalize them, it had to lend to them at the market rate, reserving Bank rate for its emergency operations.

This was desirable also on different grounds. Bank rate determined the cost at which not only British, but also foreign interests could obtain funds in the London market. If foreigners borrowed in London, the Bank of England made available to them gold or their currencies; if they lent to London, they similarly provided their British debtors with gold or their currencies. The movement of interest rates, therefore, by increasing or diminishing the attraction of London funds to foreigners, be it for investment or borrowing, affected the state of the country's gold reserve for which the Bank of England was responsible. By raising its rate, it rendered credit more expensive; foreigners, rather than pay London rates, would seek loans in Paris or New York, whereas others, with funds to lend, would place them in London to earn the higher interest. Lowering Bank rate tempted foreigners to borrow their requirements in London rather than elsewhere, while overseas surplus capital would seek other outlets as owners considered the remuneration offered by London inadequate. Bank rate movements therefore often reflected the state of the gold reserve, indicating whether the Bank of England desired foreign funds to flow in or out. The more the money market could be isolated from these fluctuations, the less did the domestic economy suffer dislocation through manoeuvres aimed purely at correcting the international distribution of capital.

In 1890 at last the Bank of England brought the period of non-cooperation with the discount houses to a close. It had always been tacitly understood that, whatever the state of day-to-day relations, the Bank of England would have to come to the money market's assistance in a crisis. Between 1866 and 1890, this understanding was not put to the test, but a panic threatened in the latter year. Prices had been on the downgrade for well over a decade; many old-established businesses had converted to joint-stock organization on imprudent terms. The main danger, however, had arisen from loans to foreign debtors of uncertain willingness and ability to repay. Among South

American republics violent government change was endemic; no new government relished the prospect of honouring financial obligations incurred by a predecessor just overthrown. This had recently happened in the Argentine; Baring Brothers, London merchant bankers, held a large portfolio of Argentine bills of exchange. If none of them were honoured, Barings doubted their ability to meet their commitments punctually. They disclosed their predicament confidentially to the Bank of England which ascertained as a matter of urgency that Barings were not insolvent, merely illiquid; though their assets exceeded their liabilities, funds immediately available did not suffice to cover current payments. The Bank thereupon arranged for a group of London bankers and discount houses collectively to guarantee Barings' liabilities; by the time the general public learnt that a crisis threatened, they also knew that their funds were in no danger and that no need for panic withdrawals existed.

By its action to prevent the Baring crisis from developing into a genuine crisis, the Bank set two precedents. First, it resumed leadership of the money market, implicitly admitting that non-cooperation had been a blind alley. Even more important, instead of mitigating the impact of a crisis once it had supervened, the Bank by timely action had headed it off; suspension of the Bank Charter Act had not been required; in fact, the Bank Charter Act was never suspended between 1866 and 1914. The Bank at last realized that its rôle as lender of last resort and guardian of the stability of the British currency required subtler tactics; in the period up to the first world war it developed and refined them. In addition to moving the Bank rate, it rendered funds more plentiful or scarcer by open market operations, mopping up surplus balances by either selling securities or borrowing on its own account, injecting additional purchasing power into the market by buying securities and thus providing sellers with cash. After 1911 the governor once a quarter met the heads of the London clearing banks, converting to a regular conference what had been a tacit agreement to concert policy. The greater importance attached to technical expertise in central banking led to a change of practice in 1920: for the first time a governor of the Bank of England was not a trader holding office for two years, but a specialist in central banking technique, Montagu Norman, who held the post for most of his working life (24 years). He considered independence of the government of the day essential for a central bank; yet such independence did not entitle the bank to frustrate the government's general policy. It was the central banker's duty to make representations, to warn, even to nag, but if these efforts did not change the Chancellor's mind, he had in the end to submit. Stressing the independence of the Bank of England, he saw nothing incongruous in a central bank owned by stock-holders to whom it paid dividends. Yet when, two years after the end of his term of office, the Bank of England was national-ized by the Labour government in 1946, this represented no more than a public acknowledgment of its long-recognized duty to follow the government's lead.

In 1810 the London clearing house had consisted of 40 members, all private bankers. Joint-stock banks, when first established, were not admitted to it by their jealous colleagues. In banking, with its need for a broad capital base even greater than in other branches of the economy, the drive towards joint-stock organization was irresistible. Only 37 private bankers survived in the whole country in 1891; by 1960 all had been absorbed. Such was the relentless progress of joint-stock banks, spreading their tentacles throughout the country, developing new services (cheque accounts, collection of dividend and interest coupons, payment against standing orders), amalgamating among themselves. Offices open for business increased tenfold between 1858 (1,200) and 1960 (over 12,000). Amalgamation reduced their numbers; there were 106 in England alone in 1891, but only 17 in the whole of Britain in 1960. Of these, the 'big five' London clearing banks accounted for 10,500 of the branches, transacting five-sixths of all British banking business already in the 1920s, when further amalgamation was in the air. On that occasion the government made it clear that it would view greater concentration with considerable misgivings. Realizing that such misgivings might be translated into action, the London clearing banks preserved their separate existences.

The central instrument of the money market was the bill of exchange. Yet already in the nineteenth century the inland bill of exchange had yielded more and more to the cheque, legally merely a form of bill of exchange, in commercial practice a far simpler and more convenient instrument. After 1914 the volume of international bills of exchange handled in London similarly underwent a shrinkage, due partly to competition from the New York money market, partly to the contraction of international trade in general, but also to the supervening habit of settling trade transactions by payment against bills of lading or by telegraphic transfers of funds. As bills of exchange receded in importance, another type of bill, that issued by the Treasury, increased its circulation. To discount houses it proved a poor substitute. The skilful dealer makes his profit by accurate assessment of the risks entailed in holding bills, depending on the creditworthiness of the signatures they bear. Treasury bills represented government debt; no skill was required to decide that they could be held without risk, nor could their quality be improved by additional signatures. With this blunt instrument occupying the centre of the stage, discount houses found themselves operating in an ever narrowing market.

The Development of Differential Taxation

Robert Lowe, a nineteenth century politician, once described the Chancellor of the Exchequer as 'an animal which ought to have a surplus'. In other words, in any one year State revenue ought to exceed expenditure. Had all Chancellors followed this golden rule at all times, no national debt would ever have come into existence. But annual budget surpluses were a counsel of perfection. On many occasions, especially in wartime, finance had to be raised more quickly than taxation collected it. The Exchequer therefore borrowed, using its revenue to repay creditors over a term of years. The national debt represented the accumulated budget deficits of the past, plus interest charges due to bondholders. A Chancellor of the Exchequer in any one year planned his revenue to cover the year's current expenditure and in addition to defray the interest on the national debt; if possible, he would also repay a fraction of it. Chancellors in a democratic régime however are not omnipotent; while they determine the amount of money to be raised, Parliament through its political decisions decrees what will have to be spent. Up to the Crimean war, at least in peacetime, Parliament respected the primacy of public revenue and did not embark upon political ventures which would have overtaxed the resources at the Exchequer's disposal. From the middle nineteenth century onwards, it reversed priorities: whatever expenditure Parliament decreed, the Treasury had to find means to pay. No wonder that a Chancellor (Randolph Churchill) resigned before presenting his first budget, disgusted or dismayed at the task imposed upon him.

Until administration is highly developed, public revenue can be raised more easily by indirect than by direct taxation. Customs and excise duties, levied at the point of entry or production, are collected from a small number of people; the taxpayers bear them in the form of enhanced prices of the goods they buy, often without becoming aware that they have been taxed. If duties are placed on luxury goods, the Chancellor earns moral approbation: taxpayers can well afford to bear the impost or else avoid it by abstaining from consumption. Duties on necessities on the other hand constitute a convenience to the Exchequer: as consumers cannot evade them, their yield can be determined in advance with reasonable accuracy. In the eighteenth century, Britain obtained the bulk of her public revenue from such indirect taxes.

In the *Wealth of Nations* Adam Smith demanded that taxation should be equitable in the sense of leaving people proportionately as well off after tax as before. This meant taxing all wealth or income at an equal rate. Indirect taxes offend against this canon of taxation by being proportionate to consumption, upon which the poor man spends a much larger part of his means than the rich. Direct taxation, whether based on wealth or income, would be more equitable. Movable property, however, was notoriously hard to assess because it could be moved; whenever a property tax had been attempted, it had sooner or later turned into a tax on land, the only type of property which could not escape the tax-gatherer's attention. Income-tax was 'repugnant to the customs and manners of the nation' (House of Commons, 1797) because of the inquisitorial methods required to ascertain liability; people looked upon it as rank confiscation of property. Not until the French wars had made the need for further resources imperative and the government had exhausted its financial ingenuity, did it overcome its reluctance to employ so draconic a device. Income-tax, as introduced in 1799, operated at the rate of 2s. in the pound. In the decade 1806–1815, it accounted for one quarter of total tax revenue, to that extent

relieving from expenditure for the war the working class whom—
with perhaps the trifling exception of a few prosperous artisans—
limits at the lower end of taxable incomes exempted from
liability. Income-tax had been granted to the government as a
war measure; not only was it repealed in 1816, but the House
of Commons ordered all returns and documents in the hands
of the commissioners for the affairs of taxes to be destroyed.
How income-tax was re-introduced after a lapse of 27 years
and facilitated reduction of tariffs, has already been discussed.

In 1874 Gladstone fought a general election on a financial
reform programme which involved abolition of income-tax. He
lost, indicating perhaps that electors realized that income-tax
had come to stay. Not that it burdened taxpayers unduly;
exemption limits confined it strictly to the middle class, who
paid in peacetime at rates varying from 2d. to 10d. in the pound,
rising to 1s. 4d. in the Crimean war. Yet income-tax was a
dangerously handy tool in the Chancellor's armoury. However
uncertain the yield of other taxes, he knew in advance the product
in any year of a 1d. rate in the pound of income-tax. Nor did
its cutting edge become blunted by restraint; provided it
operated at all, however low the rate, its administration maintained up-to-date an apparatus of collection and information
which could at short notice raise substantial funds. Even at its
modest nineteenth century level it enabled the government to
repeal an increasing number of tariffs, to relieve ratepayers of
part of the expenditure on poor relief, police, civil prisons and
main highways, while systematically reducing the national debt,
except during the Crimean war. This required considerable parsi-
mony at the centre of affairs which attempted to run a large
Empire on a shoestring—an endeavour reversed only in the
later 1880s. Two new departures in public policy, military and
social expenditure, determined the new trend. Towards the end
of the 1880s, Britain's power was challenged; around 1900 she
not only fought the Boer war, but began expensive naval rearmament in competition with Germany, terminated only by the
first world war. Social expenditure corrected what people felt
to be the maldistribution of the national income by increasing
out of the common pool the share of those inadequately rewarded.
Central government outlay on social services mounted, both as
a proportion of the budget and per head of population, especially

as the result of the Liberal social programme of 1906–11. Lloyd George interpreted the new spirit in his budget speech of 1909 in these words: 'This is a war budget. It is for raising money to wage implacable warfare against poverty and squalidness'.

Expenditure on behalf of the under-privileged out of the common pool is one way of correcting maldistribution of the national income. Graduated taxation is another; it abandons Adam Smith's canon of equitable taxation in favour of taxing the rich more heavily than the poor. Even income-tax differentiated by exempting entirely those whose incomes remained below £100 and taxing at a lower rate those whose incomes did not reach £150. In 1889 death duty became chargeable at one per cent on estates exceeding £10,000. Differentiation according to the value of the estate was further elaborated in the 1894 budget by graduating the rate from one to eight per cent. Income-tax rebates now applied to three levels of income, increased to five in 1898. Asquith in 1907 lowered the rate of tax where earned income remained below £2,000 a year; building on this precedent, Lloyd George two years later not only graduated the tax on earned income in three steps (up to £2,000, between £2,000 and £3,000, and above £3,000), but introduced an additional super-tax levied on incomes in excess of £3,000.

Wars can be financed from current revenue or borrowing. In fact, Chancellors draw on both sources. The wars of 1793–1815 and 1854–57 had been paid for in roughly equal proportions by taxation and loans; just over one third of the Boer war was defrayed from revenue. Chancellors during the first world war suffered from even greater timidity, levying less than one third of the cost in the form of taxation. By their reliance on borrowing, they added considerably to the national debt; from less than 30 per cent of national income in 1913, it grew to over 200 per cent in 1923. Even its interest and management expenses in the latter year absorbed over seven per cent of the national product. Not only was the national debt swollen out of all recognition, its wartime addition had been borrowed at high rates—up to five per cent. In spite of its reliance on loans, the government had not neglected taxation. Income-tax during the war rose to 6s. in the pound; never thereafter did it fall below 4s. 6d. Post-war governments, faced by a crippling national debt to be serviced and gradually reduced, could not afford to loosen the screw. Whereas no Chancellor before 1914 had taxed away more than ten per cent of national income, those between the wars took one quarter. In 1932 the government relieved the situation by an appeal, successful with the great majority of its creditors, for voluntary conversion of much of the public debt from a five to a three-and-a-half per cent basis, but in spite of everything done to lighten the burden, the main effort had to consist of flexing the muscles required to support it.

Throughout the nineteenth century, expenditure by the central government had increased at a slower pace than national income, though expenditure by local authorities on the other hand had grown very fast in the last quarter of the century. In the interwar years even central government spending rose more quickly than national revenue. Much of this change reflected expenditure on social services not obtainable on the cheap, such as housing and education. Other claims came from 'below the line' funds, independent bodies designed to be self-financing, but unable in a depression to maintain solvency. By far the most considerable was the unemployment insurance fund. Breaking even at an average of seven per cent unemployment among the working population, it could not survive the years after 1928, with unemployment figures climbing to three times the percentage calculated, without annual subsidies from the government—subsidies, moreover, which could never be determined in advance and which therefore destroyed all hopes of budgetary equilibrium.

Finance in the second world war avoided many of the mistakes of the first. The Chancellor relied more on revenue than in any previous war: almost 40 per cent was borne by that source in 1940, 55 per cent in 1944, 52 per cent over the war as a whole. By a cheap money policy the government prevented the public debt service from becoming a ball and chain at the ankle of the post-war economy; from beginning to end, this was a 'three per cent war'. By 1957 the national debt had shrunk to 161 per cent of national income. Greater emphasis on current revenue meant higher rates of taxation. Income-tax went up to 9s. 6d. in the pound; combined with a sur-tax (successor to Lloyd George's super-tax) rising to 10s., it left to the highest income recipient precisely sixpence out of every pound accruing.

In order to mitigate the pain of the income-tax transfusion, a system of pay-as-you-earn was devised, that is deduction at source from earned income (tax from unearned income had long been collected in this manner), on the principle that people missed money less which had never passed into their hands. Inflation during and after the second world war had the effect of thrusting direct taxation upon a larger part of the population; as more people earned incomes expressed in high money values, though not necessarily representing increased purchasing power, they became liable to taxes from which they had hitherto remained exempt. Thus income-tax during and after the second world war affected many members of the working class, while even the middle income groups of the middle class found themselves among sur-tax payers. At its highest (1944), public revenue absorbed 60 per cent of the national income, falling after the war to a level nearer 30 per cent. Even at the latter level, the intolerable height of taxation formed a common ingredient in speeches by public men, including Chancellors of the Exchequer. Though sharp increases in rates had always provoked warnings that taxation had now reached the absolute limit where it acted as a disincentive to efforts and industry, nothing is in fact known of the level of taxation required to produce this effect. What became very noticeable at post-war rates of taxation was the endeavour of business men to qualify for a fat expense account— free of tax—rather than a large salary liable to tax. Whatever the adjustments, the nation had to grow accustomed to a level of public expenditure considerably in excess of anything hitherto known, if only because certain services previously paid for out of private pockets, above all those connected with health, were now purchased collectively. To the extent to which public had merely been substituted for private expenditure, this made the burden on the citizen appear larger than it was. For the expenditure undertaken by the State, taxpayers contributed a revenue drawn in 1957–58 to the extent of 55 per cent from direct, the remainder from indirect, taxes.

Overseas Investment and the Balance of Payments

Investment means setting aside resources for production instead of current consumption. It can occur only where there are resources to spare because productivity yields a surplus over

immediate needs. Production may be undertaken by the person
with the surplus; instead of putting resources on one side for
his own use, he will often make them available to somebody else
waiting to engage in production. Such a producer may not even
live in the same country; if resources are lent by people in one
country to those in another, we speak of foreign investment. In
abbreviated language, we may say that 'Britain is investing in
the United States'. In reality, the lender is hardly ever, the
borrower only sometimes, a country; private capital owners of
one country lend, perhaps to State governments, more often
to industrial or agricultural enterprises in another. Nor does
foreign investment take place until productivity in the investors'
country affords a surplus which can safely be dispensed with
for the time being. As foreign investment is undertaken, not by
governments, but by private individuals or firms, it cannot be
expected to spring from altruistic motives. People do not invest
in other countries in order to make the world a better place,
but to use capital profitably. If risks of loss seem too high or
the rewards offered inadequate, they will not invest.

Borrowers for purposes of production want resources—manpower to labour, engineers to build dams and bridges, iron and
steel to make rails and rolling stock, bulldozers to clear primeval
forest for plantations. The investing country may supply some
or all of these *desiderata*, but not usually as part of the same
transaction. It is far more convenient to transfer to the borrower
purchasing power over all goods and services and let him select
them from such sources and in such proportions as he chooses.
As generalized purchasing power takes the form of money,
foreign investment is always expressed in money terms—the
only common denominator to which heterogeneous goods and
services can be reduced. That should not hide the fact that the
essence of overseas investment does not lie in pounds, shillings
and pence, but in the myriad real resources which producers
require.

Owing to her high development of trade and some industries,
Holland had been the great foreign investor of the seventeenth
and eighteenth centuries; the proportion of the British national
debt in the hands of Dutch bondholders in the later eighteenth
century had provoked comment at Westminster. The Napoleonic
wars put an end to Dutch hegemony in this field. Hostilities

brought Britain a great influx of foreign capital; but this was not genuine investment, but 'hot money', short-term funds which rich people sought to anchor in the safest haven they could find. Such capital could do little to fertilize the British economy; it flowed out again as soon as it anticipated no further danger of pillage or confiscation in continental countries. As British industry had meanwhile outstripped all others and produced the largest surpluses, it was to Britain that the rest of the world looked for overseas investment. Indeed, France borrowed in Britain the indemnity which the peace settlement of 1815 required her to pay to the victors.

Up to the middle 1850s Britain was the only international investor on a considerable scale. She made substantial capital exports to Europe and the United States. Though governments figured largely among borrowers, she preferred investing in industrial enterprises, especially of a public utility nature: she developed railways and built gas works in many countries. Sometimes even though they went to governments, loans were earmarked for industrial projects, the inauguration of a new industry, the opening and exploitation of mineral resources or the construction of a transport system. Investment of this nature was self-financing: by opening up new sources of goods and services, it created income out of which to defray interest or dividends on capital and eventually repay the principal. Overseas investment underwent fluctuations similar to those affecting the home capital market, due to the same causes, with the unpredictable behaviour of foreign debtors superadded. The world market was one beset with pitfalls to gullible investors insufficiently primed in political geography; the fact that a particular Central American republic represented a mere figment of somebody's fertile imagination did not prevent a loan floated in 1825 on its behalf in the London capital market from being oversubscribed. Allusion has already been made to the disinclination of revolutionary governments to accept responsibility for debts incurred by their predecessors; had every government succeeded in starting with a clean sheet, the system would have put a heavy premium on revolutions. British bondholders developed two techniques of dealing with such recalcitrant debtors. One depended on a measure of cooperation by the British government and consisted of using the navy in the capacity of a debt collector.

'Showing the flag' served an impressive reminder on forgetful countries that interest payments were overdue and that gentler methods of persuasion had met with no response. Alternatively every government sooner or later thirsted for a refreshing draught from that inexhaustible spring of funds, the London capital market. That was the moment to remind applicants of former loans which, if not repudiated, remained unserviced. How could investors be induced to part with fresh capital, with this bad example of the treatment meted out to previous bondholders clouding their view? One or the other method usually worked: most debtors at some time paid at least something of what they owed.

From the 1850s onwards, the supply side of the foreign invest-ment market ceased to be monopolized by Britain, even though she remained the world's most substantial foreign investor until 1914. France and Germany, and to a more limited extent the United States, began capital exports. Their investments followed political rather than purely economic considerations, being directed, in the case of the two former, largely to other European countries, by the latter to its North and Central American circumference. In the face of competition, British investment moved towards countries farther away and as yet less developed, including Britain's own Empire, but also much of Asia and South America. In these areas, however, the British investor faced a predicament. When entrusting resources to countries of western culture and business habits, he had usually found local talent, men who employed capital in the agreed manner; his function had been to make funds available, not to supervise their utilization. Under-developed countries had no reservoir of indigenous ability on which the British investor could rely; courts of law, so far as they existed, struck him as a travesty of jurisdiction; government officials could be actuated only by bribes. What was he to do? To risk funds without safeguards would have been irresponsible folly. At best, he could protect himself by imposing on any development project his own management, employing British consultants and supervisors, engineers and foremen on the spot. Out of this need for close control arose the system of dual boards: a board of directors, domiciled in London, responsible for policy and finance, and a board of management on the spot, dealing with actual construction or operation and day-to-day affairs. At worst, protection against predatory activities of indigenous governments and their servants required extra-territorial rights, if not outright usurpation of governmental functions; far from trade following the flag, the flag reluctantly moved in whither trade had led. Thus territories whose trade had been by charter reserved to companies of merchants turned into colonies and Britain added considerably to her Empire.

As the result of overseas investment, some countries had become indebted to Britain. International obligations are redeemed by the supply of goods and services; money is acceptable only insofar as it represents power to purchase goods and services wanted in the creditor country. The international system being multilateral, the debtor need not supply goods or services to the creditor direct; if he furnished them to a third party, that country in its turn might—direct or through further links in the circuit of international trade—achieve an export surplus with the original creditor. Whether on a bilateral (direct) or multilateral basis, Britain had to accept payment of interest or debt redemption in the form of goods. Her free trade policy testified to her acquiescence in this system and steadied the structure of overseas investment which she had erected. It enabled countries to sell to Britain any goods which they produced; what Britain did not wish to consume herself, she re-exported. By growing accustomed to an import surplus throughout the nineteenth century and down to 1914, Britain kept her doors wide open. From being the workshop of the world, she now became the world's market place where the whole earth's produce could be bought and sold freely, affording considerable profits to British shipping, commerce, credit banking and insurance in its passage across her shores. Many countries owed their main debt to Britain and sold most of their exports to Britain. As they met their obligations and collected their earnings in sterling, the rate at which their currency exchanged for sterling concerned them much more than that for gold. They preferred a fixed sterling rate, even though this left the gold value of their currencies to depend on that of sterling. Around Britain the sterling area came into existence, a group of countries adopting the pound sterling as the external standard of their currencies' value, investing their reserves in

Britain where most of their international transactions took place. In effect, the Bank of England's gold, from safeguarding the parity of the pound sterling, had become the reserve for the whole of the sterling area, whose participants relied in a panic on exchanging their currencies into pounds, while the Bank of England on demand had to provide gold for every pound, whether held in Britain or anywhere in the sterling area. Economists from the 1870s onwards expressed anxiety about a gold reserve, proportioned to the needs of a single trading country, now called upon to serve an area exceeding in size even the Empire.

No disadvantage attended the insufficiency of the gold reserve up to 1914. The international gold standard worked, not because all major trading nations paid in gold—this created confidence and facilitated the calculation of currency conversion values, but could not prevent disequilibrium in individual countries' balances of payments—but because Britain acted as a safety-valve; though its participants did not realize it, international trade was based on a sterling, not a gold standard. It functioned because any disproportion in the multilateral flow of goods and services was corrected by the two components of British policy: acceptance of imports in unlimited quantities without hindrance, and provision of capital for any foreign country in need of funds. Britain ran an import surplus with all the world's major trading areas, except the Tropics; to these, chiefly to India, she sold more than she bought from them. India in her turn produced commodities which, even in an era of increasing tariffs, penetrated into most countries, thus balancing part of the stream of goods into Britain. Whatever could not be offset in this manner was financed by dividends and interest owed to Britain by other countries, which reached her in the form of foreign goods. It was a precariously balanced mechanism; yet it appeared to function automatically and with amazingly little friction.

The first world war put an abrupt stop to it. Not only did the stream of capital exports from Britain cease to flow for four years, but it was reversed. In order to finance the imports required for her war effort, Britain had to liquidate about 15 per cent of her total foreign investment. Inevitably, the needs of the hour subjected her to something in the nature of a forced sale. The United States, hitherto on balance an international borrower, had an opportunity of developing her economic activities to a new pitch of efficiency, first to supply belligerents, after 1917 to support her own war effort; in the process her industrial productivity far outstripped that of Britain. When the smoke of gunfire cleared, it revealed therefore a novel international constellation. France and Germany, hitherto among suppliers of long-term capital, were licking their wounds; in order to repair war damage, they had, at least temporarily, joined the queue of applicants for international help. Britain, while not moving from one camp to the other, needed her funds at home and could not afford to pour them out prodigally, as she had done. Her capitalists might still have been tempted by high yields to invest abroad rather than at home; to prevent this, the government had to continue the wartime measure of controlling access to the capital market by anybody outside the country. Only approved issues could henceforth be floated in that market; even these had to be marshalled by the Bank of England into an orderly queue designed to prevent drying up available supplies by a too rapid succession of offerings. Policy varied; as a general rule, Commonwealth securities gained approval, loans of foreign governments only if issued under the auspices of the League of Nations.

Countries which had hitherto looked to Britain for long-term capital, naturally now addressed themselves to the United States. That country, having not only escaped military devastation, but on the contrary gained economically through war orders, responded generously, if not always wisely. Large American funds poured into Europe in the form of post-war help, first as outright gifts, later as reconstruction loans, followed by lending on commercial lines. But the 1920s remained overshadowed by the problem of reparations and war debts. Germany and her allies owed reparation to countries which the war had drained of blood and treasure; all belligerents had moreover relied on foreign war supplies to be paid for at a future date. Ultimately the United States was by far the largest creditor on the latter account, though she had sold to some countries, especially Russia, through Britain, leaving Britain to collect the debt for onward transmission to the United States. The refusal of Soviet governments to acknowledge liability for debts incurred by Czarist Russia weakened British solvency and showed the forethought by which the United States had safeguarded herself from loss. Britain was typical of several nations in an intermediary position: they relied on incoming payments to settle their own obligations. As long as their debtors did not default, they could maintain an unblemished record. This complicated war-born interdependence was superimposed upon the foreign investment pattern of the 1920s.

Irrespective of cross-currents or eddies, the main stream of resources was designed to flow from those owing reparations via various intermediaries to the universal creditor, the United States. Whatever its moral justification, this pattern made no economic sense; the United States was the chief repository of resources which most other countries lacked to a greater or lesser degree. As long as the United States lent to others on a scale sufficient to keep them alive and enable them to meet their obligations to the lender, the system worked, though merely by means of a circular flow: loans from the United States helped debtors to pay reparations and interest which by various detours made their way back to the United States. But when in 1929 loss of confidence in the New York capital market scared American investors into withholding funds, the whole artificial structure collapsed: if the United States did not provide the wherewithal to satisfy United States creditors, all international debts remained unpaid. Britain, foreseeing this situation, had long sponsored a proposal by which she waived all claims to war debts in proportion as the United States abated demands on Britain, but the United States demurred. In insisting on her pound of flesh, the United States was within her rights. But a claim in law is not a pound of flesh in economic reality. The whole apparatus of international payments merely ground to a standstill.

Even before this paralysis occurred, Britain's had been an unusually difficult task. Hampered in her post-war recovery by the loss of competitive efficiency on the part of both industry and agriculture, burdened by heavy taxation, she yet endeavoured to return to her pre-war status. This implied readoption of the gold standard, abandoned for the duration of the war, and resumption of international lending under a system of free trade enabling her debtors to pay what they owed. Only by re-establishing the gold value of the pound sterling could a firm foundation be laid on which to base the reconstruction of an international payments system. That stabilization would require severe domestic readjustments was clear both to those who advocated and those who opposed it; much consideration and discussion preceded the decision in 1925 to restore the pound to its pre-war parity, equivalent to $4.86. In the light of subsequent events, much criticism has fastened on this rate, on the grounds that it overvalued sterling, tempting British consumers to buy from abroad rather than at home, causing foreigners to look askance at British goods priced in dear sterling. The substance of these complaints is irrefutable, but it is open to question whether a lower parity would have avoided Britain's plight. Both France and Belgium stabilized their *francs* at a later date; both undervalued them in order to stimulate their exports at the expense of those of Britain. Had sterling been fixed at a lower parity, these countries would still have secured comparative advantages merely by undervaluing even more; Britain did not have it in her power to influence their decision, short of not stabilizing the pound at all.

This focuses attention on the decision to return to gold rather than on the rate at which it was implemented. So strong had been the position of London as an international financial centre before 1914 that the gold standard had functioned with a minimum of friction, cushioned by the ready availability of sterling loans or payments for goods. If the gold standard required adjustments, individual countries had to make them; their impact was not felt at the hub of the wheel, but only at one or the other point on the rim. The world war had eroded British strength; far from being able to lend support to an international gold standard, she could no longer right her own payments position. Former customers, especially India, having begun to manufacture their own cotton and to buy other industrial goods from Japan, Britain's one pre-war export surplus—that to tropical areas—had vanished. Her import surplus remained as pronounced as ever, though less overseas income accrued to finance it. Britain made considerable efforts to rebuild her overseas investment, but though its total by 1929 equalled the pre-war figure, it yielded a lower income much depreciated in purchasing power. The rules of the free trade game favoured consumers, as they had always done; it was the

British producer, even more the would-be producer, unable to find employment for his services or capital, who could no longer sustain it. When most countries experienced a minor boom in the later 1920s, Britain failed to register its impact at all. The world excess of agricultural commodities, the crash on Wall Street and the cessation of international payments were merely the climax of a decade of makeshifts and narrow escapes.

Political events contributed to economic difficulties. Germany and Austria in 1931 sprang a surprise on the world by announcing that they contemplated a customs union. This angered France, ever apprehensive of the growing strength of her eastern neighbour. By insisting that Austria render in gold certain payments due to her, she brought about the downfall of the principal Austrian bank which in turn involved a Dutch bank; a few days later the German government had to proclaim a moratorium which temporarily closed all that country's banks, thus gaining time to ascertain which of them were solvent, which required aid from public funds. Once started, the crisis threatened to engulf all creditors whose debtors could not meet their obligations promptly. A 12 months' moratorium on intergovernmental debts, adopted at the American President's suggestion, while easing the problem for some debtors, aggravated it for nations like Britain which were owed payments, now postponed, by debtor governments, but which continued to be liable for prompt remittances to non-government creditors. Nor was Britain the only country to dip into the Bank of England's exiguous gold reserve; the whole sterling area and all other foreign investors in Britain at this critical juncture relied on converting pounds into gold.

Inevitably the situation of Britain in mid-1931 gave cause for much alarm. She was losing gold at a rate which could not continue for long without drawing down the reserve below the indispensable working level. To eke out supplies, the Bank of England obtained emergency loans of gold from other central banks, but this did nothing to staunch the drain. Insofar as foreign investors genuinely required gold to meet obligations, the view which they formed of conditions in Britain did not influence or motivate their withdrawals. But others turned the movement into a flight from sterling, scared by portents that all was not well within Britain. Two official reports to the government did much to cause their disquiet, one stressing the inadequacy of the gold reserve, the other criticizing budgetary policy and strongly urging fiscal economies. In accordance with the latter's recommendations, the government imposed cuts on unemployment benefits and the pay of teachers, civil servants and the forces. Sailors stationed at Invergordon retorted by a refusal to man their ships—a brief demonstration soon followed by negotiations, yet in the nature of a mutiny. What prospects of stability remained if the British navy no longer obeyed orders?

'Hot money' precipitately sought a safer haven. A Labour government, always more suspect to financial interests than a Conservative administration, at a time of heavy unemployment and considerable suffering faced the threat to the country's gold reserve. A drastic rise in Bank rate would have been the time-honoured device for reversing the flow of gold by making investment opportunities in London more attractive than in other markets. For two reasons, the government could not take that course: capital was fleeing, not to seek higher rates of interest, but to escape the risk of devaluation—a fear which no raising of Bank rate could banish. Unemployment in the country had already reached a disastrous level, one of every five of the employed population being out of work; to increase the cost of credit at that moment would have added to the difficulties of economic enterprise and deepened the depression. On the contrary, the revival of economic activity had to be the government's prime concern; if this could not be done within the framework of the gold standard, then the gold standard had to be abandoned. Meanwhile, however, the government needed the means to tide the country over the immediate crisis and asked for a substantial loan from the United States. American capitalists agreed to furnish the funds, provided the British government undertook to balance its budget and live within its income; as a result, they were accused of tampering with British sovereignty. Was it then suggested that they had no right to attach conditions to a loan granted at an awkward moment and on rather shaky security? But the change in the course of the British ship of State had become entangled in a change of crew, though not immediately of pilot: the Labour government which had initiated steps to end the crisis was replaced in the middle of negotiations by a National government formed by the same prime minister, Ramsay MacDonald; controversy over the ethics of this operation obscured economic realities.

Like all other countries which threw overboard the gold standard in the crisis, Britain experienced the immediate relief which came from ceasing to be 'crucified on a cross of gold'. Her balance of payments improved, but never again to an extent which would have allowed her to resume overseas lending on a substantial scale. In the 1930s, there was little incentive to do so; prospects for profitable investment hardly existed, and most countries scared away would-be investors by freezing the transfer of foreign funds. In the second world war, Britain disinvested on an even larger scale than in the first, liquidating holdings and incurring obligations to a total of £4,200 million. Viewed against an estimate of the capital value of her overseas investment in 1938 amounting to £3,240 million, this represented a worsening of her international payments position by 130 per cent. Nor were British assets disposed of at prices which reflected their intrinsic value; in spite of efforts by economists like Keynes, assisted by Britain's American agents, losses could not be avoided where purchasers of Britain's foreign assets knew of the urgency of her need. Very cautiously, on the basis of individual licensing of each transaction, did the government after the war allow British capitalists to resume financing ventures abroad—not because it doubted the value of overseas investment, but because foreign exchange reserves permitted of no greater liberality. British exporters of capital, as much as British importers of goods, had to keep their eyes continually on the balance of payments, the sole indicator which could guide the scale of their operations in an era when Britain had to heed, rather than determine, the scope and magnitude of international economic transactions.

IX | STANDARDS OF LIVING

The Growth of Industrial Towns

How people earn and spend their incomes at different times constitutes the core of economic history. Governments and central banks, wars and trade treaties form part of the story through their effects on the satisfaction which men derive from life. Standards of living are the central theme of economic history, to which all subjects treated in previous chapters contribute explanations or glosses. Considering the crucial importance to economic history of the standard of living, it is astonishingly difficult to outline a picture at all precise or definite for the earlier period. There is no 'common man', although generalizations always refer to him; each of us is an individual, cherishing different expectations and applying his own scale of values. From the lily of the field or the helpless invalid whose comforts depend entirely on the generosity of poor relief to the tycoon pressing for a reduction of taxation on high incomes stretches a broad belt of population groups with standards of living which will change differently if the community adopts a new social philosophy. Collective opinions as well as collective resources mould standards of living. Nor are they established once and for all, but improve greatly over time. Discomforts and inconveniences inseparable from the existence of a Tudor king would have appeared intolerable to an unemployed worker in the 1930s. As the range of available commodities increases, so does satisfaction for those able to purchase them; it also fans the discontent of those who would like to indulge in the wider choice, but cannot afford it. People demand a level of comfort appropriate to contemporary conditions. Man is an envious animal; he does not glance down the family tree nearly as often as over his shoulder; not that he lives far better than his grandfather, but whether he is keeping up with the Joneses, colours his view of his standard of existence and his satisfaction with the social structure. Comparison with the Joneses suggests a standard of living prevailing somewhere in Wales which at most times would differ significantly from that of a Londoner. Not only temporal, but regional variations have to be considered.

Outlines are similarly blurred on the supply side by doubts on what we ought to take into account in determining 'income'. Man does not live by bread alone, but necessities of life must claim first attention. We have records of wage rates for the period after 1750, but they do not tell us much until we ascertain what men could buy with these wages and how regularly they earned them. Beyond money wages we enter the shadowy but important realm of non-monetary advantages and disadvantages attaching to work, be it in the shape of remuneration in kind (meals supplied by employers, tied cottages, free or reduced fares, goods obtainable at rebates, etc.) or of a subtler nature. Many gained their bread by their chosen occupation which gave them satisfaction; others laboured for excessively long hours in uncongenial, depressing and unhealthy conditions at a job they hated. Of the latter, some drew comfort from a happy home set in pleasant surroundings; others returned to ill-equipped, poorly furnished and overcrowded houses where disease was rife. Opportunities for refreshing or creative use of leisure time, relief for aged dependants, educational facilities for children— there is no end to the considerations which enter into living standards.

For 100 years up to the middle eighteenth century, workers had enjoyed approximate wage stability in the face of slightly falling prices. Though the difference between the two levels had not been very marked, it had served to improve their real wages (wages in terms of what they will buy) and consumption standards, not only in quantity, but also in quality. The paucity of statistics, coupled with the different interpretations to which they lend themselves, renders measurement of this trend difficult. It was however during this period that wheaten bread became the staple food of workers in Southern England and that tea established itself in general favour. This movement towards a higher standard of living came to a halt during the 1760s when prices for the first time in a century showed a long-term upward trend sustained, in spite of minor fluctuations, up to the end of the French wars. Wages failed to catch up with this rise in the cost of living which became more pronounced in the middle 1790s; though direct taxation did not reach down to workers, they helped to pay for the war in the form of lower real wages because prices rose, as the result partly of wartime scarcities, partly of additional customs and excise duties.

Many accounts of eighteenth century change presuppose an idyllic past, dating back vaguely to Queen Elizabeth and not essentially modified until the Industrial Revolution, of the yeomen of merry England engaged in a little hunting or farming in the intervals of feasting on roast beef and ale or dancing round maypoles. This contrasts with the dark satanic mills not only disfiguring the landscape, but coercing men into living and working in insanitary and oppressive towns. Nothing could be more misleading. Thomas Hobbes was not thinking of his contemporaries when he described life as '. . . poor, nasty, brutish and short', but his words are no inappropriate summary of seventeenth century existence. If more cultivators in the following century left the countryside, they sought a divorce from the soil because the marriage had ceased to satisfy their aspirations; they repudiated its bonds in the search for a future which held better prospects. Of country dwellers displaced by changes in the agricultural structure, it was the more enterprising who migrated to the towns. No doubt they harboured ill-founded hopes—if not of riches, at least of regular employment. But the attractions which drew them to urban areas were as potent as the forces which extruded them from the countryside.

Towns of the Industrial Revolution grew without planning or preparation. A manufacturer established a mill in a location favourable to his production. He needed workers. These had to live close to the works, as local transport did not exist, clocks were expensive luxuries and in order to start punctually a worker had to dwell within the sound of the factory whistle or the reach of the man who indicated by knocking at his window with a long pole when it was time for him to get up. Once a working force had established a community, shops would set up; a public house might open. Other manufacturers would settle in the neighbourhood to take advantage of the presence of a labour supply. Without anybody realizing it, what had been a nondescript part of the country or an inconspicuous village grew rapidly into an industrial town—a town unexpected, unplanned, sprawling far and wide as long as anybody decided to add to it. Workers had to have houses; they needed them quickly and were neither able nor willing to pay for good-quality accommodation. Somebody—either employers or some builder—had to provide them. Many have been described as 'jerry-built'. The word has no precise meaning, but so far as it goes, it signifies houses constructed flimsily of bad materials. Considering the length of time which such buildings survived, the description is singularly inappropriate. Inconvenient, insanitary, cheerless, inadequate they certainly were, but they lasted only too well.

Poor housing was aggravated by 22 years of almost uninterrupted warfare. Imported building materials, especially timber, became exceedingly scarce; its priority user, the royal navy, released only lower qualities or less useful grades for civilian consumption. The government financed a large and sustained war effort to a considerable extent by indirect taxes, greatly increasing excise duties on bricks, glass, windows and many other appurtenances of house building. War made capital scarce and dear; usury laws limited the interest permitted to be charged to five per cent. The need to keep to the legal form of mortgages prevented builders from circumventing the embargo on higher rates by fictions used for other types of loans, hence credit for building dried up. Manpower remained in much demand for alternative uses; industrial enjoyed precedence over residential building. Some at least of the back-to-back houses of towns in the North or the houses built round a courtyard with only a single common exit to the street owe their construction to the long drawn-out hostilities. The arrears of residential building caused by the war made a contribution to the housing shortage for some decades.

From the end of the French wars to the middle of the nineteenth century, standards of living did not improve much, though groups of workers in favoured and rapidly expanding industries—cotton being the most notable example—did rather better than the average. This contrasts with the increase in the productivity of British industry and suggests that workers obtained less than their share of the benefits which it yielded. Though the long-term trend of prices during the period was downward, wages showed a similar tendency due, especially at the beginning, to large-scale demobilization of service men who suddenly invaded the labour market after 1815. High birth rates and heavy Irish immigration kept up competition for jobs; even those who found work suffered from considerable irregularity of earnings, being dismissed, suspended or put on short time during the frequent depressions which formed part of short-term cyclical fluctuations. Tariffs and excise duties continued to burden the cost of consumer goods, especially food which more than anything else determined the standards of the mass of labouring people. Employers, though steadily increasing the capital value of their establishments, often lived lives no less hard and frugal than those of their workers. In the absence of a well-organized market for long-term credit, self-finance remained the most widely used source of funds; only unremitting reinvestment of current revenue pointed the way to expansion. Where employers denied themselves the enjoyment of higher consumption, they often overlooked that their workers had no similar motives for abstinence.

Urbanization made great strides as the result of the Industrial Revolution. The larger the scale on which industry could profitably operate, the greater the attraction of a location favoured by easy access to fuel or raw materials. Fuel always, raw material frequently, served the needs of, and acted as a magnet for, more than one industry. While the movement of workers to towns increased in a similar proportion to industrialization, it did not necessarily confine itself to areas of industrial concentration. Industry had not only to be carried on, but to be serviced; commercial cities and seaports grew as far and as fast as manufacturing towns and presented as many problems. Indeed, the nature of their immigrant population rendered Britain's large West coast ports more difficult to police than any centre of industry. The most serious instances of overcrowding in England occurred in London, an agglomeration of people which antedated modern industrial development. Apart from county and other inland towns by-passed by the expansion, populous centres of every kind found themselves faced with unaccustomed problems, though they became most acute in manufacturing towns and seaports. Urbanization had another side: the establishment of residential towns and holiday resorts where people congregated, not to work, but to play or enjoy life. If they had the means and the desire to provide amenities, the result could be very pleasant, adding to existence comforts and interests which the countryside could not afford. But town life of this quality remained the prerogative of a small minority.

When towns grew suddenly and unexpectedly, responsibility for social organization did not automatically devolve upon anybody. Where houses clustered round a single factory, its owner became the community's obvious leader, often providing common facilities and amenities. Responsibility remained diffused where a town originated from the aggregation of a number of enterprises with no single person emerging as head. Such communities suffered from the absence of local government. Where dwellers in a place many centuries ago had possessed sufficient money and civic pride, they had purchased a royal charter which turned their town into an incorporated borough. This enabled its burgesses to govern themselves effectively. But borough status had not been adjusted to subsequent growth or decay. Old Sarum had continued to be a borough even when all but two of its inhabitants had migrated to neighbouring Salisbury; Manchester remained at the mercy of a lord of the manor. Whether in a borough with a rotten administration or in an unincorporated township with none, local government functions suffered from neglect. Nor did the Municipal Corporations Act of 1835 effect more than a partial reform. It cleared away a thick undergrowth of misuses and sinecures in incorporated boroughs, but proved far less effective in substituting positive measures. Its provisions for establishing new boroughs were exceedingly cumbersome and expensive; only a few determined towns succeeded in obtaining corporate status in subsequent decades.

Nothing prevented groups of public-spirited or self-interested citizens from petitioning Parliament for a private Act permitting them to levy a rate for the purpose of improving their amenities. So far as local administration existed, it had mainly been created by this procedure. Improvement commissioners or commissioners charged with particular services, such as paving, cleansing, lighting public thoroughfares, providing sewers or water supplies, had been established in many communities. That citizens should have put themselves to the trouble and expense of securing an Act augured well for their reforming zeal. But often they concerned themselves with the amenities of a small and affluent section rather than those of the community at large, arguing that the poor would not appreciate a gratuitous service as they could not afford to pay for it. Moreover, successors to the original commissioners frequently valued the power to levy rates above the mandate to improve or maintain amenities. Subsequent generations of office holders became lethargic, if not positively corrupt. The existence of a statutory authority for special purposes provided grounds for hope, but no certainty that its activities were adequately discharged. Nor was the distribution of such authorities anything but haphazard, depending as it did on past initiative; while the parish of St. Pancras in London boasted 19 commissions charged with different aspects of improvement—though bearing few traces of their work—many areas had none at all.

Owners of land who were not also occupiers looked upon rates as financial burdens not offset by tangible benefits. To increase the amenities enjoyed by their tenants might appear a desirable and worthwhile endeavour where the landlord-tenant relationship had a personal basis. In poor properties let on weekly terms, mobility of tenants was high; landlords faced constant changes of occupants, often accompanied not only by defaults on rent, but by thefts of any fixtures which tenants could hope to turn into cash. Landlords refused to equip fourth-class houses with good-quality water taps or ballcocks for flush lavatories when they found themselves at the expense of replacing these fittings on an average once a month. Where private property was subject to so much misuse, little confidence existed that public amenities would experience better treatment. Most of them required space; urban land had risen in value so quickly and extensively that its sterilization in the form of parks, playgrounds or public works seemed a sheer waste. Making the most of urban plots by crowding them with houses met not only the interests of landlords, but also those of tenants anxious to find accommodation close by at the lowest possible rental.

Absence of local government left towns free to grow as accident decreed. But even had there been effective administration, it would have been difficult to prevent many dangers to public health. Until urbanization develops, a community does not acquire knowledge of the sanitary hazards which it entails. Food is something a countryman grows for himself or obtains from the actual producer; he does not buy it in a shop, in ignorance of how it has been processed or how long and in what conditions it has been stored. A generation reared in the country and transplanted to towns may well continue to share living quarters with livestock and accumulate excrements, both human and animal, looking upon them as manure too valuable to be flushed into sewers and wasted. How could men know that what was safely done in a country cottage gave rise to grave risks in the crowded quarters of a town? That this changed not only the quantitative aspect, but called for a different approach, only gradually dawned on a few social reformers, the most progressive minds of their day. But even they were puzzled by lack of precise information. Was it accumulation of filth which bred disease? Did the threat of epidemics come from the contamination of the air rather than of the water? How important was personal compared to public hygiene? If a microscope showed living organisms to inhabit a drop of water, did this indicate its natural composition or proof of its contamination? Science had not yet advanced to the point of returning unequivocal answers to such questions.

Reasons for the unsatisfactory and unwholesome conditions of towns are not difficult to find. This did not relieve the discomfort of those who had to live in them. They had come, dreaming of streets paved with gold, to streets often not paved at all; believing towns to offer them a better future, they had not envisaged risks to their health. Nor had they ever given thought to spare time pursuits, taking it for granted that the pleasures of the open country would still be available. Instead of being men and women, they now merely represented 'labour', factory 'hands': not their personalities, only their working capacity were in demand in these unfamiliar communities where nothing made life gracious or easy, where they had to fashion their own amusements in unpropitious surroundings, where, apart from the chapel, the public house represented the only community centre not established for purposes of work. They could neither reason with their fate nor understand their own part in contributing to the squalidness of their surroundings, but were angry and resentful. They felt socially disintegrated and rebellious. Their bitterness coloured early trade unionism and poisoned political disputes. In the tangle of slum streets, they had lost their way, even though they dimly preserved a sense of direction.

That direction was towards progress, partly technical through providing better equipment, partly scientific by adopting new methods. The industrial revolution helped greatly by making available cheaply a variety of products. Quite apart from personal hygiene discussed in the chapter on population, cast iron made water pipes which did not rot and produced appliances leading or keeping rain water out of houses. Water supply for a long time remained the responsibility of private enterprise, but a few municipalities began, if not to render this service themselves, then at least to supervise its performance by commercial suppliers. Scavenging, paving, lighting, sewering, especially the provision of covered-in drains—all these began to attract the attention of reformers. Municipalities often required much persuasion that such reforms were worth substantial expenditure. Epidemics proved a blessing in disguise by showing that the absence of health measures spelt danger. From a focus in the slums they spread to the quarters of the rich; nobody could purchase immunity at the price of refusing to become his brother's keeper. 'Whereas it has pleased Almighty God to visit the United Kingdom with the Disease called the Cholera . . .', ran the preamble to the Cholera Acts of 1832. Men with an interest in social medicine like Dr. Percival in the late eighteenth century, Dr. Kay, Dr. Southwood Smith and Edwin Chadwick in the nineteenth, persuaded their contemporaries that the responsibility did not fall on God, but on their own improvidence. The last-named, through his monumental *Inquiry into the Sanitary Condition of the Labouring Population of Great Britain* in 1842 startled responsible opinion. Associations came into being to propagate the health of towns; social and medical statistics were collected. When cholera threatened the country anew in 1848, the government was stirred into passing a public health Act which granted drastic powers to a general board of health during epidemics. Much of the history of 100 years of haphazard town building had been written in bricks and mortar and could not be easily eradicated, but at least by the middle nineteenth century the public conscience had begun to prick.

Poor Relief

Men depend on relief for three different reasons: they cannot work, cannot find work or have no wish to work. Social psychology needs to be highly developed before it distinguishes confidently between these groups, because the work-shy pass themselves off as members of one of the other categories. Even communities which pride themselves on the care taken of their helpless members rightly fear the demoralizing effect of harbouring parasites; no society ever completely succeeds in eliminating the determined idler who will resort to any amount of deception, equivocation and evasion rather than do an honest day's work. His shadow darkens the administration of relief throughout the ages.

Elizabethan legislation had enshrined the principle that the 'impotent poor', those unable to work through extreme youth or age, physical or mental infirmities, were entitled to relief. The condition and generosity of their maintenance could be debated, but the principle remained beyond dispute. In the absence of local agencies of central government, relief devolved upon parishes which annually elected honorary overseers of the poor; justices of the peace supervised their work and heard appeals from aggrieved parties. Parish responsibility extended not only to the disbursement, but also to the collection, of relief funds. Strengthening of local against national powers at the Restoration had led to the settlement legislation. A 'settlement' denoted the right to relief from a particular parish. People obtained a settlement by birth, parentage, marriage or prolonged residence; the law was not merely complicated, but sufficiently obscure to lead to many uncertainties and contradictions. A parish obligation to relieve absolved other parishes; anybody not a substantial land holder could at any time suffer removal to the parish of his settlement, if he found himself in a parish afraid that he might at some future time claim relief. Alternatively, some parishes pulled down any cottages which stood empty and prevented the building of new dwellings so as to frustrate the creation of new settlements. As a settlement could be acquired by residence over a period, people tried to move to a parish surreptitiously, without the overseer's knowledge. Parishes countered this deception by initiating legislation which made the qualifying period run only after official notification of a person's arrival had been received. Theoretically at least, all these devices could have completely immobilized the whole population.

A number of remedies prevented the practice from degenerating too far. By issuing a 'removal certificate', a parish could acknowledge its liability to maintain; a person thus certified moved about the country without difficulty. Some parishes, rather than receiving back paupers resident elsewhere, compensated the parish of domicile for administering relief. Many parishes, particularly in newly developed towns, needed labour; they could not afford to frighten away immigrants. Powers of removal constituted a threat rather than a much-used weapon, the last resort of a desperate parish if all its relief funds had been used up in the depth of a depression. Yet that was not the full measure of the social damage. While parishes welcomed healthy young males with good expectations of earning their living, they chiefly removed the old and ailing or families with many young children; above all, the full severity of the system was visited upon the unmarried mother about to be delivered of a child, as he acquired a settlement in the parish of his birth. Settlement laws prevailed upon employers to engage employees for 11 months, dismissing them before the year was up when they would have gained a settlement in the parish; some masters employed apprentices in their own, but lodged them in a neighbouring, parish to prevent them from acquiring a settlement where the master contributed to the rates. Legislation in 1795 reduced abuses by allowing nobody to be removed unless he became actually chargeable on the rates and by making any removal a liability of the removing parish instead of the parish of settlement.

' Setting the poor on work' had been the Elizabethan device designed to make the able-bodied unemployed defray, or at least contribute to, their upkeep; workhouses had been established and raw materials, especially for textile production, purchased for them. Gradually the workhouse came to serve as a test of their willingness to work. In order to prevent the work-shy from treating workhouses as homes of rest, overseers selected the most menial, unpleasant and degrading tasks. However legitimate the attempt to force a habitual loafer to earn his own living, such methods had no place in a system designed to support those unable to work or to find employment. Whenever the distinction between different categories of paupers became blurred, there was danger of injustice being done, humiliation and hardship being inflicted on helpless victims.

Workhouses existed only in a minority of parishes; even where they provided materials for the employment of paupers, they did not usually replace the stock once it had been exhausted. Thereafter poor relief had to be defrayed entirely out of rates levied on parish members—a burden of uneven incidence, heavy in parishes unfortunate enough to be settled with a large number of paupers. Ratepayers looked upon this imposition as a form of arbitrary taxation rather than emergency assistance due to their less fortunate fellow men; it caused much resentment: 'hate of the poor' poisoned the social atmosphere. In order to reduce the cost, assistance often took the form of out-relief, periodical payments in kind or cash to paupers maintaining their own households. Out-relief foreshadowed the solution of a problem which reached serious proportions during the French wars.

'The poor' was a description rather loosely used. In a social survey on *The State of the Poor* in the 1790s, Sir Frederick Eden discussed the family budgets of labourers earning low wages. A pauper was a person with no income or property from which to support himself. But 'the poor' often earned incomes inadequate to maintain themselves and their families; did this, or did this not, entitle them to poor relief? The question became urgent in 1795, when two years of warfare had driven up food prices. Agricultural labourers could no longer afford to buy their requirements, so they rioted, plundered shops and took by force what they needed. Magistrates holding the commission of the peace had to deal with the situation. That the rural poor had been goaded to violence by necessity was obvious. Higher wages enabling them to keep up with the cost of living would have been the surest remedy, but magistrates had power to assess wages only once a year, far too clumsy and slow an adjustment to a volatile price level. Moreover, this power derived from the Elizabethan Statute of Artificers, a law of 1563 discredited by non-use and disapproved of by modern economic thought. To put the rioters down by force would have dealt with symptoms, not causes, as well as presenting great difficulties in the absence abroad of most of the troops. Besides, agricultural labourers were food producers, essential workers in times of war. It would not do to muzzle the oxen when they treaded out the corn.

The name attached to the solution adopted is that of Speenhamland, a suburb of Newbury, where Berkshire magistrates met in 1795 and adopted a minimum scale of subsistence for the poor within their area. They realized that money values would not remain stable in a world of shifting prices. In the absence of an official measure of changes in the price level, they pressed into service bread as the foodstuff on which the working man spent most of his income. Aware that his commitments determine his needs, they provided a minimum for each member of a family, fixing a scale of maintenance proportionate to the price of the loaf of bread on the one, the number of dependants on the other, hand. To ensure the minimum to every member of the community, the magistrates ordered that, wherever a man's earnings did not reach this scale, they should be made up out of the parish rates. This has come to be known as the 'Speenhamland system'. The rate in aid of wages was not new; it had already been tried in other areas. But the magistrates promulgated a convenient scale which their colleagues in southern and eastern counties of England adopted. Isolated instances of it, chiefly to subsidize displaced craftsmen, whose earnings were no longer adequate to support them, could be found in the North, but it never became general there. No law ever sanctioned the practice, nor had it been designed as a permanent measure; in its inception it represented an *ad hoc* response to an urgent wartime emergency.

To have anticipated the need for a cost of living index and family allowances, suggests a modern approach to social problems on the part of Berkshire magistrates. The quality of their economic reasoning did not match their social understanding. By ordering wages to be made up out of parish rates, they provided a subsidy ultimately to employers, not to workers. If a worker had his subsistence guaranteed, why should his employer pay him a living wage? The less a worker drew in wages, the more came from the rates; his total receipts remained the same. But only the largest and richest members of any parish employed wage labour, whereas everybody contributed to the parish rates; hence the Speenhamland system involved the payment of subsidies by small to large ratepayers, regressive taxation at its worst. The moral effect was more disastrous than the financial. From being merely poor, labourers had become paupers, recipients of relief—in the absence of wage rises, of permanent relief. Never again would they earn their own living, let alone put anything back for old age. They had no more incentive to work; minimum maintenance was guaranteed, irrespective of employment. A number of devices, each more degrading and impractical than the last, attempted to prevail upon men in such conditions not to prefer idleness to work.

Temporary wartime measures have a habit of enduring beyond the emergency which created them. During the agricultural distress which followed in the wake of the French wars, the Speenhamland system spread; it enabled employers to replace female labourers by demobilized servicemen without incurring higher costs, the rate fund bearing the difference. To small farmers hard hit by the slump in agricultural prices, increased rates represented the last straw. Relief administration became harsh and unsympathetic. Parishes had to provide minimum maintenance for paupers, but at what level? The Speenhamland scale rested on the price of the wheaten loaf of bread; but did southern paupers have to be fed on wheat when bread could be baked of rye, when North Britain looked upon oatmeal as the staple food and when Irish peasants subsisted on potatoes? Without repudiating their basic responsibility or even the Speenhamland system, parishes could reduce the standard of life of paupers. In southern agricultural counties they drove labourers to despair, eventually to revolt. In 1830 riots took place in several parts of the country. They were hardly organized and achieved nothing, amounting to no more than the burning of crops or stocks of some large farmers and the manhandling of a few overseers of the poor. But the government took fright. Apart from punishing the guilty, it resolved upon root-and-branch reform. In 1832 a Royal Commission was appointed to enquire into the poor law. Its report—20 volumes of blue books impressive in length and thoroughness— formed the basis of the Poor Law (Amendment) Act of 1834.

The architects of the new poor law were Nassau Senior, an

economist, and Edwin Chadwick, a social reformer—the latter originally not a full member of the commission, but an assistant commissioner whose work had commended him to the main body, to which he had subsequently been appointed; most of the report came from his pen. Apart from investigations undertaken in the field by assistant commissioners, the commission had distributed questionnaires, distinguishing between rural and urban parishes, though taking no account of differences in the nature of pauperism arising where industry had changed from a putting-out system to factory production. The majority of commissioners were followers of Malthus. As such they regarded poverty as a warning-sign of Malthusian overpopulation endangering the community's means of subsistence and were horrified at a system which, by increasing relief in proportion to a man's dependants, provided an incentive to reproduction. The only solution which could commend itself to logical Malthusians was the termination of systematic poor relief. That would soon show how large a population the country's food supply could support. Those unable to find sustenance would disappear, leaving those fit to survive in full possession of the means of livelihood. Had it not been for Chadwick, these might well have been the lines along which the commission would have framed its recommendations.

Chadwick was a typical social reformer—a fearless seeker after the truth as he saw it, single-minded, impatient of opposition, unwilling to consent to half-measures, a doughty fighter, but a poor tactician, completely without a sense of humour, unable to keep friends. Men like him get things done, though they cause a maximum of friction and bad blood; they are as unable to compromise as to comprehend the psychological harm which ruthlessness engenders even in a good cause. It is always remembered against Chadwick that he would not let bells be tolled at a pauper's funeral; few give him credit for his stand against the majority of the royal commission preparing to consign paupers to starvation. Chadwick held that the situation called for no such drastic expedient: the social evil was not the existence of a pauper population, but a system which pitted rate-supported paupers against free labourers. Where the former could afford to accept a lower wage, the latter were doomed to lose in competition, sinking in their turn into dependence on relief; this gradually pauperized the population until there would be no free labour left. It was this vicious circle which Chadwick set himself to break.

To put an end to the rate in aid of wages, Chadwick proposed to terminate all out-relief at some future date. Thereafter all persons requiring relief would have to enter workhouses. Here they would be segregated: the old, the ill, children and pregnant women could be provided with more wholesome surroundings and skilled care in centralized institutions than in insanitary dwellings barely maintained by their inadequate efforts. The appropriate régime for the able-bodied whose desire to find outside employment had to be stimulated by all means would be wholesome but restrictive, designed to render their existence less pleasant than that of the humblest labourer struggling to remain self-supporting; he called this the principle of 'less eligibility'. The able-bodied pauper would be set workhouse tasks to test his willingness to labour. In the absence of out-relief, no employer could retain labourers unless he paid them a living wage. Workers in occupation without a future as well as children would be trained in workhouses for industries in which they could expect to find employment. From the nature of relief, Chadwick turned his attention to administration. Parishes were too small, their overseers too inexperienced, to cope with the task. A few had voluntarily combined into unions for relief purposes under an Act of 1782; all should now be forced to follow that example. Copying a further precedent from this Act, the ratepayers of each union should elect a board of guardians to supervise the administration of relief by paid staff. To ensure uniformity of national standards, a permanent poor law commission would be established in London, with over-riding powers to determine policy and supervise practice.

Chadwick's proposals, though harsh, were a good deal less severe than the remedies which had suggested themselves to his fellow commissioners. Moreover, they might well have solved part of the problem, had they ever been put into operation. But two obstacles presented themselves. Chadwick's scheme envisaged a number of workhouses in each union, one for each category of paupers; only thus could appropriate treatment for each group be ensured. Such buildings did not exist; they would have been expensive to erect and difficult to administer; some would have been temporarily overcrowded, others permanently under-occupied; families would have had to be dispersed on admission, then reunited by simultaneous discharge. Ratepayers were unwilling either to provide the funds or work the complicated arrangements required. Hence workhouses remained what they had always been: receptacles for the poor of every category, unable to provide different treatment or separate accommodation for the old and the young, the healthy and the sick, the criminal, the pregnant and the work-shy; all they usually achieved was a segregation of sexes introduced, contemporary opinion was convinced, to prevent the poor from propagating their kind. Failure to provide segregated workhouses frustrated Chadwick's most constructive proposals, those devoted to appropriate treatment of the 'impotent poor' and industrial training of the able-bodied. His poor law commission came into being, but did not correspond to his expectations. Poor law commissioners drew substantial salaries from public funds; as such their appointments were part of government patronage. Social affiliation rather than suitability for the post guided the appointments; Chadwick's background did not commend him to the government. Of the three commissioners, only one had had any experience of poor law administration; the other two neither understood the law they were asked to put into execution, nor approved of as much of it as they grasped, nor had the courage of their convictions if their policy incurred public criticism. As a sop to his injured pride, Chadwick received appointment as secretary to the commission. No body could have had a worse secretary. Chadwick knew himself to be the author of the law to be administered; he had fashioned its motives and its aims. He set himself to carry out the policy it had been framed to achieve, irrespective of the commissioners' intentions or resolutions. The discord between them and Chadwick rendered the commission an unhappy as well as an ineffective body; not until Chadwick's energies had been side-tracked into a study of public health problems, could the commission speak with a single voice.

Another weakness of the commission lay in its lack of representation in Parliament. This was due, not to an oversight, but to deliberate policy; had it had a spokesman in Parliament, he would have been exposed to pressure by other members for favours to be afforded to constituents in their capacity as ratepayers. It had therefore been decided to remove temptation by keeping the commission's day-to-day conduct free from parliamentary control. This however deprived the commission of a platform from which to explain and defend its policy. There could be no immediate reply to parliamentary allegations of mismanagement or abuses; in the absence of an effective medium of publicity, the commission's case often went by default.

Even Chadwick had foreseen a solution for only part of the problem of poor relief. The new poor law aimed at pauperism as it existed in agricultural areas, where men stayed in their parishes of settlement, clinging to the right to relief where they could not hope ever to find more than seasonal employment. To disperse such clots of immobile labour to industrial areas which experienced at least periodically a shortage of hands, was one of the merits of the new poor law. It came into effect at a time of lower food prices and increasing demand for railway construction labour; thus, although poor rates in agricultural areas eased after 1834, the relief cannot be exclusively attributed to the effect of the new poor law. But in areas of factory industry able-bodied poverty presented itself in a different guise. Cyclical fluctuations brought periodical bouts of trade depression, paralysing whole towns whose entire labour force found employment in the same industry. To such 'flats in trade', the new poor law had not even sought, let alone found an answer: if the wheels had stopped turning, owing to complete failure of demand for a particular type of output, denial of out-relief could not remedy the situation. It would have been neither practical nor useful to maintain workhouses large enough to accommodate all inhabitants of a town in a slump and discharge them when business revived. Attempts were made, in disregard of this incongruity, to introduce workhouses in the industrial North, but workers there looked upon them as a personal insult and reacted so violently that the application of the new poor law remained in abeyance for many years, in some instances for several decades. Chadwick would have refused to strike his flag in the face of resistance, but the commissioners thought it wiser to bow to circumstances and forestall a revolution.

For a decade and a half, the commission, aided by peripatetic assistant commissioners, tried to impose a national pattern of poor relief. Apart from accounting improvements, it failed. Boards elected by ratepayers looked upon themselves as guardians of funds raised locally and expended them generously or parsimoniously, in accordance with their electors' wishes; they lent a grudging ear or remained deaf to advice poured out by circulars or emissaries from Somerset House. The industrial North treated the poor law commission as a sinister Malthusian conspiracy employing workhouses to starve or poison the poor out of existence and thus reduce the population to the proportions tolerable to Malthusians. Political agitators eagerly seized upon the indignities of the poor law to generate heat and fury among the masses. While their more extravagant claims can easily be discounted, there is no doubt that, at a time when the humblest free labourer often experienced great privation and near-starvation, it was difficult for workhouses to pursue a policy of less eligibility without arousing suspicion that the preservation of their inmates' lives could not be their prime consideration. Not only did outdoor relief continue; it gained rather than lost ground, because it was cheaper than indoor relief and more appropriate in trade depressions. The controversies within the poor law commission eventually came into the open, as the result of a scandal over conditions in the Andover workhouse leading to a public enquiry; the commission was dissolved in 1847 and replaced by a ministry of the central government, the poor law board, whose president sat in the House of Commons. Chadwick lost all official connection with the poor law and in the following year became a member of the general board of health.

Social Theories of the Early Nineteenth Century

It was Benjamin Disraeli, the novelist, who first drew attention to 'the state of England' question and publicized the contrast of 'the two Englands'; as Disraeli, the politician, he aimed to narrow the gap between the two. The gulf between classes had slowly widened over at least a century. When industrialization of many areas changed the face of England, the rulers remained landed proprietors, living in the country in the intervals of attending to politics in London, the only large town with which they were familiar, having little knowledge of, and taking less

interest in, the new problems and tensions produced by industrialization and urban conditions. New modes of living made
small impression on the unreformed House of Commons; a
minority of some 50 business men, mainly merchants, represented the employing interest. Only occasionally did a stray
social reformer turned politician espouse the cause of the
workers. Little of what preoccupied the labouring masses of
industrial towns ever reached the ears of those who made the
country's laws. Nor did they like the sounds they heard. During
more than two decades of war with France, their preoccupation
was with national security. Murmurs of discontented industrial
workers implied threats to safety at a time when military forces
were fully deployed fighting the external enemy. Ruthless
suppression of internal dangers seemed the only possible policy—
a policy pursued not only during, but for another decade or
more after, the war. Trade unions remained forbidden until
1824; troops broke up demonstrations of unemployed handloom
weavers, such as the march of the blanketeers in 1817; many
civil liberties were suspended by the six Acts two years later,
and the nervousness of a militia commander led to bloodshed
at a protest meeting of Manchester workers in 1820, causing
deaths which made history commemorate the event as the
Peterloo massacres. Only when memories of the wars faded
and men realized that social discontent could be as potent a
threat to political stability as a foreign enemy, was this course
abandoned.

Even among the ruling class, many pursued more enlightened
policies. Richard Oastler, the first effective protagonist of factory
reform, and Michael Sadler, its advocate in Parliament, anticipated Disraeli in believing that, though their class had been
born to rule, they had to deserve this station in life by rule of a
quality commending it to those governed. The greatest and
most famous of Tory reformers was a typical land-owning
aristocrat brought up in the depth of rural Dorset, the seventh
Earl of Shaftesbury, active not only on behalf of factory and
mining legislation, but of better care for the mentally sick,
public health measures in industrial towns, improved lodging-
houses, ragged schools for the poorest children and suppression
of the iniquitous practice of sending small boys up chimneys to
clean them. Reform had its advocates among the upper class,

but they pursued reform from above, reform on their own terms, actuated by their duty towards God, by Christian charity and a sense of obligation, not by a mandate entrusted to them by their fellow men. Such reformers could not be swayed by the workers' wishes and demands; they would go only as far as their conscience commanded. While helping them to better conditions, most upper class reformers disapproved of collective attempts by workers to help themselves. So the workers took what was offered, then clamoured for more.

The nineteenth century was pre-eminently the era of the middle class. Not that a way of life intermediate between the ruling aristocracy and the masses of labouring people had not existed before; at all times we can discern the substantial farmer or small squire in the countryside, the prosperous merchant or professional man in towns. But such men, though midway between upper and lower class, hardly formed a middle class. They looked upon the station they had reached as a mere halting place on their way up, eager social climbers hoping to graduate into the upper class, the indolent and incapable always in danger of submersion in the great anonymous mass. Industrialization from the middle eighteenth century onwards widened the scope of occupations suitable for men with a modicum of education, men not only literate, but familiar with the network of laws, regulations and customs which kept society moving, men who, though not themselves initiating policy, could take routine decisions within a framework of rules laid down for them. In civil service terminology, this grade is described as executive, but its representatives multiplied not only in government offices, but also in manufacturing, transport, commerce and banking. More schools came into existence to supply the type of education needed by the large number of recruits required to fill these posts; the middle class—whether defined by income or more subtle sociological criteria—in the nineteenth century grew by leaps and bounds. It became a class-conscious middle class, composed of people who not only occupied an intermediate position between upper and lower classes, but wanted to remain in that station, who did not dream of coronets or broad acres; if they cherished ambitions, these extended no further than a seat on the local bench or in the

House of Commons. This middle class in the early nineteenth century generated its own philosophy.

The school of philosophers which formulated middle class outlooks on life with particular force and effectiveness is known as the philosophical radicals or utilitarians. Its founder, Jeremy Bentham, looked upon himself as a law reformer, but his and his followers' ideas coloured contemporary thinking in many fields. Instead of veneration of traditional customs and rules, they judged measures purely by their usefulness—hence the name 'utilitarians'—and made the greatest happiness of the greatest number the aim of government. When they attempted translation of this aim into practical politics, a split appeared among utilitarians—a split of which only the latest and greatest of their number, John Stuart Mill, became aware. How and by whom was the greatest happiness of the greatest number to be defined? Happiness cannot either be measured or compared as between different individuals: if a criminal is apprehended, does his unhappiness outweigh the happiness of the law-abiding population at seeing justice vindicated? Moreover, is an individual the best judge of his own happiness? If so, the greatest happiness of the greatest number is achieved by enabling as many people as possible freely to pursue their own aims; philosophical radicalism on this interpretation becomes pure *laissez faire*. Many utilitarians argued along those lines; others looked upon happiness as the condition which an enlightened ruler would consider most advantageous for the greatest number; ardent social reformers like Chadwick, who as a young man had been Bentham's private secretary, would not trust people to decide what was best for them. Though united on a common formula for their aim, utilitarians did not in substance agree on what it meant.

Less social importance however attached to the ends they pursued than to the means they employed. Public administration as hitherto carried on by *dilettanti*, appeared to them an amateurish and bungling performance. They demanded that government should become a scientific pursuit, on a par with physics or chemistry and yielding equally precise and predictable results. What impeded the achievement of such perfection was the inadequacy of the tools hitherto employed, the unqualified administrators—justices of the peace drew their particular scorn

—being the most obvious. The call for expert executives fore-shadowed selection of civil servants for their qualifications instead of by patronage, achieved only in the second half of the century. The need for experts did not brook so long a delay. There appeared in the hierarchy a novel and unfamiliar grade, the inspector, an interim answer to the demands for an expert bureaucracy. Recruited *ad hoc*, often from those who advocated social reform from the side-lines, he made his mark in the 1830s and 1840s, either as an inspector—of factories, prisons or coal mines—or as assistant poor law commissioner; without suspecting Sir Robert Peel of being a utilitarian, we may add to the list his creation of the metropolitan police in their capacity as inspectors of potential criminals.

For the examination of contentious issues of public policy the utilitarians adapted the royal commission of enquiry. Commissions and committees of enquiry were not new, but nobody had hitherto consciously shaped them into scientific instruments for investigating problems. Commissioners appointed because of their concern with, or knowledge of, public policy in the field to be surveyed, invited everybody with views or suggestions on the subject to place them before the commission and submit to interrogation, while securing further evidence, whether oral, written or by investigation in the field, from whatever quarter considered appropriate. Having covered the ground as thoroughly as possible, the commissioners deliberated on their findings and rendered a report—if they could not agree, majority and minority reports—to be placed before Parliament and published. Reports were reviewed by newspapers and discussed by the public. Guided by public reaction, the government inaugurated a debate in Parliament, indicating whether and to what extent it accepted, and intended to act upon, the commission's findings. Yet another utilitarian device was administration through local boards elected by ratepayers under the supervision and guidance of a central government authority, as provided for in both the poor law amendment Act of 1834 and the public health Act of 1848.

Utilitarians were not philosophers of the first rank, but follow-ed the great tradition of British philosophy established by Locke and Hume—the tradition of ordering society from the point of view of the reasonable man, of keeping free from fanaticism, of maintaining a sense of proportion. They inherited from their philosophical forebears a disregard of social realities. Stressing the political and legal equality of all men, they under-estimated the importance of social inequality; they therefore never sufficiently appreciated the need for protection of the weak and poor. Adopting the economic theories of Adam Smith and Malthus, they did not see how the condition of the working masses could be significantly improved while so many labourers competed for a limited volume of employment. Their teaching had little comfort to offer to workers, even to those few who could read and understand it; their following remained almost exclusively middle class. The man in the street found their benevolence generalized and chilly, their teaching too much concerned with questions of principle, too little with specific issues. He preferred doctrines which appealed more particularly to the working class.

The giant among early English socialists was Robert Owen, a man of working class origin, who by native ability made himself manager of a Manchester cotton mill before he was 20. In 1801 he became part owner of a similar establishment at New Lanark which during the next 25 years he turned into a model factory. By long-term planning he secured regularity of employment for his workers, avoiding dismissals during slumps. New Lanark was a community centred on a single factory, depending on the factory owner's initiative. Owen built a model housing estate, comprising a community centre, schools for his employees' children, even a district heating plant. 'The philanthropic Mr. Owen' attracted distinguished sightseers from all over the country and beyond. However, he stressed that the New Lanark enterprise combined good working conditions with moderate profits. Thinking about his venture led Owen to formulate new theories. He regarded men as conditioned by environment rather than heredity, considering the competitive atmosphere inseparable from capitalism the worst possible environment for the formation of character. Competitive capitalism should therefore give way to cooperative production, especially as the value of any article, according to Owen, consisted of nothing but the labour devoted to its production. If the price of a commodity exceeded the aggregate wages of all workers who had contributed to its making, the excess represented 'surplus value' unjustifiably withheld from them. Capitalist society paid this surplus value in the form of rent, interest and profits to those who had contributed land on which production, storage or sale took place, capital which provided the equipment and financed the duration of production, and risk bearing in case the goods should find no buyer; Owen wanted to do away with the rewards accruing in respect of these services. The publication of such views made him appear to the government less in the guise of the philanthropic Mr. Owen than in that of a red-hot socialist agitator. Owing to disagreement with his co-proprietors in 1827, he withdrew from New Lanark and for a few years conducted a settlement on communist lines in the United States. Returning to Britain in the early 1830s, he threw himself with renewed vigour into propaganda for socialism.

None of Owen's creations endured for long. He established 'labour exchanges'—retail store associations where any member could deposit articles he had produced, receiving credit for the number of hours he had laboured to make them; with this credit, less a small deduction for expenses, he could buy other goods in the store. For a year or two, 'labour exchanges' functioned successfully before becoming choked by a surfeit of unsaleable goods. Owen persuaded the trade union of building operatives to cease working for employers and undertake contracts on their own account; the builders' guild carried on for 12 months before becoming insolvent. Owen's greatest venture was the Grand National Consolidated Trades Union of 1833 which has already been mentioned.

Owen in his manufacturing activity amassed a considerable fortune which he lost by subsidizing his various projects. In spite of his remarkable capacity for management, he was by nature a philosopher rather than a business man; with advancing years the visionary strain in him became uppermost. Nor had he diplomatic gifts; he made enemies not only of landowners, capitalists and employers with whose services he wanted to dispense, but of the government which feared his influence on the masses, and of the church which disapproved of his views on religion and marriage. Revolution he did not expect in the form of a violent uprising, but as a peaceful process of persuasion; yet though he laboured long and devotedly to convert others to his views and never refused a hearing to an opponent, his own mind was closed to ideas which differed from his. He swayed men by the power of his oratory, speaking often for hours on end and arousing violent enthusiasm; his hearers would follow wherever he might lead. But Owen's fertile brain never could concentrate on any one scheme for long; when he took up another of the irons he had in the fire, those he left in charge of previous projects lost interest or enthusiasm and let them founder. More fundamentally, Owen relied excessively on the basic goodness of human nature, a goodness expected to persist in prosperity and adversity, to carry ventures not only through the experimental stage, but through many years of monotony and routine. His economic thought paid too much attention to supply and too little to demand, making no provision for establishing equilibrium between them.

A monument to Owen survived where he would have least expected it. Cooperation to Owen had meant cooperative production; he had assigned a very subordinate part to consumers' cooperation. Inspired by him, countless cooperative societies started in the early nineteenth century in industrial towns with ambitious manufacturing programmes, among them a group of flannel weavers at Rochdale in 1844, the Rochdale Equitable Pioneers. By luck or good sense, they concentrated on a single one of their aims to the exclusion of all others: the sale of foodstuffs to their members. In other words, they became a cooperative retail shop. This limitation avoided the scattering of inadequate managerial talent and even scarcer funds among an excessive number of activities. Nor did cooperative retailing neglect the demand aspect. At a time when urban workers suffered from insufficient purchasing power, the system of paying dividends on purchases strengthened them financially. Shopkeepers often sold unwholesome, stale, even adulterated foodstuffs; by attending to quality, retail cooperatives ensured good value for money. Robert Owen's theories of cooperation inspired the founders of the great Cooperative Movement which grew up in the second half of the nineteenth century. Once firmly established, retail cooperatives could support one another in financial difficulties; growing stronger, they could erect a superstructure of joint activities ranging from wholesaling to manufacturing, from banking to insurance. But the movement continued to rest squarely on the pillars of retail cooperative shops selling groceries in the back streets of industrial towns.

Of early nineteenth century movements aiming to improve working class conditions, chartism was the least philosophical. The six-point charter to which it owed its name constituted a straightforward programme of political reforms, well ahead of progressive thought in its own day, however mildly democratic it appears in ours: a vote for every man, annual elections to Parliament, an equal number of electors in each constituency, secrecy of ballots, members to be paid for parliamentary service and to qualify for election without having to possess landed property. Behind these demands lay the deep discontent of industrial workers with their conditions. The middle class had used the vote obtained by the great reform Act of 1832 to achieve redress of its grievances; realization of the charter would have enabled workers not only to vote for, but send their own representatives to, the House of Commons where they would have drawn attention to working class complaints. Political reform was a means to economic ends; chartists referred to their demands as a 'knife-and-fork question'.

Chartists were united on a political programme and economic discontent, but on little else. For agreement on positive measures the movement was too heterogeneous. Its adherents in London complained of irregularity of employment more than of working conditions; in addition, they demanded better education for workers. Not only skilled craftsmen, but even a section of the middle class, joined the chartists in the Midlands; their leader, a Birmingham banker, Thomas Attwood, advocated government stimulation of employment by means of a managed currency instead of the gold standard. Grievances of the factory operatives determined the mood in South Wales, the industrial North and Scotland, where low wages, factory conditions and the new poor law embittered chartists against employers. Feargus O'Connor, their leader, reflected their feelings by the slogan 'peaceably if we may, forcibly if we must!', a sentiment not shared by their fellow chartists further south who had no stomach for violent insurrection. Chartism was a movement born of distress; it flared up whenever the business cycle entered a trough and died down whenever an upswing of trade opened more promising avenues of reform. Hence three phases of chartism can be discerned: it originated in 1836, regained vigour in the early 1840s and blossomed out into an Indian summer in the late 1840s. Having considered and discarded as ineffective armed violence and runs on the banks, chartists sought to move the government by general strikes and mass petitions to Parliament, but none of these succeeded. Their last attempt occurred in 1848, a year of political revolutions all over Europe, when the British government feared that the great chartist demonstration called in London to adopt the petition and present it to Parliament heralded its overthrow; it took unprecedented precautions to prevent violence. They proved unnecessary. Chartism focused the dissatisfaction of the working class but had not the strength to project it into action. To do so, would have required agreement on aims and dynamic leadership; moreover, violence seemed backward-looking and unwise in the middle of the nineteenth century when at last the standard of living of the population as a whole was moving vigorously upward. More and better production had been achieved; collective agreements towards a juster distribution were on the way. Neither employers nor the men combining in new model unions had any use for chartism. Yet it would be unjust to dismiss chartism as a movement which utterly failed. Four of the charter's six points were realized within three-quarters of a century; the remaining two ceased to interest even reformers. Conditions castigated by chartists improved, some before the movement petered out, others soon afterwards. Though chartism seemed ineffective in its lifetime, its protest was not in vain.

The Growth of Social Policy

Prices moved upward during the third quarter of the nineteenth century. Whenever that had happened before, money wages had lagged behind, reducing the real income of the working community. This pattern could possibly have repeated itself in the decade after 1850, but certainly not beyond; on the contrary, between the middle of the century and 1875 the standard of living of workers rose by roughly one third. In the face of mounting prices, this could be achieved only by money wages overtaking them in the upward movement. That they did so furnishes evidence of the greater productivity which British workers achieved, thanks to larger amounts of capital at their elbows and better methods of organizing production; evidence likewise of the existence of trade unions obtaining in at least a few industries recognition of the workers' share in such increased productivity. Urban artisans obtained the vote in 1867; this enabled their grievances to be aired in Parliament. A population which in the earlier nineteenth century had subsisted chiefly on hopes deferred at last saw some of its expectations come to fruition. A relaxation of social tension resulted. Industrial conflicts became less frequent; where they occurred, they led to neither violence nor court proceedings. Owenite socialism and chartism did not endure; labour preferred to seek progress through collective organization and industrial conciliation. The greatest happiness of the greatest number seemed on the way to being realized faster than ever before.

A higher standard of living represented increased purchasing power, but the worker could exercise this only over the range of available commodities and services. As yet this was not very varied; more abundant provision of the necessities of life constituted the major gain. Clothing in particular could be obtained more easily and cheaply, owing to the great improvements in textile manufacture. Free trade and better transport brought to the shops a greater quantity and choice of foodstuffs at or near world market prices. The evidence is least convincing as regards shelter: at no time in the nineteenth century did the level of rents fall significantly, and public or benevolent efforts to improve working class housing never touched more than the fringe of the problem. The well-paid artisans whom Richard Cobden persuaded to invest their savings through the medium of building societies in the purchase of homes of their own could only have represented a tiny proportion of all workers. Among modest beginnings of semi-luxuries, railway travel for pleasure at least had become available to a much larger sector of the working class—harbinger of a more varied and interesting future existence.

These were substantial gains, but how far did they extend? Good wages, collective organization, better opportunities for leisure pursuits—did these satisfy any but those with the capacity to achieve them? Such benefits did not yet have any impact on unskilled or agricultural workers, even less on those who could not work at all. If a civilization be judged by the provision it makes for its helpless members, little progress had yet been achieved. The poor were kept from starving; beyond that point, society trusted to private charity. That this did not suffice to fill gaps in social provision became apparent through the exertions of amateur social statisticians who had begun in the 1830s and 1840s to collect factual information and to measure needs in quantitative terms. Sometimes a journalist like Henry Mayhew publicized the condition of the poor; subsequent social surveys, combining quantitative and interviewing techniques, enabled towards the end of the century men like Charles Booth for London or Seebohm Rowntree for York to produce evidence that nearly a third of the town population remained below the poverty line. Sometimes the plight of a particularly under-privileged group—ex-servicemen after the Crimean war, pros-titutes and people without an abode, homeless children—moved contemporaries to initiate institutions to help them, such as the Corps of Commissionaires, the Salvation Army or Dr. Barnardo's Homes. People still believed that extraordinary measures could deal with the victims of oversight on the part of an otherwise comprehensive system of constant social improve-ment, but as evidence of more and more oversights accumulated —whether rooms serving as permanent sleeping quarters for more than two people, numbers of newly-weds marking the marriage register with crosses in lieu of signatures, scarcity of hospital beds or the masses of volunteers for military service in the Boer war rejected as physically unfit—the belief faltered. Many of the hands pointing at these omissions were female. Middle class women, debarred by custom and position in life from money-earning activities, long required an outlet for their intelligence and energies. Not permitted to compete with men, they made voluntary social work their own sphere. Elizabeth Fry around 1800 had agitated for prison reform; in the middle nineteenth century Mary Carpenter concerned herself with the education of juvenile delinquents, Florence Nightingale re-organized hospital administration, Louisa Twining, engaged in after-care of women discharged from workhouses, found them reduced to prostitution. Writers joined in these protests; every novel from Dickens's pen constituted an eloquent denunciation of some social evil.

The wheel turned once again in the middle 1870s which ushered in two decades of falling prices. Manufacturers, hit for the first time in 100 years by effective foreign competition, found profits harder to earn; though they did not reduce the scale of their operations, they believed themselves to be passing through a great depression. Unemployment, as recorded by trade unions, showed a slight increase, but there is good reason to believe that these statistics referred to an unrepresentative section of the working population and that real employment improved rather than fell off, owing to the better and more regular utilization of the services of those in work. The standard of living of moderately skilled urban workers in full employment increased faster than before; their real wages rose by approximately 40 per cent between 1880 and 1896. Unskilled and agricultural labourers did not share equally in this improvement, though falling prices helped to augment their purchasing power and the parliamentary franchise was extended to them in 1884—an indication that their case would not in future go by default. Much upgrading took place, re-classifying workers into occupations entitled to higher rates of pay, an improvement not reflected in statistics of money wage rates. Workers had little cause to feel depressed in the last quarter of the nineteenth century.

Until the 1870s many members of the middle class continued to believe that poverty dogged the steps of only the most improvident or unlucky. Twenty years of poor profits and trading difficulties, of low agricultural rents and effective foreign competition shattered that illusion. Many business men whom nobody suspected of laziness or incompetence yet found their existence threatened. Conditions such as these gave rise to doubts whether 'the greatest happiness of the greatest number' was an adequate basis for social policy, even more whether the greatest number could achieve much happiness unaided. Faced with difficulties which transcended the power of the individual to overcome, men remembered the arguments put forward by social reformers in the earlier nineteenth century in favour of collective action. Trade depressions, epidemics, unemployment in particular industries owing to the adoption of new techniques —none of these were new, only the latter more widespread in the last quarter of the century than previously, but more often now did they prompt the question whether there was a case for State interference.

In the individualist system favoured in the earlier nineteenth century, the State played only a subordinate part. Many argued that it had been reduced to the rôle of the nightwatchman, enabling citizens to sleep soundly by maintaining against law-breakers at home a network of police and courts of justice, a diplomatic corps and armed forces against those abroad. In economic affairs, this left the State to ensure that no competitor stole a march over the others until all had cleared the starting line; it then stood aside and allowed the best man to win. This concept of the State came under severe challenge in the 1870s and 1880s from groups of philosophers tracing their theories back to Hegel, but pursuing them to divergent conclusions. According to the metaphysical view of the State as developed at Balliol College, Oxford, by the disciples of Benjamin Jowett, however important the interests of any one, the interests of several individuals outweigh that of a single person. All members of the community add up to the State; hence the interest of the State must take precedence over that of individuals, giving the State a right to interfere with, and coerce, anybody if a conflict of interests develops. To the individual forming part of the State, his true interest, though he may not realize it, is the general public interest; by allowing the State to coerce him, he follows his enlightened self-interest, whatever his transient selfish motives at the moment may suggest.

Socialists converted to the theories of Karl Marx, whose *Kapital* was translated into English in the 1880s, saw the problem from a revolutionary rather than metaphysical angle. To them the State represented the apparatus of power, embodied in the courts of justice, the police and the armed forces, employed by the ruling class to keep itself in the saddle. Individualism, democracy, philosophical radicalism were mere smokescreens hiding the sole economic reality: the relationship to the principal means of production. As long as this had been land, the class which owned it had dominated the community in a feudal order. When capital had replaced land as the principal means of production, the mantle of the feudal owner had fallen on the capitalist, to whom the economy had become enthralled. To break his hold on society, the working class had to capture the machinery of power, conquer the State; once the guns had been reversed to point at those who had hitherto directed them, the domination of society by any one class would be broken for good.

However narrow the common ground which existed between

the idealist philosophers of Balliol and Marxist socialists, both cast the State for a far more crucial and positive rôle than it had hitherto played. The change in thought permitted, even challenged, the State to become more active in social policy where it had hitherto taken only hesitant and tentative steps. When it ventured into the field of public health in 1848, it passed legislation for five years only; had it not been for an outbreak of cholera in 1853 which killed 30,000 fewer persons than the epidemic of 1848, the general board of health might have expired unsung; though this testimony to its efficacy prolonged its life for the moment, it was nevertheless permitted to lapse at the first convenient occasion, its functions being split up among three unenthusiastic government departments: explosives and nuisances to the Home Office, quarantine to the War Office, the residual tasks to the Privy Council. Had not its chief medical officer of health, Sir John Simon, engaged in public health research at the Privy Council and provided year by year new blueprints in advance of more energetic action, the government's record in public health would have been negative for another 15 years. In 1871, however, the government took a new step: it amalgamated the existing public health and poor law administrations under a single authority, the Local Government Board.

It was a step, but hardly a step forward. The new government department was ill-conceived. The poor law administration still adhered to principles of deterrence: paupers should not seek relief, unless they had lost every chance of fending for themselves. An apparatus of officials trained in this policy could not operate successfully a system of public health designed to give of its best if the largest possible number of people used its services. Public health specialists functioned at headquarters as expert advisers; at local level the department operated through the network of boards of poor law guardians and their staff. In the circumstances, though an effective and fairly comprehensive public health Act was passed in 1875, the development of public health owes little to the Local Government Board, a good deal more to municipal initiative and experiments by individual reformers. Where pioneers had shown the way, others were made to follow: permissive legislation up to the 1860s, allowing local bodies to provide for the health of their citizens, was replaced in the last quarter of the century by mandatory measures, requiring action to be taken. The all-purpose medical officer of health was supplemented by a number of specialists in various aspects of the wide field. By the end of the century a few forward-looking municipalities had passed beyond environmental improvement to the experimental provision of personal services.

Though local variations in the administration of the poor law continued, the general attitude towards poverty tended to become more sympathetic and understanding. The upper classes had lost their fear of the poor, especially after the quick and peaceful subsidence of the chartist movement. The overall proportion of pauperism was decreasing: from having formed ten per cent of the population of England and Wales in 1831, recipients of relief never rose to three per cent again after 1884. Social reformers shifted their attention from the problem of relief to that of prevention. Bernard Shaw sounded the new note when around 1900 he proclaimed in the East End of London that he hated the poor who were 'useless and dangerous and ought to be abolished'. Poverty, unless due to incapacitating illness or unemployment, fell into a regular pattern: a young couple, recently married, earned adequately while both partners worked, but suffered financially as soon as the birth of children terminated the wife's paid employment; especially if they had a large number of young children, they required much outside help towards maintenance. The growth of children to wage-earning age would ease the situation, especially as long as they lived in the parental household and contributed to its expenses; but even when they left to establish families of their own, the parents could make ends meet until they grew too old to work; then destitution supervened once more and, unless kept by their children, they were doomed to pass their last days in the workhouse. Observers of this typical course of industrial working class life isolated its danger spots: incapacity of wage earners and the number of young children.

Standards and methods of relief benefited from a more enlightened approach. The board had laid down that paupers should be maintained at a level sufficient not to endanger life. Precise determination of the standard of provision which implemented that rule would have been difficult in any case;

in practice, a level which just failed to endanger survival hardly preserved a worker's strength and energy enough to fit him for employment even if it became available. For practical reasons alone the régime had to be made adequate to preserve health and bodily fitness for self-support. Social psychology, gradually developing in the nineteenth century, showed that the rule forcing a seeker after relief to enter the workhouse stamped him a pauper not only in the eyes of the poor law, but also in his own; by changing his whole way of life, it made him feel that he had lost the battle and struck his flag. If instead he received assistance towards maintaining his own home and keeping up his accustomed mode of living, he would look upon it as a bad patch he had struck and which he might pass; his self-respect would remain unimpaired. Out-relief, administered at all times by local boards anxious to save money, now acquired enhanced status as a method which might have social value. Around 1900 the Local Government Board for the first time recommended it, at least for old people of good character, instead of merely closing a reluctant eye to it.

By the twentieth century, views about relief policy conflicted as much as practice throughout the country. The government believed the time ripe to consider the subject afresh. A Royal Commission wrestled with the poor law from 1905 to 1909. None of the commissioners approved of the practice as it prevailed, but beyond that point unanimity did not extend. A majority would have retained a single authority in charge of relief and continued the principle of deterrence at least sufficiently to stimulate endeavours on the part of the poor to help themselves. The minority—whose report reflected principally the views of its most prominent member, Beatrice Webb— condemned the approach to relief as a single problem: there was no single group in the community labelled 'the poor', but people rendered destitute for a variety of reasons—illness, old age, incapacity or large numbers of children. By dealing with the origin of poverty in each category, the minority commissioners suggested, poor relief as a whole could be abolished; the community had a social obligation to prevent destitution arising from emergencies which citizens were powerless to avoid. Though the government remained uncommitted to the view of either side, the minority suggestions were in practice adopted.

Social legislation in the early twentieth century provided help on a national basis for large sectors of the population hitherto resorting to poor relief. Children were summarily removed in 1915 from workhouses as places unsuitable for their upbringing. In 1929 boards of guardians were dissolved and county councils took over relief duties; when a new facet of poverty, that of long-term unemployment, made its impact felt in 1934, a central government authority, the public assistance board, assumed responsibility for its relief. Official repeal of the 1834 law did not take place until 114 years after its enactment, but by that time only a few shreds remained to be interred in a grave marked by no cross and watered by no tears.

Little progress was made in housing until late in the nineteenth century. The rapid increase of the population rendered accommodation a continual problem; buildings which had been inconvenient and insanitary at the time of their erection deteriorated by occupation on the part of generations of impecunious tenants. At no time was the great mass of the working class housed at a standard which satisfied those concerned with public health; though voluntary associations and charitable trusts provided model tenements and houses, the financial effort required far exceeded their means and left them to nibble at the fringe of the problem. Public opinion saw no more cause for subsidizing a working man's accommodation than his food or clothing and objected to public money being spent on it. Urban housing by the 1880s reached the proportion of a public scandal; books like *The Bitter Cry of Outcast London* and *In Darkest London*—the latter by William Booth, the founder of the Salvation Army—stirred the public conscience. Deliberations of a Royal Commission from 1884 onwards accurately reflected the cleavage in public opinion, one section despairing of any effective remedy through collective action, but relying on supply and demand eventually to re-establish the balance between houses and the need for accommodation, the other section insisting that only municipal provision could get the working class adequately housed. The latter prevailed: an Act in 1890 placed upon local authorities the duty to clear and replace slums by better accommodation—the basis of council housing in the twentieth century.

Local rather than central government pioneered collective

action in the social field. Birmingham showed the way in the 1870s, when Joseph Chamberlain, at the head of the Radicals, demonstrated during his mayoralty how reform could turn a large town into a model municipal enterprise. Birmingham at his initiative purchased its gas supply and controlled its water works; he provided parks, museums, galleries and libraries for the citizens' leisure time and edification, established cattle markets and slaughter houses to improve their meat supply; their health benefited from municipal baths and washhouses; not content with building artisans' dwellings, Birmingham even opened a savings bank. Though a Radical, Chamberlain in municipal reform found common ground with the Fabian Society, a group of intellectual socialists established in 1883, whose idea of common ownership was often labelled gas-and-water socialism. In 1882 Parliament permitted local authorities to levy rates and make provision for any services which their citizens wanted; no longer did a municipality have to apply for a special Act of Parliament if its enterprise wanted to break new ground. The chief obstacle remaining lay, not in the powers, but in the constitution of local authorities. Though the public health Act of 1875 had covered the country with a network of sanitary boards, these could not fulfil all local government functions; for many tasks they were too small. The country required better and financially stronger local authorities. Local government became an effective, capable and non-corrupt instrument of collective action, instead of an irregular medley of *ad hoc* authorities, through the Acts of 1888 and 1894, the former creating counties and boroughs, the latter turning the sanitary boards into urban and rural district councils. Only at the lowest level did the parish survive into the new and improved local government structure. Thus equipped for reform, the country could shoulder the tasks awaiting it in the twentieth century.

The Welfare State

The early twentieth century experienced an upswing of prices, emphasized by the first world war and extending to 1920. Except during wartime, people in work found some compensation in a modest amount of increased leisure, including the coming of holidays for a minority, but the fact that the consumption of necessities, including fuel, showed hardly any increase, does not suggest a significant improvement in general living standards. At most times, rising prices had implied falling real wages. Up to the war, real wages oscillated rather than fell; in 1914 they had returned to the level of 1896, after having remained below it for most of the intervening years, except for three-year periods from 1899 to 1901 and from 1907 to 1909. The former indicates that the Boer war did not represent a major economic effort, else the real income of the population would have suffered, as it did in the world war. However, even to retain their previous gains, workers in the decade preceding the first world war had to fight hard. Industrial relations deteriorated seriously; improvement in the social field made itself felt in the shape of legislative reform rather than collective agreements.

Reform in the nineteenth century had come piecemeal; whenever an evil had become too clamant, remedial action had been taken. Reformers had been pragmatic rather than doctrinaire: though the middle nineteenth century might be considered the heyday of *laissez faire*, it had witnessed the first effective State interference in working conditions and public health. The same men had often pioneered not only in one, but in several sectors of social reform: Dr. Kay, who had investigated the spread of cholera in Manchester in the early, and worked as an assistant poor law commissioner in East Anglia in the later, 1830s, as Sir James Kay-Shuttleworth subsequently helped both in an official position and by private experiments to reform primary education; Chadwick, while still secretary of the poor law commission, had been led, by an investigation of the contribution of physical incapacity to destitution, to concern himself with environmental health problems; Octavia Hill, from a preoccupation with cramped working class accommodation, had come to insist on the value of open public spaces and commons for recreation. From being isolated emergency operations, measures of social reform merged into a larger pattern: a general scheme of welfare which the community undertook to guarantee to all its members.

The government in the first decade of the twentieth century grasped the nettle. If there was to be a minimum standard of living for all citizens—in Winston Churchill's phrase, a Plimsoll line below which nobody should be allowed to sink—a coherent programme of social reform would implement it better than piece-meal measures. Between 1906 and 1911, Campbell-Bannerman's and Asquith's governments passed a series of laws which added up to such a programme—laws which provided meals and medical inspection at school for children who needed them, labour exchanges as well as better guarantees of compensation in the event of industrial injury for workmen, statutory wage fixing in occupations where workers remained insufficiently organized to bargain collectively with employers, non-contributory pensions for the aged, social insurance in the form of health insurance for all and unemployment insurance for some. Both in what it did and in what it did not provide, the programme reflected the philosophy of its authors. They accepted the community's obligation to relieve genuine need, but looked upon it as exceptional, upon relief as a lifebelt thrown to a weak swimmer in a sea where most people kept afloat unaided. Not only could the majority maintain themselves without help, but the incentive to do so was carefully preserved: labour exchanges could render service only to those who exerted themselves to seek employment. Health insurance was based on a weekly contribution of 4d. on the part of the insured, to which his employer added 3d. and the State 2d.; his weekly payment of 4d. secured for him—though not for his dependants who did not similarly contribute—benefits based on a 9d. a week premium, yet coming to him in response to his own exertions. Subsidies went to trade unions which ran their own unemployment insurance schemes; the State assisted contributories who were faced with this endeavour to provide for themselves. It gave unconditional relief only to the helpless: those incapable of work because they were too old or too young, injured in industrial accidents or unable to organize in their own defence. Unemployment insurance independent of trade union schemes covered workers in a few capital goods industries especially exposed to cyclical fluctuations: the law enumerated building and construction, ship and vehicle building and repair, mechanical engineering, iron founding and sawmilling. No relief went to the undeserving: old age pensions became payable to the respectable poor above the age of 70, provided they were in need.

The programme had hardly been completed when the first

world war broke out. The depression of the interwar years exposed it to great strain. As soon as war scarcities had been overcome, the terms of trade turned once more in Britain's favour, owing to worldwide overproduction of food and raw materials: a given quantity of industrial goods exchanged for an ever-increasing volume of primary commodities. In his capacity as a producer of manufactured articles, the British worker saw his standard of living rising again as it had done for over a century. But to do so, he had to remain in employment, and unemployment had by now assumed dimensions which the country had never previously experienced. The average proportion of the employed population out of work, estimated at roughly six per cent for the three decades before 1914, remained in excess of ten per cent from 1922 until the second world war; at its peak in 1932 the figure topped 22 per cent. Nor did percentages reveal the full impact of the scourge. One in every five of the unemployed had been out of work for 12 months or more, many of them young workers leaving school and joining the queues at employment exchanges without ever taking home a week's wages. North of a line drawn from the mouth of the Severn to the Wash unemployment was twice as severe as south, showing the unevenness of geographical incidence.

Such conditions made unemployment into a cloud which cast a heavy shadow even over trades relatively less severely affected; the scourge had become general, and unemployment insurance had to be extended to all manual workers. As the unemployment insurance fund could not for long finance benefits on this scale, especially when the crisis lasted beyond anything that had been known in the nineteenth century, the government's anxiety about the fund's financial position grew. Its policy aimed at limiting calls on assistance by all means at its disposal. This could be done only by whittling away the claims of the unemployed wherever a loophole presented itself, either by refusing them benefit in respect of the first two days of any period of unemployment, by investigating not only the means of the claimant, but those available to his family as a whole before granting assistance, or by considering insured benefits as exhausted after six months of unemployment when claimants were placed on a lower scale of 'uncovenanted benefits' administered more strictly. When the Borough of Poplar under the leadership of George Lansbury, the Labour politician, paid out more in relief than its rate fund could afford, arguing that the emergency hit working class, far more severely than middle class, boroughs and that some method of equalizing burdens ought to compensate Poplar for its excess expenditure, the government resisted, but had eventually to give way in the face of Lansbury's determination to go to prison rather than yield.

The extent of unemployment and distress called for urgent action. The government took the view that workers as a whole had it in their power to create more employment. In a depression employers suffered because machinery stood idle, raw materials remained unused. Workers whose real income had increased through the fall in the cost of living had to make their contribution. The government would have liked them to accept it in the form of lower wages; this would have reduced production costs, enabling employers to offer their output at lower prices, especially in foreign markets, in the hope of stimulating demand, attracting new orders, creating employment. Much as it wished this to happen, the government could not force workers to accept lower wages; trade unions had grown strong enough to resist wage cuts, if workers resolutely backed them. However, this did not allow workers to contract out of the depression, at least not all workers. Those who remained in employment did not suffer. But with wages staying at previous levels, production costs did not fall, British goods could not be offered in world markets at lower prices, no new orders came to this country, employment did not improve. Instead of all workers accepting a small fall in their standards of living, they deflected the full impact of depression to those whom it deprived of employment and robbed of the whole of their purchasing power.

The Labour opposition interpreted the situation differently. A working man, having no property or reserve to fall back on, was far more vulnerable to depression than an employer, capitalist or landowner. The wages which he had not earned on any one day were irretrievably lost; though he could earn tomorrow's wages tomorrow, nothing could bring back today's. He and his family depended on uninterrupted sale of his services; if such a sale discontinued, they had to go short.

Hence he could not be expected to bear his share of the depression, but had to be enabled to contract out of it. Basically it was on this issue that the trade unions fought the general strike of 1926, even though it broke out over a conflict in the coal mining industry. Owing to the fact that the unions lost that fight, the government's view prevailed throughout the interwar years.

John Maynard Keynes did not agree with either government or opposition, but his *General Theory of Interest, Employment and Money* did not appear until the trough had been passed. The fault of both arguments, according to Keynes, lay in sharing out a depression instead of fighting it. Keynes assigned the key rôle in the battle to the government. It was only common prudence on the part of any private individual whose income had been cut to reduce his outlay. But governments did not resemble private individuals; they alone could safely create debts on a large scale without having present means to pay for them. To every newly incurred government debt corresponded a claim by the holder of its promise to pay; government debt therefore scattered among the community new purchasing power which, if exerted, translated itself into demand and thus primed the pump, showing producers that goods were wanted. Where the government had led, private industry would follow, and thus by a policy of deficit financing the government could lead the country out of depression. When Keynes's *General Theory* appeared, rearmament had already got under way; the government placed new orders for political as much as economic reasons. This did not enable the theory to be put to the test before the second world war broke out.

The lessons of the 1930s however were not forgotten. Even in the middle of the war, the government sought to guard against any recurrence of the distress through which the country had passed. Keynes was not available, being on wartime service with the Treasury in an attempt to safeguard the British currency at a time when essential imports could not even remotely be balanced by exports. The government turned to Sir William Beveridge, an economist already renowned for his work in the social field; he had analysed the evils of casual employment in dock work, investigated the problem of unemployment and introduced labour exchanges to Britain. In response to the government's request, Beveridge in 1942 produced a plan which bears his name, a scheme for social security which he defined as 'security for the individual, organized by the State, to take care of risks which even good social organization cannot eliminate'. This struck the new mid-twentieth century note: if even good social organization left risks which individuals could not avoid incurring, then their assumption by the State neither disgraced nor demoralized the individual. What were these risks? In a picturesque illustration, Beveridge outlined five malignant giants: want, poverty, ignorance, idleness and squalor. A welfare State would have to dig a ditch which would keep each of these giants henceforth at bay.

Policy along the principles, if not in accordance with every detail, of the Beveridge report formed part of the programme of every post-war government; the electorate would have refused endorsement to any Parliament which repudiated this commitment. It fell to the Labour government between 1945 and 1950 to take the decisive steps, though some of its measures had been foreshadowed in preparations undertaken by the coalition government which preceded it. Family allowances for every child, bar the first, took care of one cause of poverty; retirement pensions, plus a comprehensive national assistance system, of another. Nationalizing not only environmental, but also personal, health services entitled everybody to the attention of doctors, hospitals and ancillary medical services without specific payment in respect of treatment received. Free secondary education in accordance with ability aimed at creating equality of opportunity at the starting point. In stipulating for the maintenance of full employment, with unemployment insurance compensating for frictional or transitional loss of earnings, Beveridge incorporated the Keynesian lesson in his own plan. Local authorities were encouraged by State grants to build houses and clear slums as fast as resources could be made available. All basic legislative measures towards the implementation of the welfare State had been passed by 1950; the programme was on its way.

Until the early 1950s, the British economy suffered from war and post-war shortages; though nobody went hungry, life remained shabby and drab. Ration books dominated relationships between housewives and their food shops; most articles of daily use, made of cheap and substitute materials, had a short and unsatisfactory life. Capital resources remained scarce; investment had to be restricted; buildings and plant, whether destroyed by enemy action or overtaken by technical innovation, could not be replaced as fast as their owners or users desired. Wartime austerity, adopted originally in response to necessity, threatened to become a national habit; some of the more imaginative and artistic spirits used the national exhibition of 1951, staged to commemorate the centenary of its famous predecessor, to strike deliberately a gay, many-hued, almost fanciful note—anything to repudiate drab, functional, uninspiring articles of use. Yet while economic activity lacked the variegated pattern of pre-war days, everybody welcomed one fundamental change: there was full employment. Post-war governments had taken the Keynesian lesson, reiterated by Beveridge, to heart. During the period of replacing war damage and satisfying pent-up demand no difficulty existed; once this source of employment slackened, the need for rearming on up-to-date lines eased the task. Keynes had ordered a blood infusion while the patient had passed through an unprecedented phase of economic anaemia; he did not live to explain whether he had meant his prescription to apply to a patient afflicted with high blood pressure. Interwar social insurance had paid for itself on the assumption of unemployment not exceeding seven per cent. Post-war arrangements took two to be a normal percentage; even on this basis the fund accumulated considerable reserves, as only once for a short time in the 1950s did the average national figure rise to that level. Over the country as a whole, though not in every part, two vacancies competed for the services of every person wishing to change jobs—a state of overfull employment.

This condition continued as the country moved into a high-consumption economy towards the middle of the decade. Balance of payments crises at fairly regular intervals notwithstanding, the domestic consumer lived in a permanent boom. Shortages of commodities had been wiped out, ration books consigned to the war museums; new materials and cost-reducing production methods developed during the war now made their impact on civilian supplies. The greatest changes occurred in the field of durable consumer goods: hire purchase brought motor-cars, refrigerators, washing machines, vacuum-cleaners, wireless and television sets, hitherto luxuries not available below middle class levels of income, within the reach of most workers. Goods became plentiful and elaborate, highly processed and specialized. Consumers enjoyed greater variety than ever before, attractively displayed for their choice through the arts and wiles of an advertizing industry which had at all times worked through the most up-to-date media: newspapers and periodicals, outdoor hoardings and circulars in the nineteenth century, films and radio in the early twentieth, television transmissions, aerial loudhailers and displays after the second world war. Though more skill went into making the consumer's mouth water, the durability of the goods he—or more often she—was persuaded to buy rarely matched pre-war standards. This hardly caused regret; many who formerly spent their time washing, mending and patching to give used articles a new lease of life, much preferred casting away and replacing commodities once they had lost the sheen and veneer of novelty.

Progressive taxation, the erosion of savings by inflation and differences in the speed at which incomes could be adjusted to upward movements in the price level all contributed to a permanent change in the distribution of the national income by allotting to the working class a larger share at the expense of the upper and middle classes and by diminishing the difference between the largest and the smallest incomes. All these devices, however, levelled down far more effectively than they levelled up. Any attempt at a crude classification of the population ignores those in each class who failed to share the benefits of rising standards of living: pensioners, widows or deserted mothers with young children, the crippled or mentally handicapped. Sometimes falling on bad days after being accustomed to easier circumstances, they had never pictured themselves as recipients of what they still privately termed relief. Though social services were provided for all members of the community, these formed the group for whom the standard adopted was crucial. In an atmosphere of prosperity and luxury, at what level should minimum provision be made? Should it rise in proportion to general consumption or remain tied to the standards of austerity which its designers had visualized? At a period of constant inflation, the cost of social services had to increase in money terms in order to maintain its proportion of the national product, but as those called upon to bear the burden of these services as tax or rate payers advanced to higher levels of affluence, ought they to be asked to divert a more generous share of it to those less fortunate?

Perhaps the most intractable problem arose in medicine. New and powerful drugs, discovered during and after the war, prolonged life at a cost far exceeding that of medicaments hitherto in use. With the community footing the bill, should such drugs be made available in unlimited quantities to all old persons likely to benefit, or only to some; if selectively, on what principles could a choice be made? Drugs proved more efficacious in postponing death than in preserving or restoring the faculties which made life enjoyable; did this justify more sparing use? In the days of private medicine, patients or their families had made their own choice by paying, or refusing to pay; now responsibility devolved upon the community which left it to the doctors. The medical profession had no desire to become the bearer of the nation's moral responsibility, but no other agency volunteered to share it.

An approximately stable population enjoying a rising standard of living, including an unprecedented variety of goods produced by an industry on the brink of utilizing new sources of power, foodstuffs of which a larger proportion than before was provided by home agriculture working within an overall plan agreed with the government and selling increasingly in new, safer and more lucrative mass markets, motor-cars for the masses and aerial transport at a speed not dreamt of in previous centuries— these were highlights in the picture of Britain embarking on the 1960s. Compared to the 1930s, she made better provision for her population, pursued more purposeful and self-confident economic and social policies which influenced more deeply the lives of most of her citizens. The State made its will felt more incisively in domestic affairs, except in the field of industrial relations where anarchy was only narrowly staved off, officially by a variety of precarious devices, in fact by the resistance on the part of men of good will and moderation on both sides of industry to the influence of evil-intentioned agitators and hotheads. Internationally the economic stature of Britain had shrunk—not indeed to a proportion of her geographical size in the world context, yet sufficiently to confine her investors and traders to a much smaller share in international transactions than had been theirs for a century and a half. Even to become one of the leading players of a company in which she had been the unrivalled star proved a bitter pill; in Britain's instance, it required adjustments to the domestic economy which no country could find easy, adjustments all the harder to make at a time when more and more of her colonies progressed to independence and separated their economies from that of the former mother country. Moreover, new standards of living in Britain had moral implications for which the population had not been fully prepared. Material advance, real though it had been since the second world war, by itself could not act as a substitute for the solution of these problems, but their discussion does not fall to the lot of the economic historian.

APPENDIX | TIME CHART

1756–1763 Seven Years' War

1757 Sankey Navigation opened

1769 James Watt's first steam engine

1773 Corn Law

1776 American *Declaration of Independence*. Adam Smith publishes *The Wealth of Nations*

1783 Britain recognizes the independence of the United States

1789 Beginning of the French Revolution

1793–1802 Britain at war with France

1795 Berkshire magistrates draw up Speenhamland scale

1797 Suspension of cash payments

1799 Passage of first Combination Act. Introduction of income-tax

1800 Union of Great Britain and Ireland

1801 First census of population

1803–1815 Britain at war with France

1806 Berlin decree

1807 Orders-in-Council passed. Abolition of slave trade in the British Empire

1812–1814 Britain at war with the United States

1814 Repeal of Statute of Artificers

1815 Corn Law passed

1816 Abolition of income-tax

1817 March of the Blanketeers

1819 Peterloo massacre; the Six Acts passed

1821 Resumption of cash payments and introduction of gold standard

1823–1827 Huskisson's tariff reforms

1823 Britain recognizes the independence of the South American Republics

1824 Repeal of the Combination Acts

1825 Financial crisis. Stockton and Darlington Railway opened

1829 Roman Catholic Relief Act passed. Metropolitan Police established

1830 Liverpool–Manchester Railway opened

1832 Great Reform Act passed

1833 Abolition of slavery in the British Empire. The first effective Factory Act passed. Owen's Grand National Consolidated Trades Union established. First government grants towards primary education

1834 Poor Law (Amendment) Act passed. First agricultural research station opened (Rothamsted)

1835 Municipal Reform Act passed

1836 Tithe Commutation Act passed. The People's Charter drawn up

1838 Anti-Corn-Law League established. The Agricultural Society of England founded

1839 Introduction of the penny post

1842 Re-introduction of income-tax

1844 Bank Charter Act passed. Rochdale Pioneers begin business

1845 Irish potato failure combined with poor harvests throughout Europe. First agricultural college opened (Cirencester)

1846 Repeal of the Corn Laws

1847 First suspension of Bank Charter Act

1848 Great Chartist petition. General Board of Health established. Gold struck in California

1849 Repeal of the Navigation Laws

1851 Great Exhibition

1853–1856 Crimean War

1856 Bessemer introduces his converter

1857 Siemens introduces the open-hearth furnace. Indian Mutiny. Second suspension of Bank Charter Act

1860 Conclusion of Anglo-French trade treaty

1861–1865 American Civil War

1862 Legislation on limited liability companies consolidated

1866 Overend Gurney crisis; third suspension of Bank Charter Act

1867 Franchise granted to urban workers. British North America Act passed. Bradford Boilermakers' judgment

1868   First meeting of Trades Union Congress

1869   Suez Canal opened

1870   Elementary Education Act passed

1872   Secrecy of ballot introduced. First trade union organization of agricultural workers

1875   Disraeli buys Suez Canal shares. Plimsoll's Act against unseaworthy ships passed. First effective Public Health Act

1879   Gilchrist Thomas introduces basic steelmaking

1883   Fabian Society founded

1884   Franchise granted to workers in villages. Gold discovered in Transvaal

1888   Establishment of county and borough councils. 'Fair trade' agitation

1889   London dock strike

1890   Baring crisis. The first effective Housing Act passed

1894   Establishment of district and parish councils. Death duties differentiated according to value of estate

1895   Jameson raid

1897   Workmen's compensation improved

1898   Imperial penny postage established

1899–1901   Boer War

1901   Commonwealth of Australia established. Taff Vale judgment

1902   Local education authorities constituted

1903   Tariff Reform League founded

1906   Trade unions freed from liability for acts committed by their agents

1907   Workmen's compensation further improved. Private limited liability companies legalized. First census of production

1908   First Children's Act passed

1909   Labour exchanges and trade boards established; non-contributory old-age pensions introduced; Lloyd George budget. Osborne judgment

1910   Union of South Africa proclaimed

1911   Health and unemployment insurance introduced

1914–1918   First World War

1921   Secession of Southern Ireland from the United Kingdom

1925 Return to the gold standard

1926 General strike

1929 Great slump spreads from New York stock exchange

1931 Abolition of gold standard. Introduction of protection

1932 Ottawa agreements. Peak of unemployment (22 per cent)

1936 Keynes publishes *General Theory of Interest, Employment and Money*

1939–1945 Second World War

1942 Beveridge publishes his plan

1946 Bread and flour rationed

1947 Temporary rationing of potatoes. Nationalization of coal mines takes effect

1948 Nationalization of the British Railways takes effect. Electricity industry transferred to national ownership. End of bread and flour rationing

1949 Devaluation of the pound sterling from $4.03 to $2.80

1951 Festival of Britain

FURTHER READING

General

Ashton, T. S., *An Economic History of England: the Eighteenth Century*. (Methuen. 1959.) A lifetime's research in the economic history of the eighteenth century summed up by the greatest authority in this field.

Ashworth, W., *An Economic History of England, 1870–1939*. (Methuen. 1960.) A new interpretation, based on recently accumulated quantitative evidence, of a period scamped by most economic historians.

Clapham, J. H., *Economic History of Modern Britain*. (Cambridge U.P. 1939–1951.) Three volumes packed with a wealth of contemporary evidence on which practically every subsequent economic historian has drawn.

Court, W. H. B., *A Concise Economic History of Britain from 1750 to Modern Times*. (Cambridge U.P. 2nd ed. 1958.)

Hancock, W. K. and Gowing, M. M., *The British War Economy*. (H.M.S.O. 1949.) The introductory volume of the United Kingdom official history of the civil aspects of the second world war, summing up war experience in the economic field and pointing the contrast to that of the first world war.

Population

Report of the Royal Commission on Population, 1949. Cmd. 7695. (H.M.S.O.) A Blue Book to which the country's outstanding demographers contributed their services and which, in order to advise the government on population policy, analyses population development of the last two centuries.

Agriculture

Ernle, Lord, *British Farming Past and Present*. (Longmans. 5th ed. 1936.) The standard work on the history of agriculture.

Harvey, C. N., *The Farming Kingdom*. (Turnstile Press. 1955.) While the second half is devoted to current questions, the first half provides a brief, but stimulating interpretation of the agricultural past.

Murray, K. A. H., *Agriculture*. (H.M.S.O. and Longmans. 1955.) The agricultural volume of the official history of the second world war, showing the complete change of government policy towards agriculture during the period it reviews.

Ojala, E. M., *Agriculture and Economic Progress*. (Oxford U.P. 1952.) A technical and very revealing economic analysis of productivity and reward in various agricultures, of which the British is one.

Industry

Allen, G. C., *British Industries and their Organization*. (Longmans. 4th ed. 1959.)

Dunning, J. H. and Thomas, C. J., *British Industry: Change and Development in the Twentieth Century*. (Hutchinson. 1961.) Highlights some of the characteristic changes of British industrial structure between the wars and after the second world war.

Plummer, A., *New British Industries in the Twentieth Century*. (Pitman. 1937.) Illustrates the rise of a new sector of British industry chiefly between the wars.

Industrial Relations

Cole, G. D. H., *A Short History of the British Working Class Movement, 1789–1947*. (Allen & Unwin. 1960.) One of the two standard works on the history of trade unionism, but by no means short.

Hutchins, B. L. and Harrison, A., *A History of Factory Legislation*. (P. S. King. 3rd ed. 1926.) The standard work on its subject.

Roberts, B., *The Trades Union Congress, 1868–1921*. (Allen & Unwin. 1958.) Uses the organizational history of the T.U.C. as a peg on which to hang a general interpretation of the development of the trade union movement.

Sharp, I. G., *Industrial Conciliation and Arbitration in Great Britain*. (Allen & Unwin. 1950.)

Thomas, M. W., *The Early Factory Legislation*. (Thames Bank. 1948.) Traces the development of factory legislation to 1850 on the basis chiefly of the minutes of the meetings of the early factory inspectors which the author unearthed in the Home Office records.

Webb, S. and B., *A History of Trade Unionism in England to 1921*. (Longmans. 4th ed. 1950.) The other standard work on its subject.

Webb, S. and B., *Industrial Democracy*. (Longmans. 2nd ed. 1919.) Having written a standard history of trade unionism, the authors in this work felt free to disregard chronological order for the sake of philosophical clarity in interpreting the same material.

Transport

Jackman, W. T., *The Development of Transportation in Modern England*. (Cambridge U.P. 1916.) An old work, but still the best comprehensive survey in its field.

Jeffreys, W. R., *The King's Highway*. (Batchworth Press. 1949.) A spirited account of the road *v.* rail controversy by one of the protagonists on the side of the roads.

Trade

Benham, F. C. C., *Great Britain under Protection*. (Macmillan. 1941.) A critical survey of the trade policy of the 1930s by one of our foremost economists.

Fuchs, C. J., *The Trade Policy of Great Britain and her Colonies since 1860*. (Macmillan. 1905.) Translation of a work by a German scholar written at the end of the last century, but still informative because it conveys the views of a disenchanted outsider.

Imlah, A. H., *Economic Elements in the Pax Britannica*. (Harvard U.P. 1958.) The author, an American scholar, is the foremost authority on British overseas trade and foreign payment balances from the later eighteenth century onwards. This book summarizes his conclusions.

Jefferys, J. B., *Retail Trading in Britain 1850–1950*. (Cambridge U.P. 1954.) The only work on a much neglected subject. Especially traces the growth of department store, co-operative, multiple and chain store retailing.

Kahn, A. E., *Great Britain in the World Economy*. (Pitman. 1946.) An economist's analysis of the British position in the world from the late nineteenth century onwards, highly technical, but very revealing.

Banking, Investment and Fiscal Policy

Cairncross, A. K., *Home and Foreign Investment, 1870–1913*. (Cambridge U.P. 1953.)

Clapham, J. H., *The Bank of England: a History*. (Cambridge U.P. 1944.)

Evans, G. H., *British Corporation Finance, 1775–1850*. (Johns Hopkins U.P. 1936.)

Hargreaves, E. L., *The National Debt*. (Edward Arnold. 1930.) The standard work on its subject.

Hicks, U. K., *British Public Finances: their Structure and Development, 1880–1952*. (Oxford U.P. 1954.) A historical discussion by the leading economist in this subject— the first to take local as well as national public finance fully into account.

Hobson, C. K., *The Export of Capital*. (Constable. 1914.) The earliest full treatment of a field rendered exceedingly difficult by the lack of reliable quantitative data.

Hunt, B. C., *The Development of the Business Corporation in England, 1800–1867*. (Harvard U.P. 1936.) Especially valuable in tracing the evolution of the joint-stock organization for every type of business.

Jenks, L. H., *The Migration of British Capital to 1875*. (Cape. 1938.) An exceedingly readable account of British overseas long-term lending seen through the eyes of an American scholar.

King, W. T. C., *History of the London Discount Market*. (Routledge. 1936.) The most authoritative treatment of a highly technical and difficult subject, written by the Editor of *The Banker*.

Rees, J. F., *A Short Fiscal and Financial History of England, 1815–1918*. (Methuen. 1922.) Succeeds in treating this technical subject in a manner understandable even to the non-economist.

Thomas, S. E., *The Rise and Growth of Joint-Stock Banking. vol. I. Britain to 1860*. (Pitman. 1934.)

Standards of Living

Ashworth, W., *The Genesis of Modern British Town Planning*. (Routledge & Kegan Paul. 1954.) The only account of the subject written from the social historian's rather than the town planner's angle. The first third is concerned with unplanned urban spread.

Beer, M., *A History of British Socialism*. (Bell. 1929.)

Beveridge, W., *Full Employment in a Free Society*. (Allen & Unwin.) The first interpretation of the Welfare State by the man whose plan formed its chief blueprint.

Cole, G. D. H., *Chartist Portraits*. (Macmillan. 1941.) Not a systematic history of the Chartist movement, but far livelier and more interesting than the more orthodox books on this subject.

Halévy, É., *Growth of Philosophical Radicalism*. (Faber. 2nd ed. 1952.) In analysing the philosophy, gives a history of the movement and the contemporary problems which it attempted to solve.

Titmuss, R. M., *Essays on the Welfare State*. (Allen & Unwin. 1958.) A discussion on the philosophies underlying the Welfare State by one of its architects.

Webb, S. and B., *History of the English Poor Law*. (Longmans. 1927–1929.) Of the three volumes of the standard history of the poor law, only the last two deal with the period treated in this book.

INDEX

Acid Steel, 64, 76
Act(s) of Parliament. *See* Law(s)
Advertizer(s), Advertizing, 80, 82, 265
Adviser(s) (Agricultural), 42
Aeroplane. *See* Aircraft
Africa, 21, 160, 173, 270
Age, Age Distribution, 14, 16–19
Agricultural Labourer(s), 28, 29, 37, 39, 40, 43, 44, 102, 110, 111, 140, 232–234, 249, 251, 270
Agriculture, Agriculturist(s), 2, 3, 6, 13, 22–46, 50, 52, 55, 80, 158, 163, 174, 177, 183, 210, 216, 218, 223, 234, 238, 251, 266, 269
Aircraft, 155–157
Air Transport, 42, 81, 155–157, 266. *See also* Transport
Alien, 84
Allotments, 43
Amalgamated Society of Engineers, 104, 110
Amalgamated Society of Railway Servants, 113, 114
Amalgamated Unions, 104, 105, 112. *See also* Craft Unions; New Model Unions
America(n), 12, 42, 43, 68, 74, 76, 79, 81, 84, 145, 158–163, 172, 174, 190–192, 202, 211, 212, 215, 216, 218–220, 268, 269. *See also* United States
Andover, 239
Animal(s), 3, 23, 25, 26, 30, 32, 47, 61, 131, 157, 204, 221. *See also* Livestock
Anti-Corn Law League, 36, 37, 269
Apprentice(s), Apprenticeship, 82, 89, 90, 98, 99, 103, 231
Arable, 30, 34, 36, 44
Arbitration, 115, 122–127
Arbitrator(s), 98, 122–124, 126
Arch, Joseph (1826–1919), 40
Architect(s), 41, 132
Argentine, 176, 202
Aristocracy, Aristocrat, 240, 241

Arkwright, Sir Richard (1732–1792), 53, 54, 60, 65
Armaments, 5, 77. *See also* Rearmament
Asia, 21, 212
Askwith, Sir George Ranken, Baron Askwith (1861–1942), 123
Asquith, Herbert Henry, 1st Earl of Oxford and Asquith (1852–1928), 207, 259
Assembly Line, 67, 86
Associated Electrical Industries Ltd., 81
Atlantic Ocean, 42, 145, 151, 156, 158, 190. *See also* Ocean Transport
Atomic Energy, 84, 86. *See also* Power
Attwood, Thomas (1765–1838), 247
Australasia, 42, 73
Australia, 166, 270
Austria(n), 68, 218
Austria-Hungary, 168
Automatic Machinery, 65, 67. *See also* Machinery
Automation, 86, 120
Azores, 163

Babies, 6
Bakewell, Robert (1725-1795), 26
Balance of Payments, 159, 178, 209–220, 264
Balance of Trade, 161, 173–178
Balliol College, 252, 253
Baltic, 166
Bananas, 145
Bank(s), Banker(s), Banking, 13, 69, 167, 169, 179–220, 241, 246–248, 257
Bank Charter, 188
Bank Charter Act, 188–190, 199, 202, 269
Bank Notes, 182, 184–188, 190
Bank of England, 182, 183, 186–190, 198–203, 214, 215, 218
Bank Rate, 198-202, 219